The Swift™ Developer's Cookbook

The Swift™ Developer's Cookbook

Erica Sadun

Addison-Wesley

Boston • Columbus • Indianapolis • New York • San Francisco • Amsterdam • Cape Town
Dubai • London • Madrid • Milan • Munich • Paris • Montreal • Toronto • Delhi • Mexico City
Sao Paulo • Sidney • Hong Kong • Seoul • Singapore • Taipei • Tokyo

For information about buying this title in bulk quantities, or for special sales opportunities (which may include electronic versions; custom cover designs; and content particular to your business, training goals, marketing focus, or branding interests), please contact our corporate sales department at corpsales@pearsoned.com or (800) 382-3419.

For government sales inquiries, please contact governmentsales@pearsoned.com.

For questions about sales outside the U.S., please contact international@pearsoned.com.

Visit us on the Web: informit.com/aw

Library of Congress Control Number: 2015953712

ISBN-13: 978-0-13-439526-5

ISBN-10: 0-13-439526-3

Text printed in the United States on recycled paper at RR Donnelley in Crawfordsville, Indiana.

First printing: December 2015

Cover image is the Phú Mỹ bridge, Ho Chi Minh City, Vietnam.

Editor-in-Chief
Mark Taub

Senior Acquisitions Editor
Trina MacDonald

Senior Development Editor
Chris Zahn

Managing Editor
Kristy Hart

Senior Project Editor
Betsy Gratner

Copy Editor
Kitty Wilson

Indexer
Tim Wright

Proofreader
Sarah Kearns

Technical Reviewers
Kevin Ballard
Sebastian Celis
Alexander Kempgen

Editorial Assistant
Olivia Basegio

Cover Designer
Chuti Prasertsith

Compositor
Nonie Ratcliff

Contents

Preface

More than a year after its introduction, the Swift programming language is still growing and evolving. While it seems a bit ridiculous writing a book about a language that's not fixed, final, and polished, that's exactly what *The Swift Developer's Cookbook* does. Swift is not so raw and young that even in its ever-changing state, it doesn't know what it's trying to achieve for its audience of Apple developers. A modern type-safe language, Swift already has locked down its fundamentals, even as its specific implementation details resolve over time.

Swift is simply a joy to program in. Its constructs and libraries present you with new ways to craft code, handle data, and perform the endless daily tasks that make up a programmer's life. From protocol-oriented and functional programming to first-class closures and algebraic data types, Swift offers a fresh and exciting take on programming. The more time you spend developing in Swift, the harder it becomes to return to older languages that don't offer these powerful features.

This book is not a traditional tutorial. It's written for programmers both experienced and new who are looking to push existing aptitudes into a new arena. Each concept-focused chapter covers a practical skill set. These chapters guide you to mastery over those essential Swift development tasks. You needn't read this cookbook from cover to cover (although you are more than welcome to do so). Instead, dive into whatever topic you want to learn about and uncover key insights to bring away with you from each discussion.

The Swift Developer's Cookbook has been an amazing project to work on. I hope you enjoy reading this book half as much as I've enjoyed working on it.

How This Book Is Organized

This book offers a practical survey of key Swift development topics. Here's a rundown of what you'll find in this book's chapters:

- **Chapter 1, "Welcome to Modern Swift"**—This chapter explores the kinds of applications you can build using this new modern type-safe programming language. Working in a new and changing language isn't always smooth sailing. Since Apple introduced Swift, the language has remained in constant flux. From beta to beta, dot release to dot release, new features and updated syntax mean source code that compiles in one release might not in the next. In this chapter, learn what it means to work in an evolving language and how to migrate your code as the language updates.

- **Chapter 2, "Printing and Mirroring"**—Although programming focuses on crafting artifacts through code, it's important to remember that code serves the developer as well as the end user. Code doesn't just need to compile: It should communicate clearly, coherently, and effectively as well. The features discussed in this chapter cover the gamut of output scenarios that range from user-facing write operations to developer-facing debugging support. This chapter surveys these technologies and explores how to precisely build feedback, documentation, and output to fit your development and debugging needs.

- **Chapter 3, "Optionals?!"**—Unlike in many other languages, in Swift a nil is not a pointer. Using it is a safe and expressive way to represent the potential for both valid and invalid values within a single construct. Learning how to recognize and use optionals is an essential step in mastering the Swift language. This chapter introduces optionals and surveys the supporting constructs you need in order to create, test, and successfully use optionals in your code.

- **Chapter 4, "Closures and Functions"**—Lexical closures provide the basis for methods, functions, and "block" parameters, all of which power the Swift applications you develop. By encapsulating state and functionality, they promote behavior to first-class constructs. This chapter explores closures, showing how they work in Swift and how to best incorporate them into your applications.

- **Chapter 5, "Generics and Protocols"**—Generics help you build robust code to expand functionality beyond single types. A generic implementation services an entire group of types instead of just one specific version. A combination of generic types and protocols (behavior contracts) establishes a powerful and flexible programming synergy. This chapter introduces these concepts and explores how you can navigate this often-confusing development arena.

- **Chapter 6, "Errors"**—In Swift, as in any other programming language, things fail. In daily development tasks, you encounter both logical errors—that is, things that compile but don't work the way you expect them to—and runtime errors that arise from real-world conditions such as missing resources or inaccessible services. Swift's response mechanisms range from assertions that fail fatally to error types that support recovery, enabling you to track what went wrong, and offer runtime workarounds. This chapter introduces errors and helps you understand how to handle many kinds of failure.

- **Chapter 7, "Types"**—When it comes to types, Swift offers three distinct families. Its type system includes classes, which provide reference types, and enumerations and structures, which are both algebraic value types. Each provides unique strengths and features to support your development. This chapter surveys some of the key concepts used in the Swift language and explores how its types work in your applications.

- **Chapter 8, "Miscellany"**—Swift is a vibrant and evolving language with many features that don't always fit tidily under a single umbrella. This chapter introduces an assortment of topics that could not find proper homes elsewhere in this book but that still deserve your attention.

About the Sample Code

You'll find the source code for this book at https://github.com/erica/SwiftCookbook on the open-source GitHub hosting site. There, you'll find a chapter-by-chapter collection of source code that provides examples of the material covered in this book.

Retrieve sample code either by using git tools to clone the repository or by clicking GitHub's Download button. It was at the right center of the page when I wrote this book. It enables you to retrieve the entire repository as a ZIP archive or tarball.

Contribute!

Sample code is never a fixed target. It continues to evolve as Apple updates its Swift language. Get involved. Pitch in by suggesting bug fixes and corrections and by expanding the code that's on offer. GitHub allows you to fork repositories and grow them with your own tweaks and features and then share them back to the main repository. If you come up with a new idea or approach, let me know.

Getting GitHub

GitHub (http://github.com) is the largest git-hosting site, with more than 150,000 public repositories. It provides both free hosting for public projects and paid options for private projects. With a custom Web interface that includes wiki hosting, issue tracking, and an emphasis on social networking of project developers, it's a great place to find new code or collaborate on existing libraries. Sign up for a free account at the GitHub website, which then allows you to copy and modify this repository or create your own open-source iOS projects to share with others.

Contacting the Author

If you have any comments or questions about this book, please drop me an email message at erica@ericasadun.com or stop by the GitHub repository and contact me there.

Acknowledgments

My sincere thanks go out to Trina MacDonald, Chris Zahn, and Olivia Basegio, along with the entire Addison-Wesley/Pearson production team, specifically Betsy Gratner, Kitty Wilson, and Nonie Ratcliff, and my amazing team of technical editors, Kevin Ballard, Alex Kempgen, and Sebastian Celis.

My gratitude extends to everyone who helped read through drafts and provided feedback. Specific thanks go out to Ken Ferry, Jeremy Dowell, Remy Demarest, August Joki, Mike Shields, Phil Holland, Mike Ash, Nate Cook, Josh Weinberg, Davide De Franceschi, Matthias Neeracher, Tom Davie, Steve Hayman, Nate Heagy, Chris Lattner, Jack Lawrence, Jordan Rose, Joe Groff, Stephen Celis, Cassie Murray, Kelly Gerber, Norio Nomura, "Eiam," Wess Cope, and everyone else who contributed to this effort. If I have omitted your name here, please accept my apologies.

Special thanks also go to my husband and kids. You guys are the best.

About the Author

Erica Sadun is a bestselling author, coauthor, and contributor to several dozen books on programming and other digital topics. She has blogged at TUAW.com, O'Reilly's Mac Devcenter, Lifehacker, and Ars Technica. In addition to being the author of dozens of iOS-native applications, Erica holds a Ph.D. in computer science from Georgia Tech's Graphics, Visualization and Usability Center. A geek, a programmer, and an author, she's never met a gadget she didn't love. When not writing, she and her geek husband have parented three geeks-in-training, who regard their parents with restrained bemusement, when they're not busy rewiring the house or plotting global domination.

Editor's Note: We Want to Hear from You!

As the reader of this book, you are our most important critic and commentator. We value your opinion and want to know what we're doing right, what we could do better, what areas you'd like to see us publish in, and any other words of wisdom you're willing to pass our way.

You can email or write me directly to let us know what you did or didn't like about this book—as well as what we can do to make our books stronger.

Please note that I cannot help you with technical problems related to the topic of this book, and that due to the high volume of mail we receive, we might not be able to reply to every message.

When you write, please be sure to include this book's title and author as well as your name and phone or email address. I will carefully review your comments and share them with the author and editors who worked on the book.

Email: trina.macdonald@pearson.com

Mail: Trina MacDonald
          Senior Acquisitions Editor
          Addison-Wesley/Pearson Education
          75 Arlington St., Ste. 300
          Boston, MA 02116

Reader Services

Register your copy of *The Swift Developer's Cookbook* at informit.com for convenient access to downloads, updates, and corrections as they become available. To start the registration process, go to informit.com/register and log in or create an account*. Enter the product ISBN, 9780134395265, and click Submit. Once the process is complete, you will find any available bonus content under Registered Products.

*Be sure to check the box that you would like to hear from us in order to receive exclusive discounts on future editions of this product.

Welcome to Modern Swift

When Apple introduced the Swift programming language in 2014, it offered a performance-tuned type-safe modern programming language intended to supplant Objective-C. The new language included protocol-oriented development, type inferencing, automatic reference counting, generics, first-class function objects, overloading, nullability, optionals, and more. Swift overhauled control mechanisms and constructs, enhancing features like switches and enumerations to add flexibility and power to Cocoa and Cocoa Touch projects.

Lead developer Chris Lattner began Swift language development in 2010. The project grew, and by 2013 had become a major focus for Apple's developer tools group. After the 2014 launch, Chris Lattner described the design effort that fed the Swift project on his blog: "The Swift language is the product of tireless effort from a team of language experts, documentation gurus, compiler optimization ninjas, and an incredibly important internal dogfooding group who provided feedback to help refine and battle-test ideas. Of course, it also greatly benefited from the experiences hard-won by many other languages in the field, drawing ideas from Objective-C, Rust, Haskell, Ruby, Python, C#, CLU, and far too many others to list."

The language did not express its true potential until WWDC 2015. At that time, Swift evolved to version 2, with a completely redesigned error-handling system, better integration with legacy APIs, and feature upgrades that connected the language closer to its functional roots. That's not to say Swift has *arrived* yet. Swift 2 happened, but Swift is nowhere near done. A recurring theme during WWDC presentations was expressed in phrases such as "in a future update," "in a future release," and "when we get time to implement that." Huge changes happened at WWDC, not the least of which affected foundational concepts that underpin nearly every line of code you write.

Since Apple introduced the language, Swift has remained in constant flux. From beta to beta, dot release to dot release, new features and updated syntax mean source code that compiles in one release might not in the next. I expect that Swift will change every six months or so for the next few years, at a minimum, before the rate of updates begins to slow down and a stable language emerges.

Swift is now at an awkward state. It still shows rough edges, but it has too much momentum and it's too important to the Apple developer community to ignore. It's time to jump aboard if you haven't already. Just acknowledge the realities. It's been a long, tough, frustrating environment to work in.

I feel comfortable enough committing myself to an actual book project about Swift because of two things. First, Swift's most fundamental features have mostly coalesced. Structures, enumerations, and classes are unlikely to be hit hard by profound architectural redesign, although many small features continue to evolve. Second, Apple has committed to offering migration tools that enable you to upgrade your source to the latest language release. When Swift changed its basic printing function from `println()` to `print()`, Xcode's migrator was there to facilitate the change.

Developers are no longer working in such early betas that the language doesn't know what it is. Swift has reached the point where Apple is primarily updating techniques and procedures, not core language concepts—well, not a *lot* of core language concepts. Coding in early betas was ridiculous. Today's Swift is merely frustrating. It can also be greatly rewarding. The language isn't *finished*, but it is now usable, learnable, and a worthy target for your time and attention.

Apple has committed to making Swift the future. Now is the perfect time to jump on the Swift train and see where it takes you. Don't look at Swift 2 and say, "I'm too late to board this train" or "How is it possible that version 2 of a language is still beta?" I invite you to use basic Swift math to convert the latest release into its true version number:

```
Official Swift version N = Unofficial Swift(version: N * 0.1)
```

This is a silly but amusing way of saying "Version 2 still feels behind where a version 1 release should be." The numeric constant may rise over time from 0.1 if Swift continues its rapid evolution.

Migrating Code

It might seem a little odd to kick off a language book by discussing code migration, but this entire chapter is devoted to the notion that Swift is lovable, worthy, and slightly unready for prime time. Knowing how to develop in a continuously moving landscape is a valuable skill.

Xcode's Swift migration support was first introduced with Swift 1.2. A critical feature for a changing language, the assistant locates outdated syntax and offers a smooth path to modernization. The exact details for this tool may change over time, but Apple has committed to providing a migration tool to support developers from release to release.

How to Migrate

You find Convert under the Edit menu. Figure 1-1 shows this menu in a beta Xcode 7 release. Once you select Convert, Xcode steps you through the process of migrating your code for an entire target.

Refactor
Convert
Start Dictation
Emoji & Symbols
^⌘Space
To Latest Swift Syntax...
To XCTest...
To Modern Objective-C Syntax...
To Objective-C ARC...

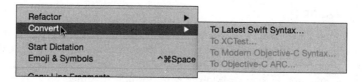

Figure 1-1 Xcode enables you to convert Swift source code to modern syntax.

Select the targets you wish to upgrade, as in Figure 1-2. You may be prompted to enable repository snapshots. Whether you use a `git` commit (you can substitute your preferred version control system) or the offered Xcode snapshot, a commit of some kind allows you to revert your project to its pre-upgrade state and is highly recommended.

Select Targets to Convert:
Hello Swift.app
Hello Swift
LibrarySupport.framework
Hello Swift

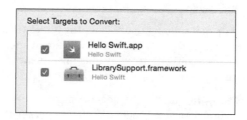

Figure 1-2 Select which targets in your project you wish to convert.

Xcode scans the files that make up your project and highlights language changes (see Figure 1-3). You approve or reject the updates by clicking Save or Cancel.

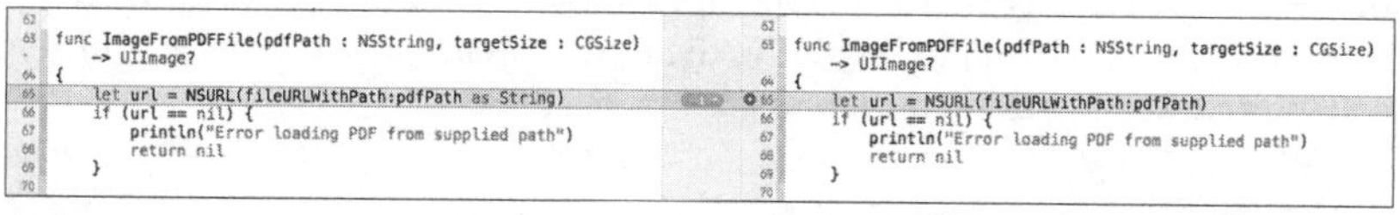

func ImageFromPDFFile(pdfPath : NSString, targetSize : CGSize)
-> UIImage?
{
let url = NSURL(fileURLWithPath:pdfPath as String)
if (url == nil) {
println("Error loading PDF from supplied path")
return nil
}
func ImageFromPDFFile(pdfPath : NSString, targetSize : CGSize)
-> UIImage?
{
let url = NSURL(fileURLWithPath:pdfPath)
if (url == nil) {
println("Error loading PDF from supplied path")
return nil
}

Figure 1-3 Xcode offers side-by-side comparisons showing the modern (After Conversion) and older (Before Conversion) syntax. The updates are to the left and the original code to the right.

Each upgrade point is marked with a red dot, as you see in Figure 1-3. The dot is paired with a small numbered gray oval. Click each dot to view a detailed explanation of the update change. Click the gray oval to discard a recommended update.

A table of contents appears at the top-left side of the Review Changes pane. It enables you to select individual files to review. Xcode presents the After Conversion and Before Conversion versions in the left and right panes. If you are at all unsure about which pane is which, check the titles at the very bottom of each pane. Xcode explicitly documents the conversion role as well as the filename. When you're finished with your review, click Save. Xcode applies its updates, and you're ready to use the code with the latest compiler.

Migration Lessons

Following the version 2 beta launch, developers started upgrading Apple-supplied playgrounds such as the March 2015 Mandelbrot sample (https://developer.apple.com/swift/blog/?id=26). Some had wasted hours trying to get the samples to work. Where possible, don't upgrade your code by hand; the migrator does a better job. It performs upgrades mechanically and has no preconceptions about the material it's working on. By re-downloading the original and automating the upgrade, those developers had code running in just a few minutes.

The upgrade process isn't a panacea. The migrator won't find logic errors or flawed coding, and it cannot account for paradigm shifts. For example, to use a rather involved Swift concept, consider the way a Swift application deals with failure conditions. The Swift migrator can't move apps away from Swift 1.2–style `if-let` pyramids to Swift 2 `guard` statements. You need to incorporate those types of transitions by hand. The paradigm has shifted, but Xcode can only adjust syntax. It cannot take into account best practices or pattern updates.

Xcode also can't upgrade code that's too far out of date. The initial 1.1 to 1.2 migrator couldn't handle 1.0 beta Swift. Keeping your code base updated and current and ready for each successive language leap forward is your job. This requires a big investment of time, but it's necessary if you're going to commit to the Swift language at this time.

Migration means review. This is the point of the side-by-side comparisons you saw in Figure 1-3. It's why you'll want to conduct general code inspections after upgrades. My experiences have been positive. That doesn't diminish the fact that language migrations involve cost both in time and loss of control.

The most important thing you can learn from Swift migration is the value of a good suite of test cases. Investing time into code validation is a critical part of keeping your libraries and applications current, modern, and running. A sufficient suite provides full code coverage and ensures that your functionality passes a minimal validation set. If your tests are written in Swift, allocate time and overhead to migrating the tests as well. Then automate your testing post-upgrade just as Xcode automates the migration itself.

Using Swift

Swift is a general-purpose language that can be compiled or run as a script, used at the command line, or used in standalone apps. From compiled apps to scripts, here's a quick survey of some ways Swift builds executable code.

Compiled Applications

Most typically, you use Swift to build applications and extensions for iOS, OS X, tvOS, and watchOS targets (see Figure 1-4). Swift is a modern, type-safe language that offers fast, efficient code generation. A complete development solution, Swift integrates with Apple's full range of developer APIs. Create apps using either pure Swift code or in hybrid language projects that bridge Swift with C and Objective-C.

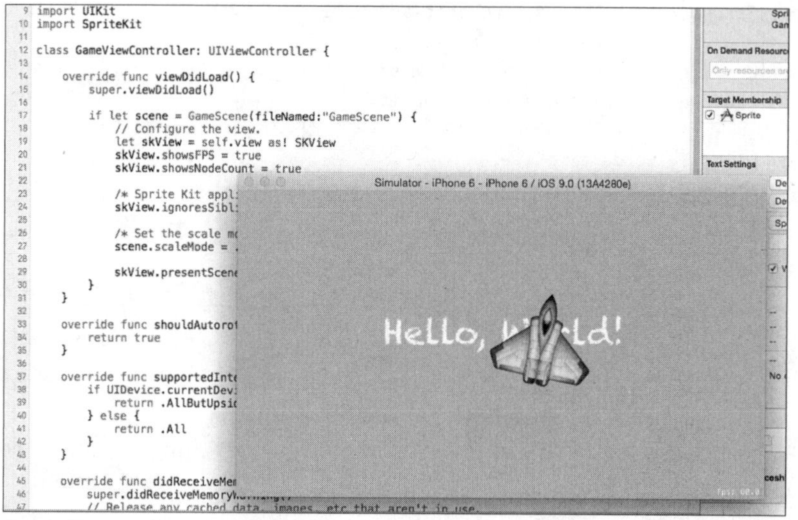

Figure 1-4   Swift is the new language of choice for Apple application development.

Frameworks and Libraries

Swift isn't just for building applications with traditional user interfaces. The Swift language enables you to create frameworks, bundles, services, and command-line utilities. (Swift does not yet support the creation of static libraries.) Xcode offers a wide range of built-in templates that support the Swift language so you can get off to a running start on your next big project (see Figure 1-5).

Scripting

Swift is also a scripting language. Use it to build quick shell utilities. The following example scrapes iTunes to look up prices of items specified with an App Store ID. Other than the shebang on the first line (the hash sign followed by the exclamation point), this script is indistinguishable from a source you'd compile for a command-line utility:

```
#!/usr/bin/xcrun swift
import Cocoa
var arguments = Process.arguments
for appID in arguments.dropFirst() {
    let urlString = "https://itunes.apple.com/lookup?id=\(appID)"
    guard let url = NSURL(string: urlString) else {continue}
    guard let data = NSData(contentsOfURL: url) else {continue}
    if let json =
        try NSJSONSerialization.JSONObjectWithData(data, options: [])
            as? NSDictionary,
        resultsList = json["results"] as? NSArray,
```

```
        results = resultsList.firstObject as? NSDictionary,
        name = results["trackName"] as? String,
        price = results["price"] as? NSNumber {
            let words = name.characters.split(
                isSeparator:{$0 == ":" || $0 == "-"}).map(String.init)
            let n = words.first!
            print ("\(n): \(price)")
    }
}
```

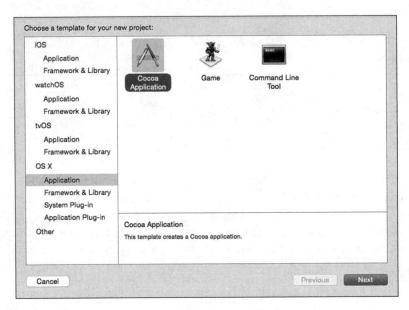

Figure 1-5   Swift builds targets like command-line utilities and frameworks.

REPL

REPL stands for "read eval print loop," an interactive top-level shell that reads user expressions, evaluates them, and prints results. The Swift REPL provides an environment for instant testing and exploration. Just run `swift` at the command line, and you enter an interactive setting.

The Swift REPL maintains ongoing state that enables you to create functions, which you can later refer to, and define structures and classes. Just type expressions for instant evaluation:

```
% swift
Welcome to Apple Swift version 2.0 (700.0.42.1 700.0.53).
Type :help for assistance.
  1> print("hello world")
hello world
  2> func greet() {
  3.     print("hello world")
```

```
  4. }
  5> greet()
hello world
  6> 1 + 2 + 3 + 4
$R0: Int = 10
```

Playgrounds

Playgrounds are Swift REPLs on steroids. They offer the same kind of immediate interpreted gratification you expect from a REPL but supplement that feedback with sophisticated visualization and documentation tools (see Figure 1-6). Playgrounds enable you to explore the Swift language, test routines, prototype quick solutions, delve into Cocoa/Cocoa Touch APIs, and create flexible interactive documents.

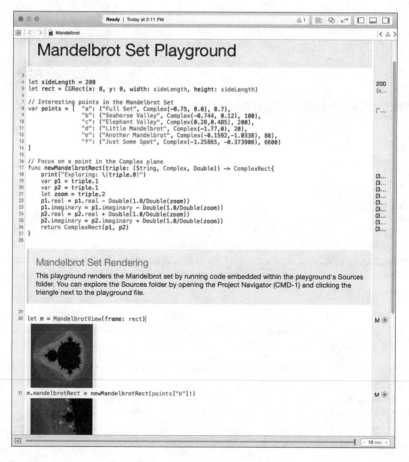

Figure 1-6   This Apple-sourced playground showcases Mandelbrot sets, complex numbers with beautiful fractal boundary features.

Other Swift

At WWDC 2015, Apple announced that Swift would be released as an open source language with Apple-sourced compilers for iOS, OS X, and eventually Linux platforms. Those who wish to explore Swift from other platforms can use online interpreters. Swiftstub (http://swiftstub. com) enables Swift programming from any web browser (see Figure 1-7).

Figure 1-7   Interact with Swift from any web browser.

Learning Swift

This cookbook is neither a "getting started" tutorial nor an exhaustive reference. Download a copy of *The Swift Programming Language*—a free ebook offered by Apple on the iBooks store—and work through the guided tour section. This ebook is regularly updated as the language evolves; an extensive Revision History section lets you explore documentation and language changes by date.

A second Apple ebook, *Using Swift with Cocoa and Objective-C*, is just as essential. It provides an overview of the topics related to interoperability between the two languages and the details of API calls. It's a much shorter volume than *The Swift Programming Language* due to its tight focus.

Both books are available on Apple's website as well as in iBooks. I prefer web-based search engines to the limited iBooks in-book tools. Web searches can use Boolean clauses and aren't limited to exact phrase matching. In contrast, iBooks searches are limited to words and page numbers. Matches against common words (think *for* or *switch*) are particularly frustrating to deal with in iBooks, which doesn't offer the context-limiting support you find with popular search engines.

Apple's online Swift Standard Library Reference (search the web for it as its URL regularly changes) provides an indispensable overview of Swift's base functionality layer. It offers an overview of fundamental data types, common data structures, functions, methods, and protocols. If you stop learning Swift at the language basics, you're missing out on this critical portion of core language expressiveness. SwiftDoc (http://swiftdoc.org) offers auto-generated documentation for Swift's standard library. This is the same documentation you find when you Command-click symbols in Xcode but presented in easier-to-read webpages. It's a terrific resource.

The Apple Swift blog (https://developer.apple.com/swift/blog/) is updated about once a month, but its coverage includes can't-miss topics related to language features and case studies. Its mission statement speaks about behind-the-scenes peeks into language design, but its focus over time has been more practical how-to articles. The blog's resources page (https://developer. apple.com/swift/resources/) further provides links to a set of essential Swift and Xcode materials, including iTunes U courses, videos, sample code, and a link to the official Swift Standard Library Reference.

The redesigned Apple Developer Forums (https://forums.developer.apple.com/community/ xcode/swift) provide access to Swift engineers, lively discussions, and up-to-date how-to information. You will also find important language information archived at the old forums site (https://devforums.apple.com/index.jspa); navigate to Developer Tools > Language > Swift.

Also amazing is ASCII WWDC (http://asciiwwdc.com). Enter keywords and search through years of WWDC talks. This website helps you track down presentations specific to the Swift language and the Xcode tools that support Swift development.

If you use Internet Relay Chat (IRC) peer support, the Freenode (chat.freenode.net) `#swift-lang` room offers access to pro-level coding advice. It's a language-specific room, so if you need help with OS-specific APIs, visit `#iphonedev` or `#macdev` instead. A final room, `#cocoa-init`, is set up specifically to help mentor developers new to iOS and OS X.

Wrap-up

With Swift, Apple committed itself to redefining its developer tool suite. Swift 2 represents the start of that journey, not the end. Its tools, modules, and the language itself will and must continue to grow in the foreseeable future. Swift is nowhere near a stopping point at this time.

As best practices coalesce and design patterns emerge, now is a great time to begin transitioning code and techniques to the new bright future. The chapters that follow in this cookbook survey key areas of Swift development. They'll enable you to cherry-pick those areas you need to learn and offer hard-won techniques for you to incorporate into your code.

Good luck on your journey.

2

Printing and Mirroring

Although programming focuses on crafting artifacts through code, it's important to remember that code serves the developer as well as the end user. Code doesn't need to just compile: It should communicate clearly, coherently, and effectively as well. Both Swift and Xcode support meta-development tasks with technologies that assist you from debugging to documentation. This chapter introduces developer-facing language features including printing, mirroring, Quick Look, and Quick Help. Each of these is a first-class element worthy of your interest and development time.

The features discussed in this chapter cover the gamut of output scenarios that range from user-facing write operations to developer-facing debugging support, particularly the latter. This chapter surveys these technologies and explores how you can precisely build feedback and output to fit your development and debugging needs.

Basic Printing

Swift's `print` function offers a simple way to display nearly any value. Here's a simple example that outputs "Hello World":

```
// Outputs "Hello World" with line feed
print("Hello World")
```

As this example demonstrates, you call `print`, supply an argument—in this case, a string—and let the function output a representation of that value. You can print any value, whether numbers, structures, enumerations, or so forth. Simply wrap the print request in parentheses, as in the following examples:

```
print(23) // prints 23

print(CGPoint(x: 50, y:20)) // prints (50.0, 20.0)

enum Coin{case Heads, Tails}
print(Coin.Heads) // prints Coins.Heads

func plus1(x: Int) {x + 1}
print(plus1) // prints (Function)
```

Some printed values (for example, `Coins.Heads`) provide more meaningful output in their default form than others (for example, `(Function)`). Apple continues to improve default print output in each Swift update.

When the content of the default output is not suitable for your needs, you can customize it. Swift has evolved quickly with ever-improving representation. Nearly all standard `print` results are now usable, if not always perfect.

Printing Multiple Items

Swift supports multiple `print` parameters. Here's what those `print` declarations look like:

```
public func print(items: Any..., separator: String = default,
    terminator: String = default)

public func print<Target: OutputStreamType>(items: Any...,
    separator: String = default, terminator: String = default,
    inout toStream output: Target)
```

In each call, the `items` label followed by the `Any...` type indicates that the function accepts variadic (that is, a variable number of) arguments. This means you can print several values at once:

```
print(value1, value2, value3)
```

The `Any` item type means you can mix and match types for a heterogeneous argument list:

```
print("String:", myStringValue, "Int:", myIntValue, "Float:", myFloatValue)
```

Unlike `printf` or `NSLog`, `print` does not use a format string and arguments to create its output. This may seem inflexible, but it offers greater runtime safety. Although the default implementation doesn't offer output precision and alignment features, you can access those through the `String` class (via a format-based initializer) or by defining custom protocols and standalone functions that manipulate values for printing.

For example, you might extend the `ConvertibleNumberType` protocol in Chapter 4, "Closures and Functions," to add a precision feature:

```
public extension ConvertibleNumberType {
    public func toPrecision(digits: Int) -> String {
```

```
      if digits == 0 {return "\(lrint(self.doubleValue))"}
      let factor = pow(10.0, Double(digits))
      let trunc = round(self.doubleValue * factor) / factor
      var result = String(trunc)
      while result.rangeOfString(".")?
          .startIndex.distanceTo(result.endIndex) < (digits + 1) {
          result += "0"
      }
      return result
  }
}
```

You can easily expand this concept to introduce padding, hex/octal/binary representation, and other standard formatting features.

Adding Item Separators

The optional `separator` parameter adds a text string between each pair of printed items. The following call prints out a comma-delineated list of integers:

```
print(1, 5, 2, 3, 5, 6, separator:", ") // 1, 5, 2, 3, 5, 6
```

Use the `separator` argument to provide a natural visual break between printed items. This argument defaults to a single space (" ") when not otherwise specified.

String Interpolation

Swift enables you to embed value output in strings with *string interpolation*. Supply a value or expression and wrap it within backslash-escaped parentheses for use in printing or creating strings to supply to other consumers. Here's an example of what interpolation looks like using basic values:

```
let value = 23
print("Value: \(value)") // prints Value: 23
let square = value * value
print("The square of \(value) is \(square)")
    // prints The square of 23 is 529
```

Alternatively, skip the intermediate variable and insert a simple expression:

```
print("The square of \(value) is \(value * value)")
```

The multiple-output example earlier in this chapter uses the following call:

```
print("String:", myStringValue, "Int:", myIntValue, "Float:", myFloatValue)
```

And produces this output, which is not particularly beautiful:

```
String: Hello Int: 42 Float: 2.0
```

The result is not improved by adding comma separators:

```
print("String:", myStringValue, "Int:", myIntValue,
    "Float:", myFloatValue, separator: ", ")
// String:, Hello, Int:, 42, Float:, 2.0
```

String interpolation shows its strength in the following tweak:

```
print("String: \(myStringValue)", "Int: \(myIntValue)",
    "Float: \(myFloatValue)", separator: ", ")
String: Hello, Int: 42, Float: 2.0
```

The `print` statement chunks labels and values together using string interpolation, and then applies the separator to the label/value pairs.

Use embedded expressions for very short, very precise insertions. Complex string interpolation provides a good way to confuse a compiler that has yet to achieve notable maturity and stability:

```
let count = "hello".characters.count
print("The count is \(count)")
```

Interpolated material inserted in a string matches the output you expect from printing. When you customize the way an instance represents itself, that description is used for interpolation as well as print output.

Controlling Line Feeds

By default, `print` appends a newline and writes to standard output. The `terminator` parameter controls a termination string. Its default value is `"\n"`, a standard newline. To print on a single line without that carriage return, assign the `print` call's `terminator` parameter to `""` or any other non-newline string. The following example joins the output from the `Hello` and `World` print requests into a line of output that ends with a single carriage return:

```
// Outputs "Hello World" followed by carriage return
print("Hello ", terminator: "")
print("World")
```

Skip carriage returns to blend multiple results together on a single line. `if` statements let you combine optional elements together. In the following snippet, a view displays tags, stored constraint counts, and external constraint references when values are significant:

```
print("[\(debugViewName) \(frame)", terminator: "") // start of line
if tag != 0 { // optional
    print(" tag: \(tag)", terminator: "")
}
```

```
if viewConstraints.count > 0 { // optional
    print(" constraints: \(viewConstraints.count)", terminator: "")
}
if constraintsReferencingView.count > 0 { // optional
    print(" references: \(constraintsReferencingView.count)",
    terminator: "")
}
print("]") // end of line
```

This next example shows how you might use the `terminator` parameter to sequentially build and combine labels and results. This snippet pulls out the long string initializer into its own `print` statement:

```
// Create star output
for n in 1...5 {
    print("\(n): ", terminator: "")
    print(String(count: n, repeatedValue: Character("*")))
}
```

This code produces labeled stars:

```
1: *
2: **
3: ***
4: ****
5: *****
```

IRC servers often require you to send both \r and \n to terminate each line. If you're writing a client, you could automate this by tweaking the `terminator` argument like so:

```
print(myText, terminator: "\r\n", toStream: &myIRCStream)
```

This example uses a custom stream destination for the IRC communications. You'll read about output streams like this in the next section.

Recipe: Printing to Custom Destinations

To redirect `print` output from its default `stdout` destination, create a construct that conforms to the `OutputStreamType` protocol. This protocol requires a single `write` function, which you implement to send string data to an output destination of your choice:

```
protocol OutputStreamType {
    /// Append the given `string` to this stream.
    mutating func write(string: String)
}
```

Here's a trivial example that uses `fputs` to write to `stderr`:

```
/// StderrStream conforms to OutputStreamType
public struct StderrStream: OutputStreamType {
    static var shared = StderrStream()
    public func write(string: String) {
        fputs(string, stderr)
    }
}
```

Use a custom standard error output stream by incorporating it in `print` statements. This snippet creates a new instance and then prints, supplying values to both the `toStream` and terminator arguments:

```
// Print "Hello World" to stderr
print("Hello ", terminator: "", toStream: &StderrStream.shared)
print("World", toStream: &StderrStream.shared)
```

This example declared `shared` as a mutable static class property. Constructs that conform to `OutputStreamType` must be mutable as each stream is passed as an `inout` argument to `print`. Use the `inout` prefix (`&`) to annotate streams in your `print` requests.

An `inout` parameter enables Swift to modify values using a copy-and-write-back mechanism. It's required for printing because output streams may mutate their targets. You encounter this mutability when you print directly to strings, as you'll read about in the following section.

Printing to Strings

The `OutputStreamType` protocol is adopted by Swift's `String` type. This conformance means you can use `print` to output to strings as well as to file streams. Here's an example that prints `Hello World` to a string:

```
var s = ""
print("Hello World", toStream: &s) // s is "Hello World\n"
print(s)
```

When this `print(s)` statement executes, it writes two carriage returns. The first is added when printing to the string; the second is added when the string is printed to `stdout`. To avoid that extra line, skip the newline either when constructing the string or when printing it:

```
s = ""
print("Hello ", terminator: "", toStream: &s)
print("World", terminator: "", toStream: &s)
print(s) // "Hello World" plus newline
```

More commonly, you'll want to use the inverse of the preceding example. Instead of suppressing new lines, add carriage returns on each print request to build a line-delimited log. Here's an example of what that approach might look like:

```
var log = ""
print("\(NSDate()): Hello World", toStream: &log)
print("\(NSDate()): Hello World", toStream: &log)
print("\(NSDate()): Hello World", toStream: &log)
print(log, terminator: "")
```

In this example, the `log` variable grows with each call. The results can be printed (as shown here), saved to a file, or sent to a consumer such as a text view. You can even use a property observer like `didSet` to update the text view each time `print` is called. Combining string interpolation with string printing gives you a simple and powerful way to iteratively grow text in your data.

Printing to Custom Output Streams

Recipe 2-1 expands the custom output stream that only printed to `stderr` to a more flexible implementation. Predefined `stderr()` and `stdout()` constructors enable you to pull ready-made streams. This listing builds two public output streams for these typical use cases.

This class can also initialize with a path and then print to that file. An optional `append` parameter (which defaults to `false`) prevents rewriting the file on open:

```
if var testStream = OutputStream(
    path: ("~/Desktop/output.txt" as NSString).stringByExpandingTildeInPath) {
    print("Testing custom output", toStream: &testStream)
    print("Hello ",terminator:"", toStream: &testStream)
    print("World", toStream: &testStream)
    print("Output sent to \(testStream.path)")
} else {
    print("Failed to create custom output")
}
```

This recipe is built around a class implementation. It adds a crucial deinitializer that closes open file pointers if they were used to construct an instance. This is a good example of a place where `deinit` wins out over `defer` statements. The lifetime of an output stream normally extends long beyond a single scope, which is the limiting factor for `defer` clean-up.

Recipe 2-1   **Configurable Output Stream**

```
public class OutputStream: OutputStreamType {
    let stream: UnsafeMutablePointer<FILE> // Target stream
    var path: String? = nil // File path if used

    // Create with stream
    public init(_ stream: UnsafeMutablePointer<FILE>) {
        self.stream = stream
    }
```

```
    // Create with output file
    public init?(var path: String, append: Bool = false) {
        path = (path as NSString).stringByExpandingTildeInPath
        if append {
            stream = fopen(path, "a")
        } else {
            stream = fopen(path, "w")
        }
        if stream == nil {return nil}
        self.path = path
    }

    // stderr
    public static func stderr() -> OutputStream {
        return OutputStream(Darwin.stderr)
    }

    // stdout
    public static func stdout() -> OutputStream {
        return OutputStream(Darwin.stdout)
    }

    // Conform to OutputStreamType
    public func write(string: String) {
        fputs(string, stream)
    }

    // Clean up open FILE
    deinit {
        if path != nil {fclose(stream)}
    }
}

// Pre-built instances
public var errStream = OutputStream.stderr()
public var stdStream = OutputStream.stdout()
```

Recipe: Printing and String Formats

Cocoa's standard logger is NSLog. Available in the Foundation framework, the NSLog utility function uses string formatting to construct log messages that are sent to standard error and the system console. Unlike print, NSLog supports standard %-delimited format specifiers as well as Apple-supplied extensions. Apple's *String Programming Guide* details its support for and extensions to the IEEE printf specification (see http://pubs.opengroup.org/onlinepubs/009695399/functions/printf.html).

You pass NSLog a format string followed by a variadic list of Objective-C-compatible parameters:

```
NSLog("Dictionary: %@, Double: %0.2f", ["Hello":3], 2.7)
```

The parameters map to specifiers embedded within the format string. The result is a string that combines the format specifiers and the arguments into coherent text.

Swift and Format Specifiers

Swift supports format specifiers as one way the standard library offers to create and initialize strings:

```
/// Returns a `String` object initialized by using a given
/// format string as a template into which the remaining argument
/// values are substituted according to the user's default locale.
init(format: String, arguments: [CVarArgType])
```

This initializer enables you to build a custom SWLog logger that mimics NSLog. Recipe 2-2 combines string formatting with Recipe 2-1's errStream to create a minimal stderr log-alike: It prints to standard error output but doesn't mirror output to the system console. This implementation also minimizes the printed time shown for each log entry to just minutes, seconds, and fractions of a second rather than the exhaustive date output provided by NSLog. For example, this:

```
SWLog("Hello world") // no args
SWLog("Formatted double: %2.3f", 5.2) // one arg
SWLog("Double plus string %2.3f, %@", 5.2, "Hello world") // multiple
```

Produces this:

```
55:40.706: Hello world
55:40.707: Formatted double: 5.200
55:40.708: Double plus string 5.200, Hello world
```

Format Limitations

You cannot use format arguments to express Swift constructs like enumerations, functions, and structs as they do not conform to the CVarArgType protocol. For example, this line results in a compile-time error:

```
SWLog("Struct: %@, Int: %03zd", CGPoint(x: 50, y: 20), 5)
```

However, you can add Swift string interpolation to format string initialization:

```
SWLog("Struct: \(CGPoint(x: 50, y: 20)), Int: %03zd", 5)
```

If your interpolated material contains anything that looks like a % token, formatting may break and possibly crash your application. It is ridiculously easy to create potential format errors that pass the compiler smell test but crash when run. Compile and execute the following example to see this issue in action:

```
let formatSpecifierInsert = "%s %ld"
let s = String(format:
    "Hello \(formatSpecifierInsert) %@", arguments: ["world"])
```

This is probably not the outcome you're hoping for.

In nearly every case, Swift printing and string interpolation is safer than using format specifiers as Swift can determine safety at compile time.

Conditional Compilation

Recipe 2-2 differentiates logging output between debug and release configurations. The build configuration test in the `SWLog` function uses command-line flags for conditional compilation (`#if DEBUG`). The function prints only when the `DEBUG` flag is set.

Figure 2-1 shows how you can add the `DEBUG` flag. Navigate to TARGETS > *Your Target* > Build Settings > Other Swift Flags. Select the Debug configuration and add `-D DEBUG`. Swift detects this flag when it compiles and uses it to include or exclude material marked within `#if` guards.

Figure 2-1   Differentiate between Debug and Release configurations by adding flags in Build Settings.

> **Note**
>
> You cannot add build configurations to playgrounds. Although you can use a predefined configuration suite for conditional playground builds, you cannot add compile-time tests that depend on developer-defined flags. Built-in tests include target OS (OSX, iOS, watchOS, tvOS) and target architecture (x86_64, arm, arm64, i386). You can combine tests using the || or operator, which is handy when you want to create cross-platform code that differentiates not just between OSX and iOS but also between the (more iOS-like) newer platforms.

Recipe 2-2   **Custom Logging**

```
internal func BuildSimpleTimeFormatter() -> NSDateFormatter {
    let dateFormatter = NSDateFormatter()
    // Alternatively pass mmssSSS. Extraneous punctuation is ignored
    dateFormatter.dateFormat =
        NSDateFormatter.dateFormatFromTemplate("mm:ss:SSS",
            options: 0, locale: NSLocale.currentLocale())
    return dateFormatter
}
internal let dateFormatter = BuildSimpleTimeFormatter()

public func SWLog(format: String, _ args: CVarArgType...) {
    #if DEBUG
        // Prints only for DEBUG build configurations
        let timeString = dateFormatter.stringFromDate(NSDate())
        print("\(timeString):",
            String(format: format, arguments: args), toStream: &errStream)
    #endif
}
```

Debug Printing

Swift's debugPrint() function offers a developer-facing alternative to the user-facing print() function. Unlike normal print commands, debug print requests show instance representations that are most suitable for debugging. With debug printing, "1..<6" becomes "Range(1..<6)", and the grinning face created with UnicodeScalar(0x1f601) becomes "\u{0001F601}". Each result offers additional utility that supports your development.

Custom Stream Output

Both print and debugPrint enable you to establish custom representations and integrate them into Swift constructs. This is not to say that Swift's default output is unacceptable. Consider the following Point structure:

```
struct Point {
    var x = 0.0
    var y = 0.0
}
```

The default description for instances of this struct looks like this: "Point(x: 1.0, y: 1.0)". This output string includes both a type name and current property values. In Swift 2, nearly every construct presents with an acceptably readable representation. However acceptable, that output carries no semantics. This string may not match the user's expectations of a traditional (x, y) point presentation nor support a developer who might require additional information computed from the point values.

Swift enables you to build use-specific representations for logging, playground previews, LLDB output, and so forth. Each technology is built using protocols. For streams and string interpolation, the `print` and `debugPrint` functions task two developer-customizable protocols: `CustomStringConvertible` and `CustomDebugStringConvertible`. As the names suggest, these protocols describe behaviors that convert values to string presentations. Each uses a custom text representation property—`description` for `print` and `debugDescription` for `debugPrint`:

```
/// A textual representation of `self`.
var description: String { get }
```

```
/// A textual representation of `self`, suitable for debugging.
var debugDescription: String { get }
```

If you implement one protocol and not the other, each one falls back to the other. So if you print and there's only a debug description, it will print the debug description in favor of the default output and vice versa. Here's how the `print` fallback cascade works:

- If an instance conforms to `Streamable`, call `instance.writeTo(s)` on an empty string s and print s.
- If an instance conforms to `CustomStringConvertible`, return the instance's description.
- If the instance conforms to `CustomDebugStringConvertible`, return the instance's debugDescription.
- Return the value supplied by the Swift standard library.

The `debugPrint` fallback cascade reverses the priority of the first three bullets. The textual representation uses the following preferences order: `CustomDebugStringConvertible`, `CustomStringConvertible`, `Streamable`. If none of these conformances are available, Swift uses a default text representation.

The following snippet implements the `Point` structure and demonstrates conformance for both `CustomStringConvertible` and `CustomDebugStringConvertible`:

```
struct Point: CustomStringConvertible, CustomDebugStringConvertible {
    var x = 0.0
    var y = 0.0
    var description: String {return "(\(x), \(y))"}
    var theta: Double {return atan2(y, x)}
    var degrees: Double {return theta * 180.0 / M_PI}
    var debugDescription: String {
        let places = pow(10.0, 3)
        let trunc = round(theta * places) / places
        return "(\(x), \(y)) \(degrees)°, \(trunc)"
```

```
        }
    }
    var p = Point(x:1.0, y:1.0)
    print(p) // (1.0, 1.0)
    debugPrint(p) // (1.0, 1.0) 45.0°, 0.785
```

Recipe: Postfix Printing

When developing and debugging, I find it handy to use a special operator that prints a value in-place. This operator passes through whatever value it's printing so it can easily be added, tested, and discarded on the fly:

```
let x = 5
let y = 3
let z = x*** + y // prints 5
let v = (((3 + 4) * 5)*** + 1)*** // prints 35, then 36
let w = 1 + z*** // prints 8, w is now 9
```

Recipe 2-3 implements two versions of the operator, one with three stars that uses standard printing and one with four that uses debug printing instead. Embed the operator to the right of any expression you wish to display. This star-delimited approach enables you to use global find-and-replace to remove or comment out print requests. As you see in Recipe 2-3, the operator implementation takes a DEBUG flag into account (like Recipe 2-2 did), preventing stray items from printing in release builds.

Nearly everyone I've shown this operator to reacts with noticeable horror, but its utility cannot be denied. It's a handy item to have in your development toolbox, especially for playground use.

Recipe 2-3   **Adding Postfix Printing Operators**

```
postfix operator *** {}
public postfix func *** <T>(object: T) -> T {
    #if DEBUG
        print(object)
    #endif
    return object
}

postfix operator **** {}
public postfix func **** <T>(object: T) -> T {
    #if DEBUG
        debugPrint(object)
    #endif
    return object
}
```

Quick Looks

Xcode and Swift implement two kinds of Quick Look technologies. *Quick Look for Custom Types* offer a way for Xcode to preview NSObject-based type instances and present them to the developer in a clear, visual, and inspectable form. Playground Quick Look (CustomPlaygroundQuickLookable) extends preview support to Swift constructs. The Swift-specific version is used only in playgrounds. The general form can be used in both playgrounds and with the Xcode debugger.

Quick Look for Custom Types

Quick Look for Custom Types was first introduced in Xcode 5.1. The Xcode debugger enables you to view variables in pop-up displays, creating a graphical rendering of object contents. Figure 2-2 shows this Quick Look technology in action.

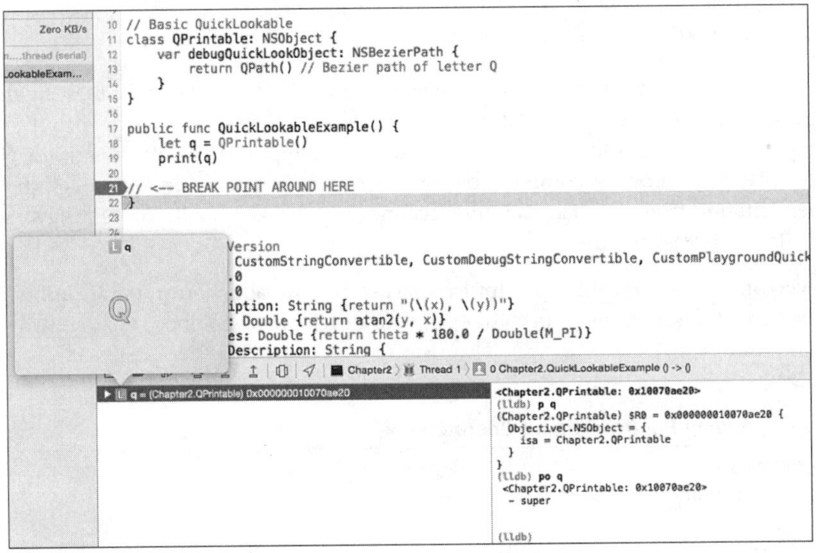

Figure 2-2   Debugger Quick Looks transform objects to custom visual representations.

Add Quick Look by implementing a debugQuickLookObject method. (There is not an associated protocol.) Your classes must be marked @objc / and descend from NSObject, which makes Quick Look of limited use for Swift development. (Your internal/public classes will be @objc by default, but private classes won't be.) The method must return a valid Quick Look type: images, cursors, colors, Bezier paths, locations, views, strings (and attributed strings), data, URLs, or Sprite Kit classes. Apple details these types in its *Quick Look for Custom Types in the Xcode Debugger* support document. Search the web for the most recent version of this document.

In this example, the QPrintable class includes a single method: the debugQuickLookObject required for Quick Look previews. It returns a Bezier path consisting of the letter Q. The p (print expression) and po (print object) commands issued in the debugger confirm that a class instance otherwise consists solely of a pointer (isa) to an NSObject superclass. When you select an instance in the debugger and press the spacebar, Xcode renders and displays the associated Quick Look to a pop-up.

Apple writes in *Quick Look for Custom Types*, "Because your debugQuickLookObject method runs in the debugger, when you are inside your paused application, it is best to be economical in your method implementation. Write as little code as needed to represent your variable's state as a useful visual graphic. Remember that running code when in a paused application can have side effects. If possible, cache the item you want to return."

Quick Looks for Custom Types in Playgrounds

Standard Quick Look also renders in playgrounds (see Figure 2-3), where it is accessed by the Quick Look button. As this figure demonstrates, Quick Look output can also be embedded into the timeline (between lines 11 and 12) using value history panes. As with the debugger, playground-sourced standard Quick Looks are limited to NSObject descendants. Fortunately, Swift now has a Quick Look protocol more suitable for non-Objective-C constructs.

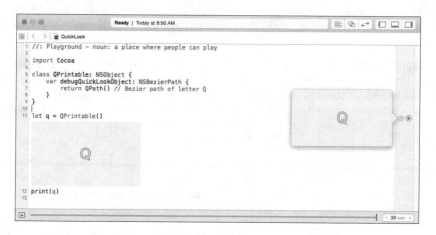

Figure 2-3   Playgrounds detect and display standard object Quick Looks.

Playground Quick Looks

Swift playgrounds can render any construct that provides Quick Look compliance. Many system-supplied structures, classes, and enumerations already offer built-in implementations. Figure 2-4 shows a playground displaying some of these ready-made Quick Looks in its timeline.

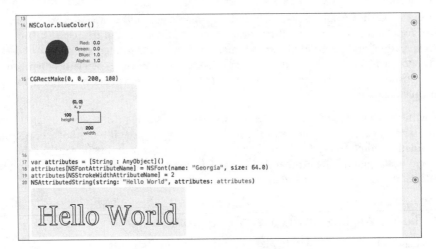

Figure 2-4   Many basic classes provide built-in Quick Looks.

From top to bottom, this playground first presents a color instance. This comprises a swatch and an RGBA channel breakdown. Next, you see a CGRect structure. Its display includes an origin along with height and width values. A proportionate preview enables you to visualize the rectangle's shape. Below that you find an attributed string with a custom font and stroke pattern.

I particularly like the output for CGRect. It provides one of my favorite built-in Quick Look previews. I cannot think of many circumstances in which you need to visualize what a rectangle looks like (think about it), but the care and layout in this overview is outstanding. The presentation provides a clear design that relates the structure's fields with its inherent geometry. Notable details include multicolored fonts that differentiate labels and values and an outline with a small dot that emphasizes the rectangle's origin.

This representation makes me want to up my game for my own Quick Look previews. Your Quick Looks can be as complex or as simple as needed (or wanted). You may want to reevaluate priorities if you find yourself spending more time building an exciting Quick Look (that your end users will never see) than on the actual class the Quick Look represents.

Creating Custom Quick Looks for Playgrounds

When your instance does not provide a built-in Quick Look option or you want to enhance a Quick Look to something more elegant, add custom support. Swift makes it easy to create Quick Look items that express constructs as images, paths, sprites, and other representations. Just conform to CustomPlaygroundQuickLookable and implement a customPlaygroundQuickLook() function that returns a member of the PlaygroundQuickLook enumeration.

It's always easiest to leverage an existing built-in Quick Look for custom constructs. In Figure 2-5, the Point class redirects to the similarly named `PlaygroundQuickLook.Point` enumeration. This abstract structure expresses a one-to-one correspondence with a built-in enumeration. That happy coincidence doesn't always work out so perfectly, but you can usually build at least a string or an image that represents your constructs in an expressive and semantically valuable way.

```
5  struct Point: CustomPlaygroundQuickLookable {
6      var x = 0.0
7      var y = 0.0
8      var description: String {return "(\(x), \(y))"}
9      var theta: Double {return atan2(y, x)}
10     var degrees: Double {return theta * 180.0 / Double(M_PI)}
11     var debugDescription: String {
12         let places = pow(10.0, 3)
13         let trunc = round(theta * places) / places
14         return "(\(x), \(y)) \(degrees)°, \(trunc)"
15     }
16
17     func customPlaygroundQuickLook() -> PlaygroundQuickLook {
18         return QuickLookObject.Point(x, y)
19     }
20 }
21
22 let p = Point(x: -3, y: 6)
```

Figure 2-5   This playground Quick Look is created around the built-in Point presentation.

Built-in Quick Look Types

Here is the current list of Quick Look types and the associated values they support:

```
/// The sum of types that can be used as a quick look representation.
enum PlaygroundQuickLook {
    case Text(String)
    case Int(Int64)
    case UInt(UInt64)
    case Float(Float32)
    case Double(Float64)
    case Image(Any)
    case Sound(Any)
    case Color(Any)
    case BezierPath(Any)
    case AttributedString(Any)
    case Rectangle(Float64, Float64, Float64, Float64)
    case Point(Float64, Float64)
    case Size(Float64, Float64)
```

```
    case Logical(Bool)
    case Range(UInt64, UInt64)
    case View(Any)
    case Sprite(Any)
    case URL(String)
}
```

You must return an enumeration instance populated with a value from your conforming type. As you can see from this list, there's a large overlap between `PlaygroundQuickLook` support and types that can be returned for Quick Look for Custom Types.

As a rule, prefer established `PlaygroundQuickLook` types when available. If you require a custom Quick Look, create a presentation such as an image, a shape, or a description and return a populated enumeration instance, as in Figure 2-6. This example replaces the point enumeration returned by `customPlaygroundQuickLook()` in Figure 2-5 with `PlaygroundQuickLook.BezierPath(path)`.

Figure 2-6   This custom Quick Look returns a path that points from the origin to a point.

The arrow path is meant to represent a vector from the origin to the point instance. A full graph with axes and scale ticks would provide an even more valuable visualization. (You would need to build an image and return `PlaygroundQuickLook.Image(image)` in that case.) Always weigh the costs and rewards of custom Quick Looks against the development support returns over time.

Third-Party Rendering

Figure 2-6's crude arrow represents a poor standard for custom playground Quick Looks. Third-party libraries and web services enable you to effectively visualize Swift constructs, as you see in Figure 2-7. This playground includes a value history Quick Look established by Google Charts. Services like Google, Wolfram Alpha, and others provide well-tested, easy-to-leverage tools that limit the effort you invest in rendering instances.

Web-based rendering involves risks such as connection errors and delays. Always prepare fall-back visualizations with off-site presentations, as you see in Figure 2-7 on line 35. Also consider the loads you will place on external servers if playgrounds continually update after edits.

Consider the real costs of tasking APIs with rate limits or pay-per-call access. You can disable real-time updates by requiring manual execution. Use the pop-up found at the upper left of the playground debug area. The debug area is normally shown at the bottom of the playground and can be opened with the View > Debug Area menu.

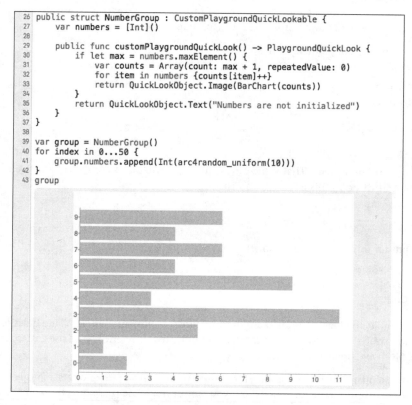

```
26  public struct NumberGroup : CustomPlaygroundQuickLookable {
27      var numbers = [Int]()
28
29      public func customPlaygroundQuickLook() -> PlaygroundQuickLook {
30          if let max = numbers.maxElement() {
31              var counts = Array(count: max + 1, repeatedValue: 0)
32              for item in numbers {counts[item]++}
33              return QuickLookObject.Image(BarChart(counts))
34          }
35          return QuickLookObject.Text("Numbers are not initialized")
36      }
37  }
38
39  var group = NumberGroup()
40  for index in 0...50 {
41      group.numbers.append(Int(arc4random_uniform(10)))
42  }
43  group
```

Figure 2-7   This Quick Look presentation was built using Google Charts. Although Charts remains active for use, it was officially deprecated in 2012.

Visualization libraries provide another worthy alternative with additional caveats. For stand-alone playground use, they must offer raw Swift sources, which Xcode compiles into the running playground page. Otherwise, you must build a workspace with a custom module and co-locate the playground within that workspace to access data presentations. Both approaches enhance your playground value presentations, regardless of whether you proceed with service-based or library-based rendering.

Using Dump Functions

Swift supports an additional mechanism for reviewing constructs. The dump() function prints to output streams, just like print() and debugPrint(), but it creates structure-specific results. Its output represents an item's mirror—that is, the description and components that represent a type, including its logical children. Mirroring functions and protocols create an alternative to simple logging by presenting a structure for inspection.

Here, for example, is a point structure:

```
struct Point {
    var x = 0.0
    var y = 0.0
    var theta: Double {return atan2(y, x)}
    var degrees: Double {return theta * 180.0 / Double(M_PI)}
}
```

You call dump() on a value. That value can be any type, whether a construct such as a class, an enum, or a struct or, in this example, an instance:

```
let p = Point(x: -3.0, y: 6.0)
dump(p)
```

The output for this request is as follows:

```
∇ Chapter2.Point
  - x: -3.0
  - y: 6.0
```

In this example, the logical children are the structure's x and y properties. Value types (enums, tuples, and structs) are automatically labeled and indented. Reference types use a more traditional Objective-C-style presentation.

Here is the standard library declaration for dump. As you can see, dump offers a fairly comprehensive list of customizable properties, but you almost never use these directly. You either dump from code (for example, using dump(x)) or you print from the debugger, as in Figure 2-8:

```
/// Dump an object's contents using its mirror to the specified output stream.
func dump<T, TargetStream: OutputStreamType>(x: T,
    inout _ targetStream: TargetStream,
    name: String? = default,
    indent: Int = default,
    maxDepth: Int = default,
    maxItems: Int = default) -> T
```

```
16
17  public func DumpExamples() {
18      let p = Point(x:-3.0, y: 6.0)
19      dump(p)
20      // <-- add break here and po p
21  }
22
```

```
▽  ➡  ▷  △  ⊥  ⊥  ⟐  ⟁  ■ Chapter2 ⟩ ■ Thread 1 ⟩ ■ 0 Chapter2.DumpExamples () -> ()

▶ ⬛ p (Chapter2.Point)                                      ▾ Chapter2.Point
                                                              – x: -3.0
                                                              – y: 6.0
                                                            (lldb)  po p
                                                            ▾ Chapter2.Point
                                                              – x : -3.0
                                                              – y : 6.0

                                                            (lldb)
```

Figure 2-8   Using po with Swift structures leverages the output from a construct's mirror.

Building Custom Mirrors

By default, dump() describes the structures of your Swift constructs. That information is helpful but limited. Custom mirrors enable you to expand output to represent the content of your instances *and* additional semantics. Consider Figure 2-9. The debugger output displays both the default dump() contents and enhanced object po / expr -o output. In addition to showing the raw x and y values, these results contain derived information: the angle of the point relative to a zero origin in both radians and degrees.

```
27  // Custom mirror
28  extension Point: CustomReflectable {
29      public func customMirror() -> Mirror {
30          return Mirror(self, children: [
31              "point": description,
32              "theta": theta,
33              "degrees": "\(degrees)°"
34              ])
35      }
36  }
37
38  func DumpExamples() {
39      let p = Point(x:-3.0, y: 6.0)
40      dump(p)
41      // <-- add break here and po p
42  }
43
```

```
▽  ➡  ▷  △  ⊥  ⊥  ⟐  ⟁  ■ Chapter2 ⟩ ■ Thread 1 ⟩ ■ 0 Chapter2.DumpExamples () -> ()

▶ ⬛ p (Chapter2.Point)                                      ▾ Chapter2.Point
                                                              – x: -3.0
                                                              – y: 6.0
                                                            (lldb) po p
                                                            ▾ Chapter2.Point
                                                              – point : "(-3.0, 6.0)"
                                                              – theta : 2.0344439357957
                                                              – degrees : "116.565051177078°"
```

Figure 2-9   Adding a custom mirror enables you to create semantically rich debugger results. Use p or expr (without the -o argument) for a complete list of fields and values.

Custom mirrors were introduced in Swift 2. Developer-designed mirrors enable you to represent both raw content and the semantic meaning of that content in terms of your application. You saw an example (involving `CustomStringConvertible` and `CustomDebugString-Convertible`) that demonstrated a transformation between structure and semantics earlier in this chapter. In the absence of custom mirrors, output works like this: Conformance to `CustomDebugStringConvertible` is most preferred, followed by `CustomStringConvertible`. When neither conformance is present, descriptions mimic Objective-C class output.

Mirrors offer two main differences. First, unlike with custom `print` and `debugPrint` output, you generally consume mirror output in the debugger or a playground and not in files or strings. Second, you typically present custom mirror output as a dictionary instead of as a string.

> **Note**
>
> Before exploring custom mirrors in the playground, comment out any custom Quick Look work you may have added. The one tends to overwhelm the other.

Build mirrors by conforming to `CustomReflectable`. As with custom stream descriptions, be flexible. Your mirror needn't adhere to the underlying data structure that powers your instance. You can add any description and information that supports understanding your construct in a way that speaks to you as a developer.

Implement `CustomReflectable` by adding a `customMirror` method. Return a `Mirror` initialized with the value you're reflecting and a dictionary composed of keys and values that describe the instance. The following reflection implementation, which you also see in Figure 2-9, breaks out the point, the angle in radians, and in degrees:

```
extension Point: CustomReflectable {
    public func customMirror() -> Mirror {
        return Mirror(self, children: [
            "point": description,
            "theta": theta,
            "degrees": "\(degrees)°"
            ])
    }
}
```

The dictionary created by this example provides greater semantic understanding of how the `Point` structure is used within an app. By raising the abstraction, this reflection is more pertinent to specific development and debugging details instead of just dumping raw values.

Recursive Reflection

There is a point where the built-in system with its mirror dictionaries doesn't really get you where you want to go. The best example of this is when you're working with a construct that uses virtual children, such as with bit flags. A bit flag is essentially an integer. It combines bit-keyed flags into a single value. There are no "real" children involved. All the semantics are embedded into the internal raw value. At the same time, you might want to create a mirror that breaks out the individual flags and represents them as part of the mirror hierarchy.

At this time, the best you can do really is to build an embedded array or dictionary in your `customMirror` implementation and present those children as strings or numbers. Although the standard library defines a `_MirrorType` protocol, this avenue is not generally accessible to developers.

Here's an approach you might use to pull out flags from the underlying integer. This method enumerates through a human-consumable array of strings, using each string's index to test a bit flag. As shown here, pass the resulting array of collected strings to a mirror dictionary to provide a more meaningful presentation:

```
public var names: [String] {
    var nameArray = [String]()
    let featureStrings = ["Alarm System", "CD Stereo",
        "Chrome Wheels", "Pin Stripes", "Leather Interior",
        "Undercoating", "Window Tint"]
    for (flagLessOne, string) in featureStrings.enumerate()
        where self.contains(Features(rawValue: 1<<(flagLessOne + 1))) {
        nameArray.append(string)
    }
    return nameArray
}
```

For example, instead of `rawValue: 34`, you'd see `[Alarm System, Leather Interior]`.

Presumably at some point in the future, Swift may support bit flag decomposition mirrors the way it automatically creates human-consumable output for enumeration members. Until then, this approach helps transition those raw values to a semantically rich member list.

Building Basic Mirror Descriptions Using Protocol Conformance

Improve your default mirror output with a simple trick I learned from developer guru Mike Ash. Consider the following otherwise identical classes. The second conforms to a protocol called `DefaultReflectable`, while the first does not:

```
public class NonConformantClass {
    var x = 42; var y = "String"; var z = 22.5
}
public class ConformantClass: DefaultReflectable {
    var x = 42; var y = "String"; var z = 22.5
}
```

As you construct and inspect instances, you see the difference. The first shows a monolithic `NonConformantClass` result in its mirror and print output. The second breaks down its class members for greater clarity. It presents the instance's individual properties:

```
NonConformantClass() // Chapter2.NonConformantClass
ConformantClass()    // ConformantClass(x=42 y=String z=22.5)
```

You basically get this behavior for free through the magic of protocol extensions. Declaring conformance is all it takes to leverage this protocol and the description property it implements. Recipe 2-4 implements the `DefaultReflectable` protocol, whose extension provides the default behavior.

Recipe 2-4   Adding Default Mirroring Through Protocols

```
// Coerce to label/value output where possible
public protocol DefaultReflectable: CustomStringConvertible {}
extension DefaultReflectable {

    // Construct the description
    internal func DefaultDescription<T>(instance: T) -> String {
        // Establish mirror
        let mirror = Mirror(reflecting: instance)

        // Build label/value pairs where possible, otherwise
        // use default print output
        let chunks = mirror.children.map {
            (label: String?, value: Any) -> String in
            if let label = label {
                return "\(label)=\(value)"
            } else {
                return "\(value)"
            }
        }

        // Construct and return subject type / (chunks) string
        if chunks.count > 0 {
            let chunksString = chunks.joinWithSeparator(", ")
            return "\(mirror.subjectType)(\(chunksString))"
        } else {
            return "\(instance)"
        }
    }

    // Conform to CustomStringConvertible
    public var description: String {return DefaultDescription(self)}
}
```

Adding Header Docs

Printing, mirroring, and Quick Looks all communicate developer-facing representations of application values. Quick Help augments that communication by adding intent to that mix. You leverage Xcode's built-in documentation system by adding Quick Help–compliant annotation to your code. This commenting technology augments your documentation. It creates well-structured usage information for yourself, for future-you (looking back at a project from the distance of time), for members of your team, and for any other consumer of your code.

Quick Help offers concise in-line reference docs for symbols, build settings, and interface objects, as well as classes, structures, enums, and their members. Quick Help annotates your code to create custom details that display via pop-ups (Option-click symbols) and the Quick Help inspector (View > Utilities > Show Quick Help Inspector).

> **Note**
>
> Quick Help enables you to document individual local constants and variables. Although Cocoa conventions encourage you to use human-readable names instead of i, j, k and x, y, z, it can be valuable to add Quick Help comments to remind yourself further down in the algorithm what you wanted to store in that symbol.

This is where you document usage, parameters, expectations, and preconditions. For example, you might note that some function `Requires: string is non-empty` or `Postcondition: memory is allocated and initialized to zero`. Specify any edge cases and list your return value types. Make sure to mention any side effects the code might produce, as well as whether the code is thread safe, and provide information about possible failure cases that might be involved when using these routines.

Keep your documentation short and clean and use consistent language and terms throughout. If you're looking for inspiration, look at similar methods in Apple's frameworks to see how they are documented. You won't go wrong by following Apple's in-house style.

Building Header Documentation

A Quick Help comment consists of either triple-slashed (as in Figure 2-10) or double-asterisked comments, as in the following examples:

```
/// This is a quick help comment

/**
   And so is this
*/
```

A Quick Help comment placed just before a function is automatically interpreted to annotate that function, whether or not the comment mentions the function by name. It probably shouldn't actually mention the name. Xcode automatically adds function names to the declaration, as you see in Figure 2-10.

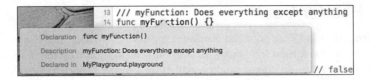

Figure 2-10   Quick Help comments are delineated with triple slashes or double stars.

> **Note**
>
> "Header documentation" remains applicable in Swift even though the language does not use header files. Follow Apple's example and document everything in your source rather than just the material intended for public consumption. You and your team are first-class consumers of Quick Help comments.

Markdown Support

Quick Help supports a robust set of basic markdown syntax, a lightweight formatting syntax developed by John Gruber that's popular on most development platforms. You can add headers, links, horizontal rules, bolding, and italics to your core description. Figure 2-11 shows marked-up output rendered by the Quick Help engine. Apple's implementation covers all the basics. It includes the features you'll find on standard markdown cheat sheets.

Figure 2-11   Markdown-delimited elements render within your Quick Help comments.

The basics are flexible. You can add code insets, as in Figure 2-12, to demonstrate usage within the Quick Help pop-up. Use the ```swift code fence or add four spaces or more to indicate code sections.

As you see in this example, Xcode treats adjacent triple-slashed comments as a single comment block. Xcode unifies the material that flows from one line to the next.

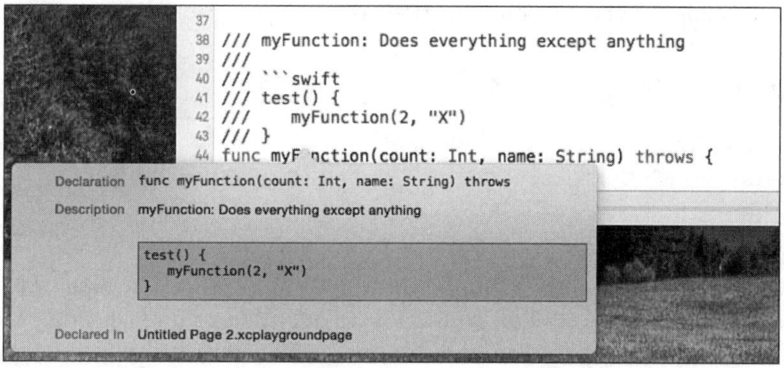

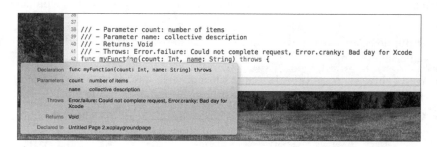

Figure 2-12   Use indentation or code fences (```swift) to delineate code sections.

Keywords

Quick Help supports parameter, returns, and throws keywords. These create category call-outs in the pop-up; you see some of these realized in Figure 2-13. These keywords are case-insensitive and preceded by a hyphen or an asterisk:

```
/// - returns: term
/// - throws: error-lists
/// - parameter term: definition
```

Figure 2-13   Special sections include Parameters, Returns, and Throws.

returns requires a colon. The colon for parameter is optional but recommended as it creates a more readable tab-aligned parameter list. Unfortunately, you cannot break out errors into lists the way you do with parameters. For example, the following does not parse properly. You end up with one of the two throws declarations eaten by Xcode:

```
/// - Throws: Error.failure: Could not complete request
/// - Throws: Error.cranky: Bad day for Xcode
```

The parameter outline syntax supports two styles. You can specify:

```
- parameter x: ...
- parameter y: ...
```

or:

```
- Parameters:
    - x: ...
    - y: ...
```

Both approaches produce equivalent output. Apple writes in Xcode's release notes, "You can mix and match these forms as you see fit in any order or continuity throughout the doc comment. Because these are parsed as list items, you can nest arbitrary content underneath them."

Other sections noted in the Quick Help template (`Availability`, `Reference`, `Related`, `Guides`, `Sample Code`, and `Related Declarations`) do not appear to be developer configurable at this time.

Quick Help recognizes several other keywords and uses bolding to highlight them (see Figure 2-14): `Attention`, `Author`, `Authors`, `Bug`, `Complexity`, `Copyright`, `Date`, `Experiment`, `Important`, `Invariant`, `Note`, `Postcondition`, `Precondition`, `Remark`, `Requires`, `SeeAlso`, `Since`, `TODO`, `Version`, and `Warning`.

The section label terms overlap with and appear to be influenced by other header documentation standards, like `Doxygen` and `reStructuredText`. There is minor overlap with Apple's older `HeaderDoc` standard for Objective-C. Here's a quick summary of the label terms and their uses:

- **Attributions** (`author`, `authors`, `copyright`, `date`) create a documentation trail for authorship.

- **Availability** (`since`, `version`) specifies when material was added to the code or updated, enabling you to lock down both release conformance and real-world time.

- **Admonitions** (`attention`, `important`, `note`, `remark`, `warning`) caution about use. These establish design rationales and point out limitations and hazards.

- **Development state** (`bug`, `TODO`, `experiment`) expresses progress of ongoing development, marking out areas needing future inspection and refinement.

- **Performance characteristics** (`complexity`) express a code's time and space complexity.

- **Functional semantics** (`precondition`, `postcondition`, `requires`, `invariant`) detail argument characteristics before and after calls. Preconditions and requirements limit the values and conditions under which the code should be accessed. Postconditions specify observable results that are true after execution. Invariant elements presumably do not change during a call.

- **Cross-references** (`seealso`) enable you to point out related material to add background to the documented implementation.

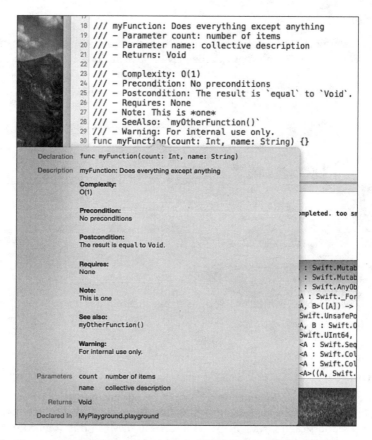

```
18 /// myFunction: Does everything except anything
19 /// - Parameter count: number of items
20 /// - Parameter name: collective description
21 /// - Returns: Void
22 ///
23 /// - Complexity: O(1)
24 /// - Precondition: No preconditions
25 /// - Postcondition: The result is `equal` to `Void`.
26 /// - Requires: None
27 /// - Note: This is *one*
28 /// - SeeAlso: `myOtherFunction()`
29 /// - Warning: For internal use only.
30 func myFunction(count: Int, name: String) {}
```

Declaration   func myFunction(count: Int, name: String)

Description   myFunction: Does everything except anything

Complexity:
O(1)

Precondition:
No preconditions

Postcondition:
The result is equal to Void.

Requires:
None

Note:
This is *one*

See also:
myOtherFunction()

Warning:
For internal use only.

Parameters   count   number of items

name   collective description

Returns   Void

Declared In   MyPlayground.playground

Figure 2-14   Common keywords are pulled out and bolded with special highlighting.

You can use a hyphen/asterisk-space-colon layout for other items, but they don't receive preferred markup, as you see in Figure 2-15. The results are simply the bulleted list you'd expect to build with markdown.

```
34 /// myFunction: Does everything except anything
35 /// - These: don't get
36 /// - Any: special highlights
37 func myFunction(count: Int, name: String) {}
```

Declaration   func myFunction(count: Int, name: String)

Description   myFunction: Does everything except anything

• These: don't get
• Any: special highlights

Declared In   MyPlayground.playground

Figure 2-15   Unrecognized markers are bulleted but not highlighted.

Special Swift Concerns

Method/function annotations appear in-line with the declaration, for example, when a function throws (see Figure 2-16). This looks a little ugly but is syntactically appropriate for Swift 2. Quick Help incorporates most declaration attributes—for example, noescape, noreturn, and so on—into the declaration line as well. You see this in Figure 2-16 with rethrows.

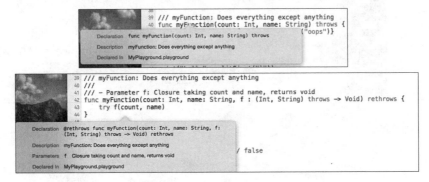

Figure 2-16   Swift function annotations such as **throws** and **rethrows** are mentioned in Quick Help.

Adding Images to Header Docs

You add images to header documentation by including URLs to assets stored on the web or to files with absolute URLs on the local file system (see Figure 2-17). Unlike rich playground comments, header docs cannot read in-app resources, but they can read from a full path to the current desktop, which is what is used in this example. Because image use is so rigid, I recommend against using them with header docs at this time as your source material may move and break links.

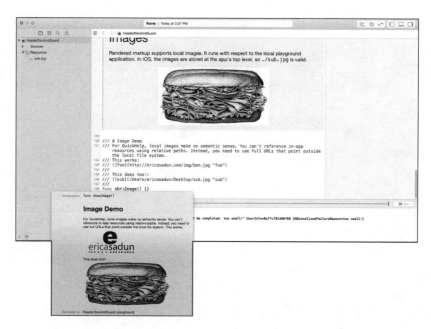

Figure 2-17   Quick Help supports image integration. (*Royalty-free image of sub sandwich by Billy Alexander via freeimages.com.*)

Wrap-up

Never forget that you are your own best customer. The time you spend building code and documentation to support your development efforts pays you back over the lifetime of your tools. While you're probably not best served by creating the most perfect Quick Look previews for in-house classes and structures, building visualizations and semantically meaningful output can dramatically decrease debugging overhead because the information you need in order to proceed is right at your fingertips.

This chapter has introduced techniques that enable you to present values that expand beyond simple raw data. With these developer-facing tools, you'll be able to get better and more meaningful feedback for your Swift development efforts.

3

Optionals?!

`nil` happens. When dictionary lookups fail, when instance properties are case dependent, when asynchronous operations have not completed, when failable initializers cannot create instances, and in dozens of other situations where values may or may not have been set, Swift may return `nil` instead of some other more concrete content. Swift provides `nil` as a powerful tool for expressing situations in which values are unavailable for use.

Swift differentiates these "no content" scenarios from error handling. In error handling, control flow changes to offer failure mitigation and reporting. With `nil`, a *value-of-no-value* represents an absence of data. It offers a testable placeholder to be used when no data is otherwise available.

Unlike in many other languages, in Swift, `nil` is not a pointer. It is a safe and expressive way to represent the potential for both a valid and invalid value within a single construct. In Swift, the `Optional` type encapsulates this concept and enables you to differentiate between successful value assignments and `nil` cases.

Learning how to recognize and use optionals is an essential step in mastering the Swift language. This chapter introduces optionals and surveys the supporting constructs you need to create, test, and successfully use optionals in your code.

Optionals 101

Question marks and exclamation points are the hallmark of Swift optionals. Any variable marked with ? may—or may not—contain a valid value. To get a sense of this language feature, consider the following example:

```
var soundDictionary = ["cow": "moo", "dog": "bark", "pig": "squeal"]
print(soundDictionary["cow"] == "moo") // prints true
print(soundDictionary["fox"]) // What does the fox say?
```

What does the fox say? In Swift, the answer is `nil`. In Swift, `nil` indicates "no value." Unlike in Objective-C, in Swift, `nil` is not a pointer. Swift `nil` indicates a semantic missing non-existence, a count of Monte Cristo, a cup of "not tea," an honest politician. A nil item means "nothing to see here, move along, move along, move along."

In this soundDictionary example, the variable stores a string dictionary. With strings for both keys and values, its type is Swift.Dictionary<Swift.String, Swift.String>. You can also represent this type as [String: String], using square brackets and a colon. Swift infers this type from the concrete data provided on the right-hand side of the soundDictionary assignment. Alternatively, you can use explicit type annotation in your code by adding a colon and a type in the variable declaration:

```
var soundDictionary: [String: String] =
    ["cow": "moo", "dog": "bark", "pig": "squeal"]
```

Although the dictionary uses String keys and values, when you look up any item in this dictionary, the value returned is not a String. It's typed String?. That question mark is critical to understanding dictionaries because it indicates an Optional type. Dictionary lookups may succeed or fail. Optional return types encapsulate both possibilities.

Contrast this behavior with arrays, where it's the programmer's job to check whether an index exists before accessing it. Both types could easily be implemented with the other convention, of course, but the Swift people chose the more likely use case for each type. Arrays are highly bounded with a small domain of legal lookup indexes. Dictionaries are often sparse compared against their possible key domain. Optionals enables dictionaries to better represent their "may or may not map to a value" results.

Confirm the return type with Quick Help. Enter the dictionary and the following assignment in Xcode. Then Option-click the sound symbol (as in Figure 3-1) or select the symbol and open View > Utilities > Show Quick Help Inspector. The declaration line in the Quick Help presentation confirms that the type assigned to sound is String?:

```
var sound = soundDictionary["cow"] // sound is typed String?
```

```
 8
 9 var sound = soundDictionary["cow"] // String?
10

Declaration   var sound: String?
Declared In   Chapter 3.playground
```

Figure 3-1   Xcode's Quick Help reveals symbol typing.

While it might appear that the dictionary returns "moo" on success or nil for failed lookups, this is actually misleading. Print the output to the Xcode console, with print(sound). A successful result looks like Optional("moo"), with its value embedded in an optional wrapper. In this case, the Optional type uses a .Some enumeration, and its associated value is the "moo" string.

You cannot use this optional directly as a string. The following example fails because you must unwrap Optional types before using their values:

```
let statement = "The cow says " + sound
```

The + operator in this case works on two string values, not on a string and an optional. Unwrapping gives you access to the string stored within the optional wrapper, enabling you to perform tasks like appending values.

Unwrapping Optionals

Optional types always return either a wrapped value or nil. Wrapping means that any actual content is stored within a logical outer structure. You cannot get to that value (in this case, "moo") without unwrapping it. In the Swift world, it is always Christmas, and there are always presents—or at least variables—to unwrap.

Swift offers a variety of mechanisms for unwrapping optionals and recovering the underlying data type stored within them. There are more ways to get at a wrapped optional value than you might expect. The expressive possibilities expanded in Apple's Swift 2 update to provide greater developer flexibility.

Forced Unwrapping

The simplest way to extract an optional value is to append an exclamation point:

```
print("The sound is \(sound!)") // may or may not crash
```

This is also the most dangerous approach, and you want to generally avoid it in production code.

If the value is wrapped (that "optional" result you just read about), the exclamation point returns the value stored within the wrapped element. If the value is nil, you experience a fatal runtime error—which is not nearly as fun or gratifying for your workday.

The nil value is the Swift equivalent of your aunt's home-crocheted vest with a large friendly moose decoration on it. It's pretty important to check whether an item is nil before unwrapping it. You can more safely unwrap with an exclamation point within an if statement because this sound is nominally guaranteed to be non-nil in non-extreme (that is, nonthreaded) situations:

```
if sound != nil {
    print("The sound is \(sound!)") // doesn't crash
}
```

Safety is a relative thing. While this forced unwrap is pretty safe at compile time and runtime in its current use, it's dangerous while editing. If you accidentally move that print line out of the if block, the compiler cannot warn you about it, and you will ship broken code.

In this example, the `sound` variable is also not `weak`. It won't deallocate between the `nil` test and unwrapping. Never use forced unwraps with `weak` variables because they may do just that.

As a rule, avoiding forced unwraps, even within `if` clauses, helps you avoid potential disasters.

Conditional Binding

Conditional binding provides a better and safer approach that avoids forced unwrapping. In conditional binding, you optionally bind (that is, assign) a value to a new constant or variable using an `if-let` or `if-var` statement. When the optional is not `nil`, Swift unwraps the value, assigns it, and executes a block of code. When `nil`, you either enter an `else` clause or continue to the next statement:

```
if let sound = soundDictionary[animal] {
    print("The \(animal) says \(sound)")
} else {
    print("Any sound the \(animal) says is unknown to modern science")
}
```

It's conventional in Swift to use identical identifiers in conditional bindings for both wrapped and unwrapped versions. In the following snippet, a `mySound` constant is unwrapped within the `if-let` (or `if-var`) scope but wrapped outside it:

```
let mySound = soundDictionary[animal] // mySound is wrapped
if let mySound = mySound {
    print(mySound) // mySound is unwrapped
}
```

Using the same identifier makes it clear that you're working with the same semantics in different states of undress. Conditional binding clauses tend to be short. This enables you to verify your overloaded symbol intent with a glance.

The right-hand value in an `if-let` assignment must be an optional. You cannot use this construct with an already-unwrapped item. The following statement leads to an error, complaining that a conditional binding initializer must have `Optional` type:

```
if let sound = soundDictionary["cow"]! { // error!
    print("The cow says \(sound)")
}
```

Conditional Binding and Type Casts

Type casting enables you to re-interpret an instance's type at runtime. Swift offers two distinct type-casting operators (`is` and `as`) with four variations: `is`, `as`, `as?`, and `as!`. These operators enable you to check value types and cast values to other types. The `is` operator checks whether you can convert an instance's type to another, typically more specialized, type:

```
let value = 3
value is Any // true
value is Int // true
value is String // false
```

The `as` operator casts to other types and can test whether an item conforms to a protocol. These are its three forms:

- The `as` operator applies direct casts. The compiler must determine at compile time that the cast will succeed.

- The `as?` variant contains a question mark. It performs a conditional cast that always returns an optional value. If the cast succeeds, it's wrapped in an optional instance. If not, it returns `nil`. This is the cast I use most often in day-to-day coding. The compiler issues warnings when it detects that a cast will always succeed (for example, `String` to `NSString`) or always fail (`String` to `NSArray`).

- The forced variant `as!` includes an exclamation point. It either returns an unwrapped item or raises a runtime error. This is the most dangerous cast type. Use it when you know a cast will always succeed or when you want your application to prematurely crash.

Conditional binding and conditional casting work hand-in-hand. Figure 3-2 demonstrates why. In this screenshot, Swift code creates a string-indexed dictionary that stores arbitrary `Any` instance types. Even when a lookup returns a valid integer for the `"Three"` key, a forced unwrap still reports `Any` type. To use this value as a number, you must downcast from `Any` to `Int`.

```
40 var dict = [String:Any]()
41 dict["Three"] = 3
42 let result = dict["Three"]! // type is Any?

Declaration   let result: Any
Declared In   Test.playground
```

Figure 3-2   Lookups from a `[String:Any]` dictionary return `Optional<Any>` values. The type remains `Any` even after forced unwrapping.

The `as?` type operator produces optionals even when used with non-optional values:

```
let value = 3 // Int
let optionalValue = value as? Int // Int?
```

Conditional binding enables you to apply a cast, test the resulting optional, and then bind unwrapped values to a local variable. In the following example, `result` is bound as an `Int` constant within the `if` clause code block:

```
if let result = dict["Three"] as? Int {
    print("\(result + 3) = 6") // 6 = 6
}
```

attern of `fetch`, `cast`, and `bind` commonly appears when working with
m web services and databases. Swift enables you to use type safety while
n key paths down to data leaves.

κccipe ɔ-ɪ scaiunes a `UIView` hierarchy, using conditional casting to match subviews against a supplied type, returning the first subview that matches that type. The `as?` type operator returns an optional, which is conditionally bound to a local `view` variable. If the binding succeeds and a type match is found, the function returns. Otherwise, it recurses down the tree in a depth-first search.

Recipe 3-1   **Using Conditional Binding to Test Types**

```
public func fetchViewWithType<T>(
    type t: T.Type, contentView: UIView) -> T? {
    for eachView in contentView.subviews {
        if let view = eachView as? T {return view}
        if let subview = fetchViewWithType(
            type: t.self, contentView:eachView) {
            return subview
        }
    }
    return nil
}
```

Binding Cascades

Although useful for accessing values, `if-let` bindings build into code structures colloquially known as *pyramids of doom*. Each successive test indents your code further and further to the right, creating a triangle of empty space to the left of the `if` statements and then the closing brackets:

```
if let cowSound = soundDictionary["cow"] {
    if let dogSound = soundDictionary["dog"] {
        if let pigSound = soundDictionary["pig"] {
            // use sounds here
        }
    }
}
```

It's the sort of code you don't want to bring home to your project manager—or your mummy.

Using multiple optional bindings within a single test enables you to avoid this structural mess. First introduced in Swift 1.2, cascading permits any number of conditional bindings tests within a unified conditional:

```
if let
    cowSound = soundDictionary["cow"],
    dogSound = soundDictionary["dog"],
    pigSound = soundDictionary["pig"] {
        // use sounds here
}
```

If any assignment fails, evaluation stops, and control moves past the `if` statement. This approach is particularly useful when working with web-sourced data, such as JSON, where each step may depend on the results of the previous conditional binding. The following example is from a script that checks prices on the iTunes App Store:

```
if let
    json = json as? NSDictionary,
    resultsList = json["results"] as? NSArray,
    results = resultsList.firstObject as? NSDictionary,
    name = results["trackName"] as? String,
    price = results["price"] as? NSNumber {
    // Process results
}
```

This code pulls data from the App Store and deserializes it with `NSJSONSerialization.JSONObjectWithData`. The results list is extracted from the JSON data, and the app results from that list, and so forth.

While this approach avoids pyramid indentation, it introduces a bad tendency toward code constipation. Increased blockiness makes `if-let` cascades hard to mentally process. Copious commenting and spacing can mitigate this. As shown here, the results are faster for the brain to parse, make it easier to spot errors, and are better for adding, removing, and reordering intermediate steps:

```
if let
    // Access JSON as dictionary
    json = json as? NSDictionary,

    // Retrieve results array
    resultsList = json["results"] as? NSArray,

    // Extract first item
    results = resultsList.firstObject as? NSDictionary,

    // Extract name and price
    name = results["trackName"] as? String,
    price = results["price"] as? NSNumber {

        // Process results
}
```

guard Statements

The guard statement was first introduced in Swift 2. It offers another way to unwrap and use optionals. Although guard is not limited to use with optionals—you can use it with general Boolean conditions as well—it provides a major development advantage that's specific to optional handling. In particular, guard statements move code out of indented scopes by offering early-return error handling.

Early-return inverts the handling of success and failure paths. Errors are handled first, enabling success code to be written at the highest possible scope. Compare this to if-let, where you cannot put the failure path first and your success conditions must be handled in a child scope. Without guard statements, all conditionally bound values must be used with the if statement code block that binds them. For example, the following snippet conditionally binds a cowSound constant using if-let, and the cowSound constant is undefined outside that scope:

```
if let cowSound = soundDictionary["cow"] {
    // cowSound is unwrapped within this scope
}
// cowSound is undefined outside the scope
```

Like if-let, a guard statement conditionally unwraps and binds optional variables. When that binding fails, it executes a mandatory else clause, which *must* exit the current scope, using throw, break, continue, or return statements. Otherwise, the guard statement unwraps the optional value and binds it to a variable you can use throughout the remaining lifetime of the current scope:

```
guard let cowSound = soundDictionary["cow"] else {throw Error.MissingValue}
// cowSound now defined and unwrapped
```

Think of a guard statement as a soldier that will not permit the flow of execution to continue forward unless its condition or conditions are met. Unlike if-let, guard does not establish new scopes. Instead, it guides traffic through the existing scope.

Like if-let, a single guard statement can express multiple conditions, separated by comma delineators. For example, you might perform multiple constant assignments:

```
guard let
    cowSound = soundDictionary["cow"],
    dogSound = soundDictionary["dog"]
    else {throw Error.MissingValue}
```

Or you might include a more general test along with assignments:

```
guard
    soundDictionary.count > 2,
    let cowSound = soundDictionary["cow"],
    let dogSound = soundDictionary["dog"]
    else {throw Error.MissingValue}
```

Implicitly Unwrapped Optionals

Swift provides a feature called implicitly unwrapped optionals, which you declare by appending an exclamation point to the end of the type. Unlike normal optionals, these versions unwrap themselves, much like a jack-in-the-box or the hired entertainment at a bachelor party. Use implicitly unwrapped optionals cautiously. They're a fairly dangerous feature as they introduce fatal runtime errors if you attempt to access values stored inside a `nil` case optional.

Here's an example of first an assignment to a normally typed constant and then to an implicitly unwrapped one. The difference is what happens when you access the wrapped value. That's where the name comes from because during access, the value is implicitly unwrapped:

```
var animal = "cow" // 1
let wrappedSound = soundDictionary[animal] // Optional("moo")
let unwrappedSound: String! = soundDictionary[animal] // "moo"

// prints: The unwrapped sound is "moo"
let soundString = "\"" + unwrappedSound + "\"" // 2
print("The unwrapped sound is \(soundString)")
```

In this example, when you use `unwrappedSound` in the string assignment, its value is not `Optional("moo")`. Its value is accessed as `moo`, and it behaves like a simple string. Implicit unwrapping extracts the value from an optional item and uses the data type you'd expect from a successful dictionary lookup. Once unwrapped, you can use the variable directly. You don't have to add that "unwrap this variable" exclamation point or use conditional binding.

A real danger arises from unwrapping `nil` values. If you replace the assignment to `animal` in the line marked 1 with `"fox"` instead of `"cow"`, this code raises a fatal error in the line marked 2. The runtime complains that it `unexpectedly found nil while unwrapping an Optional value`. With great unwrapping comes great responsibility. Take care that you properly guard these items to ensure that you don't attempt to unwrap `nil`.

Limit implicit unwrapping to when you know in advance that a variable will always have a value after some logical point. For example, if you're responding to button taps or menu clicks, you probably don't have to wonder "does this button or menu item exist?" It does. If it didn't, you would never have reached your callback.

Don't use implicit unwrapping for more general cases like dictionary lookups. That's just asking for trouble. You can, however, print unwrapped items and test them against `nil`:

```
print(unwrappedSound) // prints nil
if unwrappedSound != nil {
    print("Valid:", unwrappedSound)
}
```

An error won't be raised until you perform an operation that attempts to access the value inside.

As a rule, it is legal to assign a value, an optional value, or `nil` to an implicitly unwrapped variable. The following code is legal and will compile without error:

```
var myImplicitlyUnwrappedOptional: String!
myImplicitlyUnwrappedOptional = Optional("Value")
myImplicitlyUnwrappedOptional == "Value" // true
myImplicitlyUnwrappedOptional = nil // do not test except against nil
myImplicitlyUnwrappedOptional == nil // true
myImplicitlyUnwrappedOptional = "Value"
myImplicitlyUnwrappedOptional == "Value" // true
```

Assignments to both optional and non-optional values end with non-optional results, which you see by comparing against the non-optional string literal `"Value"`. The danger lies in the `nil` assignment. A non-`nil` comparison tries to access the value and ends in a runtime error. The win is that you can perform an assignment to either optional or non-optional values with a single assignment.

An implicitly unwrapped scenario is common when working with Interface Builder. A view *binding* is optional; it may or may not be properly instantiated in the interface file. The view *use* is normally non-optional; presumably you set up the binding correctly. Implicit unwrapping simplifies code access to views at the cost of potential crashes during development and testing.

Swift 2's one-line `guard` statement more or less offers a shorthand summary for the following initialization pattern:

```
let cowSound: String! = soundDictionary["cow"]
if cowSound == nil {throw Error.missingValue} // Handle nil case
// cowSound's value is now usable without explicit unwrapping
```

This assignment uses implicit unwrapping and then tests against `nil`. This is a safe check because the code makes no attempt to access an associated value. If the optional is `nil`, the `if` statement's conditional block executes, transferring control away from this scope. Otherwise, execution continues, and the unwrapped `cowSound` constant is now available for use.

An implicitly unwrapped approach is both wordier and less safe than `guard`. It uses multiple statements compared with `guard`'s one, and it makes no conditions about leaving the current scope. If the `throw` request were replaced with a `print` statement, the `nil` case would continue forward. In doing so, it might encounter a use of `cowSound`'s nonexistent value and a nasty runtime crash.

Use implicit unwrapping cautiously and prefer `guard` where possible.

Guarding Failable Initializers

When an initializer returns an optional instance, it's called a *failable* initializer. The initializer may succeed in establishing a new instance, or it may fail and return `nil`. For example, the following structure can be initialized only with even numbers:

```
struct EvenInt {
    let number: Int
    init?(_ number: Int) {
        if number % 2 == 0 {self.number = number} else {return nil}
    }
}
```

Mark failable initializers by appending a question mark or an exclamation point to the `init` keyword (`init?` or `init!`). The punctuation choice depends on whether the initializer returns a normal optional instance or an implicitly unwrapped one. The implicitly unwrapped variation is almost never used in real life. According to my technical editor Kevin Ballard, you might theoretically encounter one when working with legacy code ported from Core Foundation or from any unaudited Objective-C API.

Use `guard` to test assignments from failable initialization. Here's an example built around the `EvenInt` struct. When created with an odd number, an `EvenInt` initializer returns `nil`. The `guard` statement throws an error and exits the scope:

```
do {
    guard let even2 = EvenInt(2) else {throw Error.Odd}
    print(even2) // prints EvenInt(number: 2)
    guard let even3 = EvenInt(3) else {throw Error.Odd} // fails
    print(even3) // never gets here
} catch {print(error)}
```

Although you can use any approach for testing and unwrapping optionals, `guard` statements offer a natural synchronicity with failable initializers. Guarding initializers once again enables you to test for failed initialization at the point where you declare variables and constants and ensures that these bindings remain valid for the remaining scope.

Optionals and Sentinel Values

It is tempting to use optionals to signal when an operation has failed. The following snippet represents Swift prior to version 2 and is common to Apple's traditional Cocoa patterns:

```
func doSomething() -> String? {
    let success = (arc4random_uniform(2) == 1) // flip a coin
    if success {return "success"} // succeed
    return nil // fail
}
```

```
if let result = doSomething() {
    // use result here
}
```

An unsuccessful operation returns `nil`, and a successful one returns a value.

Starting in Swift 2, reserve `nil` failures for initialization (although you can also use `throws` in initializers as well as in normal code) and prefer `guard` over `if-let`. Instead of using optionals as sentinels—that is, to signal success and fail conditions—use Swift's new error-handling system. Error handling enables you to redirect the flow of control to mitigate errors and provide recovery support:

```
func betterDoSomething() throws -> String {
    let success = (arc4random_uniform(2) == 1) // flip a coin
    if success {return "success"} // succeed
    throw Error.failure // fail
}
```

```
do {
    let result = try betterDoSomething()
} catch {print(error)}
```

This refactoring skips optionals; the `nil` case is never of interest to the client code. Swift 2 error handling means you never have to unwrap.

When a thrown error is not of interest to its consumer, the `try?` operator can discard errors and convert results to optionals. This lets you integrate new-style errors with old-style optional handling. A `try?` expression returns a wrapped value for successful calls and `nil` for thrown errors:

```
guard let foo = try? somethingThatMayThrow else {
    // ...handle error condition and leave scope
}
if let foo = try? somethingThatMayThrow {}
```

The new error-handling system profoundly affects Cocoa-sourced APIs. Calls that used `NSError` pointers pre-Swift 2 change their return type from optional to non-optional, add the `throws` keyword, and eliminate error pointers from API calls. The new system sends `NSError` through `do-try-catch`. Compare the old approach with the new one:

```
// Old
func dataFromRange(range: NSRange,
    documentAttributes dict: [NSObject: AnyObject],
    error: NSErrorPointer) -> NSData?
```

```
// New
func dataFromRange(range: NSRange,
    documentAttributes dict: [String: AnyObject]) throws -> NSData
```

By introducing error handling, optionals can eliminate overloaded "failed call" semantics. It's always better to use `throws` with well-defined errors than to use optional sentinel values. When you really have no information to pass back to the caller other than "I failed," Swift 2's updated error system simplifies creating an error enumeration to explain why that failure occurred. It is ridiculously easy to add informative errors that don't require complicated `NSError` initializers:

```
enum Error: ErrorType {case BadData, MemoryGlitch, ItIsFriday}
```

Although many current APIs, especially asynchronous handlers and calls based on Core Foundation, have yet to transition to the new system, I encourage you to update your code to avoid using optionals as sentinel values. Return your optionals to the "contains a value or does not contain a value" semantics they were designed to handle.

Coalescing

Swift's `nil`-coalescing operator `??` unwraps optionals and provides fallback values for the `nil` case. This next example checks uses `nil`-coalescing to assign a value to the `sound` constant:

```
let sound = soundDictionary["fox"] ?? "unknown"
```

If the lookup succeeds and the dictionary returns a wrapped value, the operator unwraps it and assigns it to `sound`. If not, it assigns the fallback value, which is `"unknown"`. In either case, the assignment is not optional. `sound` uses a `String` type, not `String?`.

Use `nil` coalescing when you can supply fallback values that won't interrupt a normal operational flow. When you cannot, choose `guard` instead and handle `nil` as an error case in the `else` clause.

> **Note**
>
> If the optional is non-`nil`, the right-hand side of the operator is never evaluated. The operation short-circuits, as with the Boolean operators `&&` and `||`.

Optional Assignment

In `nil` coalescing, you must supply a valid unwrapped fallback value. In cases where a fallback does not exist, consider optional assignment instead. This approach shortcuts any case where an optional value is unavailable. Normally, you embed assignments into an `if-let` scope. If the conditional binding succeeds, you assign the unwrapped value.

Alternatively, you might consider creating a custom operator that conditionally assigns values to a target, as in the following example:

```
// Thanks, Mike Ash
infix operator =? {}
public func =?<T>(inout target: T, newValue: T?) {
    if let unwrapped = newValue {
        target = unwrapped
    }
}
```

This snippet builds an `=?` operator that supports simple assignment by wrapping and hiding its underlying `if-let` approach with a basic `infix` call.

The following assignments show this operator in action. The `s` string variable updates only for non-`nil` assignments:

```
var s: String = "initial value"
s =? "value 1" // value 1
s =? nil // value 1
```

Hiding `if-let` overhead makes the resulting conditional assignments cleaner and potentially more intuitively obvious to read through.

Optional Patterns

A Swift *pattern* matches a value's structure rather than just the value itself. Patterns decompose and express a data structure, including component elements. They enable you to refer to an item's subconstructs when testing instead of dealing with instances as a monolithic whole. Using patterns is a powerful and nuanced way to represent an instance, and it's extremely handy for working with optionals.

The optional enumeration consists of two cases, .None and .Some. The .Some case contains an associated value of an arbitrary type:

```
enum Optional<T> {
    case None
    case Some(T)
}
```

With optionals, pattern matching enables you to limit statements to work only with the .Some case. You can reach into that case and bind the internal value using a single declaration. Follow the `case` keyword with a specific enumeration (the .Some case) and then bind the value nestled within it using `let` or `var`:

```
switch soundDictionary[animal] {
    case .Some(let sound):
        print("Using case, the unwrapped sound is \(sound)")
    default: break
}
```

The result is an unwrapped value, ready for access.

The `case` .Some(`let constant`) expression provides a one-to-one pattern match with the underlying optional. Optionals with the None case don't match this pattern, so the `case` code need not consider `nil` scenarios.

There's no denying that the `case` (case .Some(`let constant`)) is awkward to process visually. It lacks grace. Responding to the complexity of this optional pattern-matching code, Swift 2 introduces shorthand using a postfixed question mark:

```
switch soundDictionary[animal] {
    case let sound?:
        print("Using case, the unwrapped sound is \(sound) [2]")
    default: break
}
```

This postfixed question mark is nothing more than syntactic sugar for the `.Some` case. The results are simpler and more readable because this `case` matches and unwraps its optionals.

The preceding example shortchanges Swift because there's still no major advantage in using this one-case `switch` statement over, say, if-let. When you introduce a simple `where` clause, you begin to see where pattern-matching optionals adds power and concision.

The following snippet uses a `switch` statement to differentiate unwrapped optionals whose string values are longer than five characters from those that are shorter:

```
switch soundDictionary[animal] {
case let sound? where sound.characters.count > 5:
    print("The \(sound) is long")
case let sound?:
    print("The \(sound) sound is under 5 characters")
default: break
}
```

Swift's `switch` cases may experience significant logical overlap where small details select which case to execute.

Using pattern matching with `if` statements enables you to drop `switch` statement overhead and simplify one-case code even further. You lose the default statement and the surrounding `switch`, and you reduce the check to just a simple pattern comparison with `where` clause support. This `if` statement uses both pattern matching and a `where` clause for precise testing:

```
if case let sound? = soundDictionary[animal] where sound.hasPrefix("m") {
    print("Sound \(sound) starts with m")
}
```

The `where` clause isn't limited to if-case. You can construct a similar statement using if-let:

```
if let sound = soundDictionary[animal] where sound.hasPrefix("m") {
    print("Sound \(sound) starts with m")
}
```

Pattern matching also enables you to iterate through an array and perform actions on unwrapped non-nil values. The for-case-let approach simplifies working with optional collections, as you see in the following snippet:

```
// Collect sound optionals into array
let soundOptionals = ["cow", "rhino", "dog", "goose", "hippo",
    "pig"].map({soundDictionary[$0]})
```

```
print(soundOptionals) // [Optional("moo"), nil, Optional("bark"),
                       // nil, nil, Optional("squeal")]

for case let sound? in soundOptionals {
    print("The sound \"\(sound)\" appears in the dictionary")
}
```

You can also use pattern matching with `guard` statements:

```
guard case let .Some(sound) = soundDictionary["cow"] else {fatalError()}
print(sound)
```

This example from Apple sample code uses a GameplayKit enumeration. It performs an enumeration pattern match and binds the `targetAgent` associated value:

```
guard case let .HuntAgent(targetAgent) = mandate else {return}
```

Optional Chaining

In Swift, you *chain* methods and properties by appending period-delimited selectors. Each function in the chain returns an intermediate value. This allows calls to be joined into a single statement without requiring variables that store intermediate results:

```
soundDictionary.description.characters.count
```

This approach creates a *fluent interface*, which is ideally a parsimonious and more readable expression of a set of operations you want to consider as a single unit. A danger, of course, lies in over-chaining. If you're producing enormous lines of code that are difficult to debug and hard to read and that cannot be easily commented or differentiated on updates, you're probably doing this wrong. Ask yourself, "Would I ever need to put a breakpoint in this statement or step through it?" If the answer is yes, you are over-chaining.

Swift introduces a powerful feature called *optional chaining*. Swift method calls may return optionals, and you must take this into account when forming chains. Swift provides a way that an entire chain can fail gracefully on encountering `nil`.

Optional chaining involves adding question marks after optional values. For example, you might look up an animal in the sound dictionary and use optional chaining to return a capitalized version of the sound:

```
soundDictionary[animal]?.capitalizedString // Moo or nil
```

Even though `capitalizedString` normally returns a non-optional, this chain returns `String?`. It may succeed or fail, depending on the lookup.

Add question marks to any chain participants that return optionals:

```
soundDictionary[animal]?.characters.first?.hashValue // returns Int?
```

You can add forced unwrapping to any chain item by replacing the question mark with an exclamation point. This usage comes with the same forced unwrapping dangers discussed earlier in this chapter:

```
soundDictionary[animal]!.capitalizedString // Moo or Runtime Error
```

Here's a real-world example of where you might use optional chaining to simplify an `if-let` pattern. This code extends `Array` to return the index of a possible maximum element. Swift's standard library `maxElement()` function returns an optional based on whether a sequence has values to compare (Apple writes in the standard library, "Returns the maximum element in `self` or `nil` if the sequence is empty."):

```
extension Array where Element:Comparable {
    var maxIndex: Int? {
        if let e =
            self.enumerate().maxElement({$1.element > $0.element}) {
            return e.index
        }
        return nil
    }
}
```

Introducing optional chaining greatly simplifies this code, enabling you to shortcut the `index` lookup and returning `nil` if the `maxElement` call fails. Recipe 3-2 returns the index of an array's maximum value.

Recipe 3-2   **Using Optional Chaining to Shortcut Evaluations**

```
extension Array where Element:Comparable {
    var maxIndex: Int? {
        return self.enumerate().maxElement(
            {$1.element > $0.element})?.index
    }
}
```

Extend Recipe 3-2's functionality to all collection types with the following snippet:

```
extension CollectionType where Generator.Element: Comparable {
    var maxIndex: Index? {
        return self.indices.maxElement({self[$1] > self[$0]})
    }
}
```

Selector Testing and Optional Chaining

Optional chaining isn't just about transforming your code into bite-sized lines. It also acts as shorthand to test whether an item responds to a method or property selector. Optional chaining offers a rough equivalent to Objective-C's `respondsToSelector:` method, enabling you to determine whether it's safe to execute calls on particular instances.

Commonly, you work with subclasses that are directly related to each other but that implement distinct method sets. For example, you might retrieve a collection of SpriteKit nodes from a scene and then adjust the line widths of the shape nodes. This snippet uses a failable cast followed by an optionally chained property assignment:

```
for node in nodes {(node as? SKShapeNode)?.lineWidth = 4.0}
```

This selector-testing approach also works in pure Swift, as in the following example:

```
// Root class put two subclasses
class Root {func rootFunc() {}}
class Sub1: Root {func sub1Func() {print("sub1")}}
class Sub2: Root {func sub2Func() {print("sub2")}}

// Create heterogeneous array of items
var items: [Root] = [Sub1(), Sub2()]

// Conditionally test and run selectors
(items[0] as? Sub1)?.sub1Func() // runs
(items[0] as? Sub2)?.sub2Func() // no-op, nil
```

This snippet constructs a heterogeneous array of `Root` subclasses. It then performs conditional casts and uses selector tests before calling class-specific methods.

Selector testing enables you to test whether a method exists before constructing a new instance. Adding the question mark ensures that the `NSString` call won't fail with a runtime "unrecognized selector" exception:

```
let colorClass: AnyClass = UIColor.self
let noncolorClass: AnyClass = NSString.self
colorClass.blueColor?() // returns a blue color instance
noncolorClass.blueColor?() // returns nil
```

This is a special behavior of `AnyClass` and `AnyObject` that works only with Objective-C methods, for compatibility with `Class` and `id`. These are special cases because these types return functions as implicitly unwrapped optionals. Other types don't do that.

Subscripts

Contrary to expectations, optional chaining with subscripts *doesn't* introduce safe lookups. This is an important factor that you should internalize as soon as possible and recognize in your code. In the following example, if you try to access index 8 (aka the ninth element of this six-element array), your code dies with a fatal `Array index out of range` error:

```
let array: Array? = [0, 1, 2, 3, 4, 5]
array?[0] // 0
// array?[8] // still fails
```

In this example, the question mark does not qualify the lookup for safety. It is required for subscripting after `array`, which is optional. With subscripts, you add chain annotations in-line after the optional value and before the subscript brackets.

Optional chaining is meant solely to set and retrieve values for subscripts used with optional values. It does not and cannot short-circuit failed subscripts unless you build a failable subscripting extension, as in the following example:

```
extension Array {
    subscript (safe index: UInt) -> Element? {
        return Int(index) < count ? self[Int(index)] : nil
    }
}
```

Once you add a simple array `safe-index` extension, you can optionally chain the safe version of the subscript. In the following calls, the `Element?` results of the `safe:` subscript are now optional and can be chained:

```
print(array?[safe: 0]?.dynamicType) // nil
print(array?[safe: 8]?.dynamicType) // Optional(Swift.Int)
```

Optional Mapping

Swift's `map` and `flatMap` functions enable you to conditionally apply functions to optional values. Their calls are similar, as you see in the following declarations, and both are incredibly useful tools:

```
/// If `self == nil`, returns `nil`. Otherwise, returns `f(self!)`.
func map<U>(f: @noescape (T) -> U) -> U?
/// Returns `f(self)!` iff `self` and `f(self)` are not nil.
func flatMap<U>(f: @noescape (T) -> U?) -> U?
```

The `map` closures return type `U`, which may or may not be an optional, while `flatMap` closures specifically return type `U?`, which is always an optional. This practical limitation simply means you can use `map` with closures that return non-optionals, but you cannot do the same with `flatMap`:

```
// flatMap must return optional
print(word.map({string->String in string})) // compiles
// print(word.flatMap({string->String in string})) // errors
```

Maps and Chaining

When working with optionals, `map` and `flatMap` both act like chaining, but you supply an arbitrary closure instead of a chained method name or property:

```
        String? = "hello"
     = word?.capitalizedString // Optional("Hello")
   word.map({$0.capitalizedString}) // Optional("Hello")
```

When you just want to unwrap-and-apply, use `map`. This mapping:

```
UIImage(named:"ImageName").map({print($0.size)})
```

is equivalent to this `if-let`:

```
if let image = UIImage(named:" ImageName ") {
    print(image.size)
}
```

Both the mapping and `if-let` include about the same level of code complexity for this particular example. Both unwrap the optional returned by `UIImage(named:)` and then print the size. You can argue which approach is better. Both bind the unwrapped result to a local constant whether that constant does or does not have an explicit name.

Filtering `nil` Values with `flatMap`

The `flatMap` function offers great utility both in the realm of optionals and outside it. With optionals, you can use `flatMap` to filter away `nil` values and easily convert an array of optionals to an array of unwrapped values:

```
let optionalNumbers: [Int?] = [1, 3, 5, nil, 7, nil, 9, nil]
let nonOptionals = optionalNumbers.flatMap({$0})
print(nonOptionals) // [1, 3, 5, 7, 9]
```

Recipe 3-3 uses a single `flatMap` call to eliminate `nil` instances and extract values from their optional wrappers.

Recipe 3-3   **Extracting Members from an Optionals Array**

```
func flatMembers<T>(array: [T?]) -> [T] {
    return array.flatMap({$0})
}
```

Unmanaged Wrappers

In rare cases (which are growing rarer by the day), a Core Foundation function may return a C pointer or an object reference embedded in an `Unmanaged` wrapper. You encounter these in the older, dustier, and stranger parts of Cocoa, where grues still lurk in shadows. Keychain Services is a notorious offender in this regard. You must transfer `Unmanaged` references into the normal memory management system before working with them.

An `Unmanaged` wrapper, like an `Optional` wrapper, provides a layer of safety between your code and a potentially nasty crash. The `Unmanaged<T>` type stores a pointer whose memory is not controlled by the Swift runtime system. Before using this data, you take responsibility for how this memory should stay alive.

In Cocoa, this works very much like bridging in Objective-C. Unwrap any object with an existing +1 retain count using `takeRetainedValue()`. This applies to any item built with `Create` or `Copy` in its name. Use `takeUnretainedValue()` for +0 returns.

If you have an Objective-C framework or are developing one that you would like people to use in their Swift application—and if there are methods or functions in your Objective-C framework that return Core Foundation objects—decorate your methods or function names with `CF_RETURNS_RETAINED` or `CF_RETURNS_NOT_RETAINED`. If you don't decorate your methods or functions, Core Foundation objects are returned as unmanaged.

In Swift 2, `CF-IMPLICIT-BRIDGING-ENABLED` and `CF-IMPLICIT-BRIDGING-DISABLED` automatically bridge based on Core Foundation naming conventions. So if you audit your APIs and ensure that they follow `get/copy/create` conventions, you can avoid specific method decoration.

For example, `UTTypeCopyPreferredTagWithClass` returns a +1 `CFString` instance. Assign this result with `takeRetainedValue()`, making sure to test for failed calls. Unwrapping `nil` causes nasty crashes that even blessed potions of restore life will not fix. Recipe 3-4 demonstrates how to use unmanaged wrappers by returning a preferred file extension for a given universal type indicator.

Recipe 3-4   Conditional Binding from Unmanaged Wrappers

```
import MobileCoreServices
Import Foundation

enum Error: ErrorType {case NoMatchingExtension}

public func preferredFileExtensionForUTI(uti: String) throws -> String {
    if let result = UTTypeCopyPreferredTagWithClass(
        uti, kUTTagClassFilenameExtension) {
        return result.takeRetainedValue() as String
    }
    throw Error.NoMatchingExtension
}
```

This recipe uses conditional binding. The `UTTypeCopyPreferredTagWithClass()` function returns `Unmanaged<CFString>?`, which is an optional instance. If the call fails and returns `nil`, the function throws an error. Test the recipe by passing it a few common UTIs, such as public. jpeg and public.aiff-audio:

```
let shouldBeJPEG = try PreferredFileExtensionForUTI("public.jpeg")
let shouldBeAIFF = try PreferredFileExtensionForUTI("public.aiff-audio")
```

Use `takeUnretainedValue()` to unwrap any object built by a Core Foundation function with `Get` in its name (for example, `CFAllocatorGetDefault()`) and constants passed as unmanaged objects (for example, `kLSSharedFileListSessionLoginItems`). These items are not automatically retained for you. Unlike with `takeRetainedValue()`, calling `takeUnretainedValue()` won't consume a retain upon unwrapping.

These functions follow the patterns established in Apple's *Memory Management Programming Guide for Core Foundation*, where you can read more about the "create rule," the "get rule," and other details about memory ownership policies. Search the web for the latest update of this document.

Wrap-up

Optionals are an invaluable component of Swift development. With their "possible value" semantics, they enable you to store and represent the results of lookup operations whose data may or may not exist. Optionals are a powerful workhorse construct that you regularly use in day-to-day operations.

Swift's new early-return `guard` statement is a gift that eliminates awkwardness from your code. Now you can assign, unwrap, and use values with a clear path for missing values. Between `guard` and `nil` coalescing, Swift 2 can elegantly express both fail-on-`nil` and fallback-on-`nil` scenarios with a minimum of overhead and indenting.

Swift 2's revised error handling has also started to eliminate the role of optionals as sentinel values. This usage continues to be common as it's simple to use optionals to represent fail and success states for method calls. Ideally, optional sentinels will shrivel and die as the language matures and Apple's APIs catch up with current language features. Until then, know that it's always better to use `throws` with well-defined errors than to use optional-style sentinels in the code you control.

`nil` happens. Be prepared.

4

Closures and Functions

Lexical closures provide the basis for methods, functions, and "block" parameters, all of which power the Swift applications you develop. By encapsulating state and functionality, they promote behavior to first-class constructs. Closures enable you to pass functionality as parameters and to treat actions as variables, ready for later execution and repeat use. If you're entering Swift from other languages, you might already know these features as lambdas, blocks, or anonymous functions. This chapter explores closures, showing how they work in Swift and how to best incorporate them into your applications.

Building a Function

When I first started learning Swift, I decided to see how many ways I could rewrite one basic function, a simple test that compares two integer values for equality:

```
func testEquality(x: Int, y: Int) -> Bool {
    return x == y
}
```

Like any other Swift function, this example creates a named and parameterized sequence of behaviors:

- The `func` keyword declares a new function, which is named `testEquality`.

- Parameters are listed between parentheses after the function name. These use integer type (`Int`), and a colon separates each parameter name from its type.

- The function returns a Swift truth value (`Bool`). This return type is listed after a *return token* arrow composed of a hyphen and a greater-than symbol (`->`).

- Behavior statements appear between braces.

In Swift, as in many other programming languages, there are many ways to achieve a single goal. Exploring that flexibility was a valuable learning experience for me. The following sections revisit that exercise and give you a chance to consider some of the features you'll encounter when building functionality.

Parameter Names

You call the `testEquality` function by passing to it arguments in parentheses. By convention, the Swift compiler does not create an external label for the first parameter. That's why there's no x: used in the following calls:

```
testEquality(0, y: 1) // returns false
testEquality(1, y: 1) // returns true
```

In this contrived case, the convention is a mismatch to how the function will be used. Since the way this function is named and called doesn't follow Swift convention, it should just go ahead and use x: and y: labels. Fortunately, the extra label issue is easily tweaked. Adding a second x to the function declaration instructs the compiler to require an explicit label in function calls:

```
func testEquality(x x: Int, y: Int) -> Bool {
    return x == y
}
```

Now you call the function using labels for both the x and y parameters. This promotes both labels and differentiates the values they assign:

```
testEquality(x: 0, y: 1) // returns false
testEquality(x: 1, y: 1) // returns true
```

The doubled-x solution distinguishes between *external parameter names* that are used for calling and *local parameter names* that are internal to the function. The first x tells the compiler how the function signature looks to external consumers. This overrides the normal default no-label convention. The second x provides a semantically appropriate name to use within the implementation scope. In this example, the external and internal parameters match. This is not always the case.

Label Conventions

The Swift 2 convention that skips the first label mimics Objective-C descriptive signatures that extend beyond the function name to include parameter labels. This language version matters as different rules held sway prior to the Swift 2 redesign. Swift 2 makes label rules apply more consistently across most use cases. In Swift 2 and later, you adapt a function name to incorporate the first parameter label, as you see in the following sample calls:

```
constructColorWithRed(0.2, green: 0.3, blue:0.1)
lengthOfString("Hello")
testEqualityBetweenX(3, andY:3)
```

Each of these examples encourages you to continue reading past the function name to incorporate labels into how the function describes itself. The results create descriptors that incorporate prepositions like *with*, *of*, and *between*. You "construct color with red, green, and blue," test the "length of string," or "test equality between x and y." A natural fluency relates the function name and its labels to a story about how the function will be used. The result is self-documenting, without relying on memory or lookup to determine which parameters and types are to be provided in each ordered spot.

Without this convention, calls are terser and drop helper words that encourage you to relate parameters to their roles. Here are the same calls in their less fluent forms:

```
constructColor(red:0.2, green: 0.3, blue:0.1)
length(string: "Hello")
testEquality(x:3, y:3)
```

When you use the underscore token for external labels, Swift enables you to drop the label level down further to more C-like function calls:

```
constructColor(0.2, 0.3, 0.1)
length("Hello")
testEquality(3, 3)
```

You can argue whether the context is sufficiently clear for each of the modified calls, but it's obvious that the current Swift conventions make parameter usage clearer. Although labels add overhead to your typing (ignoring the convenience of autocomplete), they encourage better communication to both future-you and to any developers who will eventually collaborate on or inherit your code. Encouraging readability and self-documentation is always a positive thing.

Until Swift 2, descriptive signatures were used primarily for *methods*, which are functions bound to a class, an enumeration, or a structure. Starting in Swift 2, the fluid convention extends to all functions, whether or not they're used as methods or declared at another scope. You can choose to override this default, as testEquality does, by adding an explicit label that instructs the compiler to require all labels, including the first one.

A fully descriptive label mandate (that is, a label for each parameter) applies to constructors, which are initializers that build type instances. Except in cases that mimic typecasting—for example, String(5) or Int("3")—initializers typically use labels for every value passed. Swift initializers are called either with parentheses following a type name or explicitly with init:

```
struct MyStruct{
    let x: Int
    init(x: Int) {self.x = x}
    func myMethod(y: Int, z: Int){}
}

let s = MyStruct(x: 1) // first label by default
// let s = MyStruct.init(x: 1) // equivalent
s.myMethod(2, z: 3) // no first label by default
```

Swift's `init`-by-label convention makes clear how each parameter will be used to create new instances and clarify which initializer will be called.

Naming Methods and Functions

Apple offers suggestions in its Cocoa coding guidelines (https://developer.apple.com/library/mac/documentation/Cocoa/Conceptual/CodingGuidelines/CodingGuidelines.html) that generally extend to Swift. The following are some of its recommendations, as passed through a Swift-centric filter.

Be both brief and clear. Add nouns to contextualize verbs and prepositions. Prefer `removeObject(object, atIndex: index)` over `remove(object, at: index)`. An excess of brevity should not compromise clarity.

Avoid abbreviations. Prefer `printError(myError)` to `printErr(myErr)` and `setBackgroundImage(myImage)` to `setBGImage(myImg)`. Apple offers a list of "acceptable" abbreviations online, but I encourage you to avoid them in Swift except for conventionally universal abbreviations like `max` and `min`.

Avoid ambiguity. Consider whether a function or method name has multiple interpretations. For example, in `displayName`, is the word `display` a noun or a verb? If it's unclear, rework the name to eliminate that confusion.

Be consistent. Use the same terms throughout your apps and libraries to describe concepts. For example, avoid using `fetchBezierElements()` in one method and `listPathComponents()` in another.

Don't reference constructs. Avoid using `struct`, `enum`, `class`, `instance`, and `object` in your names. Prefer `buildDeckOfCards` to `buildDeckOfCardsStruct`. This suggestion does not apply to collection names such as `array`, `set`, `dictionary`, and so forth, where the collection type adds valuable details about the action (for example, `sortArray` or `selectBestChoiceFromSet`).

Use lowercase for method names. Apply common-sense adjustments to this rule for functions that start with an acronym like `URLForAsset` or `QRCodeFromImage`. Although most developers use lowercase for functions outside a type scope, you *can* capitalize without committing a moral crime. Uppercase function names are immediately distinguishable from methods but are currently out of fashion. This practice was quite common up to and including name-spacing, when it suddenly went extinct. It's like a million capitalized voices cried out and were suddenly silenced.

Integrate the word `value` into a type-based label. Prefer `toIntValue` to `toInt` and `withCGRectValue` to `withCGRect`.

Skip `get`. Functions that retrieve state information should describe the thing they're returning. Prefer `extendedExecutionIsEnabled()` or `isExtendedExecutionEnabled()` to `getExtendedExecutionIsEnabled()`. When computed state information does not produce side effects or perform actions that extend beyond the instance, prefer computed properties to methods.

Use prepositions; avoid and. and is the one word that Apple specifically says to avoid. Instead of initializing with (view:, andPosition:), use (view:, position:) arguments.

If you're truly set on using and, reserve it for when there's a semantic link between groups of arguments, such as when constructing colors with "red, green, and blue" floating-point values. In such cases, it's unlikely that future keyword tweaks will interrupt the relationship between these items. Purists will continue to disapprove.

The one case where Apple endorses the use of and is when a method describes two distinct actions, as in openFile(withApplication:, andDeactivate:).

Use American phrases where standard. Prefer initialize to initialise and color to colour as these words are Apple supplied. However, feel free to accessoriseAgeingData-CentreStore.

When in doubt, mimic Apple. Search for an Apple API with a similar concept and use that method signature as a guideline. Be prepared to be inspired by Objective-C. As a rule, not all Apple APIs have been reviewed for Swift. Their automatic translation may not offer sufficiently well-considered examples.

External and Local Parameters

Separate external and local parameter names enable you to differentiate the way a function is called and consumed. The following testEqualityBetweenX:andY: example creates a function called with an andY: external parameter label:

```
func testEqualityBetweenX(x: Int, andY y: Int) -> Bool {
    return x == y
}
testEqualityBetweenX(1, andY: 2) // false
```

Internally, the function uses the more implementation-appropriate y.

Using an underscore (_) for external parameter names enables you to create label-free calls. The following example modifies testEquality to accept two no-label parameters:

```
func testEquality(x: Int, _ y: Int) -> Bool {
    return x == y
}
testEquality(1, 2) // false
```

Swift's conventions mean you only need to modify the external name for y. The compiler already expects to skip the first parameter's label.

Defaults

You make parameters optional by adding default values. Callers can provide specific custom values or skip the parameter and accept the value declared in the default argument clause. For example, you call the `flip` method in the following `Coin` enumeration with either no arguments (flips once) or an integer (the number of times to flip the coin):

```
enum Coin {
    case Heads, Tails
    mutating func flip(times: Int = 1) {
        if times % 2 == 0 {return} // even means no flip
        switch self {
            case Heads: self = Tails
            case Tails: self = Heads
        }
    }
}


var coin = Coin.Heads
coin.flip() // tails
coin.flip(50) // tails
```

If you skip the argument, the parameter defaults to 1, a single flip.

> **Note**
>
> The `mutating` keyword used in the `flip` declaration marks a method that modifies structures. Class methods can always modify instances and do not require this keyword.

Default parameters enable you to adjust Swift function calls in ways you might not expect. When you add default parameters, you can reorder arguments based on labels, as you see in the following example:

```
extension Coin {
    func prettyPrint(lhs lhs: String = "[", rhs: String = "]") {
        print("\(lhs)\(self)\(rhs)")
    }
}
coin.prettyPrint() // [Coin.Tails]
coin.prettyPrint(rhs: ">") // [Coin.Tails>
coin.prettyPrint(lhs: "<") // <Coin.Tails]
coin.prettyPrint(lhs: ">", rhs: "<") // >Coin.Tails<
coin.prettyPrint(rhs: ">", lhs: "<") // <Coin.Tails>
```

The compiler infers calling intent based on the position and labels of the arguments you supply.

The preceding `prettyPrint` example adds an external name to `lhs` (that is, `lhs lhs`) to ensure that each argument has an explicit label. Without that external name, Swift offers the following slightly bizarre behavior:

```
extension Coin {
    func prettyPrintNoLabel(lhs: String = "[", rhs: String = "]") {
        print("\(lhs)\(self)\(rhs)")
    }
}
coin.prettyPrintNoLabel() // [Coin.Tails]
coin.prettyPrintNoLabel(rhs: ">") // [Coin.Tails>
coin.prettyPrintNoLabel("<") // <Coin.Tails]
coin.prettyPrintNoLabel(">", rhs: "<") // >Coin.Tails<
coin.prettyPrintNoLabel(rhs: ">", "<") // <Coin.Tails>
```

You can still reorder arguments, and the no-label argument remains bound to the first parameter.

When you omit both external names, the Swift compiler can no longer differentiate between the arguments except by position, so it mandates specific position-to-parameter binding. The following example shows how this works in the presence of default values:

```
extension Coin {
    func prettyPrintNoLabelsAtAll(lhs: String = "[", _ rhs: String = "]") {
        print("\(lhs)\(self)\(rhs)")
    }
}

coin.prettyPrintNoLabelsAtAll() // [Coin.Tails], both defaults
coin.prettyPrintNoLabelsAtAll("<") // <Coin.Tails], second default
coin.prettyPrintNoLabelsAtAll(">", "<") // >Coin.Tails<, no defaults
```

Constant and Variable Parameters

Swift variables use `let` and `var` to indicate whether their values are immutable (cannot be changed after the initial assignment) or mutable (can be updated at will). Some developers don't realize that closure and function parameters can also be annotated by `var` and `let`. For example, the following function declaration uses `let` and `var` keywords to indicate parameter mutability:

```
func test(let x: String, var y: String) {}
```

The `let` keyword is redundant: All parameters default to constant parameters; they cannot be changed within the function scope. This compile-time check avoids situations where you mistakenly change the value of a parameter without meaning to. Mandating a `var` keyword ensures that any value updates for parameters are intentional. For example, the following snippet raises a compile-time error as you cannot assign a new value to the constant value x:

```
func test(x: String, var y: String) {x = "Hello"} // error!
```

Here's an example where assignment does work. You can adjust y to a new value because it is a variable parameter:

```
func test(x: String, var y: String) {y += " World"; print(y)}
```

Even though you tweak y within this function, the y parameter and any variable it was called with do not change outside the function. The parameter's value is copied and then updated within this scope.

Modifying Parameters

To change the value of an external variable, use Swift's inout call-by-reference copy and write-back mechanism. Add an inout keyword and pass the variable you intend to mutate by prefixing it with &. Here's an example that combines all these concepts. The adjustValues function showcases calls using each kind of parameter:

```
func adjustValues(
    var varParameter: Int,
    letParameter: Int,
    inout inoutParameter: Int) {
    varParameter++ // updates only within function scope
    // letParameter++ // compile-time error
    inoutParameter++ // updates within and outside function scope
    print("\((varParameter, letParameter, inoutParameter))")
}
var x = 10; var y = 20; var z = 30 // assign
print("Before: \((x, y, z))") // (10, 20, 30), check
AdjustValues(varParameter: x, letParameter:y, inoutParameter: &z)
    // prints (11, 20, 31)
print("After: \((x, y, z))")
    // (10, 20, 31) z has now changed and x has not
```

In this example, varParameter increases within the function but does not propagate back to the original variable. inoutParameter also increases, but that change updates the value of z. In Swift, you do not have to dereference a pointer during assignment to an inout parameter.

Now consider the following assignment:

```
let w = 40
```

You can pass w to either or both of AdjustValue's first and second parameters. Immutability outside the function scope does not affect use within the function. However, you cannot pass &w to the AdjustValue's third parameter without a compiler error. You cannot assign new values to immutable variables in this way.

Closures and Functions

In Swift, closures and functions are more or less the same thing, although slight details differentiate the two. For the most part, closures are anonymous (that is, nameless) functions, and functions are named closures. They both offer an executable block of functionality, and they both capture values from their enclosing scope.

Function Types

Every function or closure has a type. The type for the following `testEquality` function is `(Int, Int) -> Bool`:

```
func testEquality(x x  Int, y: Int) -> Bool {
    return x == y
}
```

The `(Int, Int) -> Bool` type consists of an input type tuple, an arrow token, and an output type. *Tuple* refers to a sequence of elements surrounded by parentheses that contain items separated by commas. Tuples may look a bit like arrays but are syntactically distinct from them. Tuples represent fixed-length vectors of potentially distinct types, while arrays are ordered collections of data that share a unifying type.

Confirm the type for `testEquality` by typing the function into a Swift source file or playground and then print `testEquality.dynamicType`. The console shows `(Swift.Int, Swift.Int) -> Swift.Bool`, prepending each type name with the Swift module that defines the type.

You can duplicate a method's functionality by assigning a closure instance to a constant or variable, as in the following example:

```
let testEqualityClosure = {
    (x x: Int, y y: Int) -> Bool in
    return x == y
}
```

Notice the slightly different label convention. By default, closure parameters do not use external names. This assignment adds external x and y labels, using x x and y y to duplicate the calling pattern used for the standalone function.

The closure consists of a signature that defines parameter binding and a return type followed by statements. The `in` keyword that appears after the signature and before the function statements says "use these parameters in these statements." This keyword is required whenever you add an explicit signature to the start of the closure.

The resulting assignment enables you to call the closure using the same parameter values and labels as with the function built with `func`:

```
testEqualityClosure(x: 1, y: 2) // false
testEqualityClosure(x: 1, y: 1) // true
```

> **Note**
>
> At the time this book was being written, Apple was still settling on how to have the compiler handle function type conversion. Apple writes in its release notes for an early Swift 2.1 beta, "Conversions between function types are now supported, exhibiting covariance in function result types and contravariance in function parameter types. For example, it is now legal to assign a function of type `Any -> Int` to a variable of type `String -> Any`." This behavior may change by the time you read this book.

Using Tuple Arguments

Swift allows you to pass tuples to functions and closures as argument sets. The compiler matches the correspondences between the arguments you supply and the input type tuple, which means you can pass all your parameters in a single argument.

Tuple arguments are, internally, anonymous structures with ordered members. An `(x:, y:)` tuple with `.x` and `.y` labels is essentially identical to an unlabeled tuple of matching types with implicit `.0` and `.1` labels:

```
let testArgs = (x:1, y:1)
print(testEquality(testArgs)) // prints true
print(testEqualityClosure(testArgs)) // prints true
```

In the current Swift incarnation, tuple labels must match the function or closure signature. You'll encounter compile-time errors if the expected labels do not agree.

Combine tuple arguments with Swift mapping for appealing results. For example, you can use Swift's `zip` function to create labeled tuples from parameter arrays and then apply the function or closure to each tuple pair by using map. Here's what that approach might look like:

```
let pairs = zip([1, 2, 3, 4], [1, 5, 3, 8]).map({(x:$0.0, y:$0.1)})
let equalities = pairs.map({testEquality($0)})
let equalities2 = pairs.map({testEqualityClosure($0)})
print(equalities) // true, false, true, false
print(equalities2) // true, false, true, false
```

The first statement creates labeled tuple pairs. This example compares items in the two arrays, checking whether similarly positioned items are equal. The closure passed to map redirects each `(x:, y:)` tuple. Alternatively, you can cast the `(Int, Int)` tuple to use `(x: Int, y: Int)` labels in the map closure's signature:

```
let equalities3 = zip([1, 2, 3, 4], [1, 5, 3, 8]).map({
    (tuple: (x:Int, y:Int)) in  testEquality(tuple)})
```

Using Shorthand Argument Names

When Swift knows types and positions, it doesn't really need parameter names. This next version of `testEquality` is a simple closure whose arguments are defined by position, starting with $0 for the first argument and then continuing to $1, $2, and so on:

```
let testEquality: (Int, Int) -> Bool = {return $0 == $1}
testEquality(1, 2) // false, but no labels in call
testEquality(2, 2) // true, but no labels in call
```

These positional, anonymous arguments are called *shorthand argument names*. The closure doesn't define *x* or *y* or any other parameter identifiers. In this example, the function proto-type moves outside the scope of the closure. This `(Int, Int) -> Bool` prototype declares `testEquality`'s type, enabling the compiler to match it to the behavior on the right. Without explicit typing, Swift is unable to infer the roles of the two anonymous closure arguments or determine whether they can be compared using the == operator.

To match previous examples, add external labels to the signature. The following example intro-duces labels while retaining the anonymous internal bindings:

```
let testEquality: (x: Int, y: Int) -> Bool = {return $0 == $1}
testEquality(x: 1, y: 2) // false
testEquality(x: 2, y: 2) // true
```

When using explicit typing, you can bind positions to names using a simple labels-in approach, as in the following example:

```
let testEquality: (x: Int, y: Int) -> Bool = {x, y in return x == y}
```

The compiler knows the external labels and types from the explicit type assignment. It relates these to the internal names that precede the in keyword. Compare this implementation to the following fully qualified version:

```
let testEqualityFull: (x: Int, y: Int) -> Bool = { // typed closure assignment
    (x: Int, y: Int) -> Bool in // closure signature
    return x == y // statements
}
testEqualityFull(x:1, y:2) // false
testEqualityFull(x:2, y:2) // true
```

Swift's standard library offers ways to coerce data into positional arguments. The forEach func-tion processes each member of a sequence. Use withExtendedLifetime to create positional arguments within a closure:

```
[1, 5, 2, 9, 6].forEach{print($0)}
[(2, 3), (5, 1), (6, 7)].forEach{print($0)} // pairs
[(2, 3), (5, 1), (6, 7)].forEach{print("a: \($0) b: \($1)")} // split
let a = 1; let b = 2
withExtendedLifetime(a, {print("a: \($0)")})
withExtendedLifetime((a, b)){print("a: \($0) b: \($1)")}
```

In addition to guaranteeing that values are not destroyed before the end of the closure's life-time, withExtendedLifetime's anonymous arguments enable you to capture and use values without creating intermediate variables.

> **Note**
>
> A tuple shuffle enables you to perform simultaneous permuting assignments from one anony-
> mous tuple to another:
>
>   (x, y) = (y, x)
>   (x, y, z, w) = (w, x, y z)
>
> In optimized compilation, performance is indistinguishable from that of `swap(&x, &y)` and
> `let tmp = x; x = y; y = tmp`, and the simpler declaration helps make your intent clear.

Inferred Closure Types

Use caution when creating untyped closure assignment, as in the following examples. The
compiler can infer only so much. Here are a couple of well-behaved assignments:

```
let hello = {print("Hello")}
let random = {return Int(arc4random_uniform(100))}
```

Call these functions by adding `()` after their name—for example, `hello()` and `random()`. The
first function is typed `()->Void`. It has no parameters and returns no result. The second returns
an integer between 0 and 99. It is typed `()->Int`.

> **Note**
>
> The keyword `Void` is aliased to `()`. Prefer `Void` for return types and `()` for empty parameter
> lists.

Now, consider the following more problematic declaration. The compiler cannot process it due
to ambiguity:

```
let printit = {print($0)} // this is problematic
```

Swift's compiler has no way to infer the type of the positional `$0` parameter. By default, the
compiler wants to type this no-return-value closure as `()->Void`, but the source code references
an anonymous positional parameter. This is not a good thing. The rule of thumb to take from
this is that you always want to combine positional parameters with well-typed signatures.

You use anonymous parameters almost exclusively in the realm of closure arguments rather
than standalone functions. For example, `MutableCollectionType`'s `sortInPlace` function
takes one parameter, a closure with two arguments that returns a truth value:

```
mutating func sortInPlace(isOrderedBefore:
    (Self.Generator.Element, Self.Generator.Element) -> Bool).
```

Implement the sort by passing a closure that compares the two arguments. The returned truth
value indicates whether the first argument is ordered before the second. Since the closure type
is hard-wired into the parameter, you are free to use positional parameters to return a succinct
ordering test, as in the following example:

```
let random = {return Int(arc4random_uniform(100))}
var nums = (1...5).map({_ in random()}) // 5 random Ints
nums.sortInPlace({$0 > $1}) // reverse sort
```

> **Note**
>
> Use `sort` with the same arguments to return a sorted copy of the original collection without updating the original. You cannot use `sortInPlace` with an immutable array assigned with `let`.

Because the closure is the final (and, in this case, only) parameter to the `sortInPlace` function, you may omit the parentheses that normally would surround it. Instead of this:

```
nums.sortInPlace({$0 < $1})
```

You can use this:

```
nums.sortInPlace{$0 < $1}
```

This is called a *trailing closure*. It is added outside and after any parentheses used for other arguments. Prefer trailing closures for procedural elements that do not pass through values or that will be used strictly for procedural execution (such as in Grand Central Dispatch or Notification Center). Naked braces indicate standalone scopes. Retain parentheses for any function whose scope returns consumable values. This practice instantly differentiates between procedural and functional closures, especially when chaining results.

> **Note**
>
> Some developers like to add a space to separate trailing closures from the calls they complete, like this: `functioncall {}`. I prefer the abutting format, which is what you see throughout this book. Spaces between braces and code are another common practice to add readability to single-line calls: `functioncall{ ...code... }`.

The closure for the sort-in-place example omits a *return* keyword. That's because the return can be implied from the context. When working with a closure with a return type, Swift assumes that a single line creates a return value. When used with `testEquality`, you establish an even simpler closure than the one that started this section:

```
let testEquality: (Int, Int) -> Bool = {$0 == $1}
```

Parameter Type Inference

Swift offers some interesting declaration variations. For example, you can use an already-declared closure type to infer variable roles by position. In this example, the x and y argument types are known to be integers. Swift matches them to the prototype in the variable declaration outside the closure:

```
let testEquality: (Int, Int) -> Bool = {
    (x, y) -> Bool in
    x == y
}
```

The declaration establishes the return type so you can skip the `Bool` return type inside the closure since it's redundant:

```
let testEquality: (Int, Int) -> Bool = {
    (x, y) in
    x == y
}
```

You can also squoosh all the code together if you like, so x == y appears on the same line as (x, y) in:

```
let testEquality: (Int, Int) -> Bool = {(x, y) in x == y}
```

If you *really really* are looking for the simplest possible expression, well, look no further than this example, which supplies an operator function. At this point, you've omitted pretty much every detail that can be inferred:

```
let testEquality: (Int, Int) -> Bool = (==)
```

Declaring Type Aliases

A type alias, as the name suggests, gives you an alternative way to refer to a type. You create one by using the `typealias` keyword. It's most commonly used to simplify complex types into consistent reusable components and to conform types to Swift protocols. Declaring a type alias simplifies repeated declarations, particularly when you're using closures as parameters. The following snippet declares a `CompareClosureType`, which is set to `(Int, Int) -> Bool`. Once declared, you can use the alias anywhere you'd normally specify the type:

```
typealias CompareClosureType = (Int, Int) -> Bool
let testEquality: CompareClosureType = {$0 == $1}
```

Xcode is now optimized to show originating type annotation in error messages. For example, you might try to access a nonexistent property on the newly declared `testEquality` constant:

```
print(testEquality.nonExistentProperty)
```

Because the diagnostic involves a type alias, Xcode adds a note with `aka` (also known as) and the original type:

```
error: value of type 'CompareClosureType' (aka '(Int, Int) -> Bool') has no member
'nonExistentProperty'
```

This behavior enables you to instantly see not only a direct type name but also its underlying definition.

Nested Functions

As functions are a first-class type, a function can return another function as its value. Recipe 4-1 selects and returns one of its nested functions.

Recipe 4-1   **Returning Embedded Function References**

```
// Kinds of comparison
enum CompareType{case Equal, Unequal}

// Comparison function factory
func compareFunction(comparison: CompareType) -> (Int, Int) -> Bool {
    // Function that tests equality
    func testEquality(x: Int, y: Int) -> Bool {return x == y}

    // Function that tests inequality
    func testInequality(x: Int, y: Int) -> Bool {return x != y}

    // Return a function
    switch comparison {
    case .Equal: return testEquality
    case .Unequal: return testInequality
    }
}

compareFunction(.Equal)(1, 2) // false
compareFunction(.Equal)(1, 1) // true
```

More commonly, nesting Swift functions enable you to tuck away details by providing implementation-specific utility that isn't needed at a wider scope. In Recipe 4-2, the nested `factorial` function is not exposed.

Recipe 4-2   **Basic Function Nesting for Reusable Internal Components**

```
// Return n choose i
// This is not an efficient or ideal implementation
func n(n: Int, choose i: Int) -> Int {
    // n >= i
    precondition(i < n, "n choose i is not legal when n (\(n)) < i (\(i))")

    // i > 0 guarantees that n > 0
    precondition(i > 0, "choose value i (\(i)) must be positive")

    // Nested factorial function helps organize code
    func factorial(n: Int) -> Int {return (1...n).reduce(1, combine:*)}
```

```
    // Compute the choose results
    return factorial(n) / (factorial(i) * factorial(n - i))
}

print(n(5, choose:3)) // 10
print(n(10, choose:4)) // 210
```

You can nest in closures as well as functions, as you see in Recipe 4-3.

Recipe 4-3   **Nesting Functions Within Closures**

```
let myFactorialFactoryClosure: () -> (Int) -> Int = {
    func factorial(n: Int) -> Int {return (1...n).reduce(1, combine:*)}
    return factorial
}

let fac = myFactorialFactoryClosure()
fac(5) // 120
```

Nested functions have access to variables declared in the outer function's scope. In the following example, the inner `incrementN` function modifies the n variable each time it is called:

```
func outerFunc() -> Int {
    var n = 5
    func incrementN() {n++}
    incrementN()
    incrementN()
    return n
}

outerFunc() // 7
```

Tuples

In Swift, as in many other modern languages, tuples group items. A Swift tuple appears in parentheses as a sequence of comma-delineated elements. So far, you've read a little bit about tuples and their role in working with closures and functions. This section explores these features more fully, offering a deep dive into their workings.

Tuples are essentially anonymous structures. They allow you to combine types in an addressable fashion. For example, a tuple of (1, "Hello", 2.2) is more or less equivalent to the following struct instance:

```
struct MyStruct {
    var a: Int
    var b: String
    var c: Double
}
let mystruct = MyStruct(a: 1, b: "Hello", c: 2.2)
```

The `(1, "Hello", 2.2)` tuple doesn't use labels, while the struct does. You access the tuple properties with `.0`, `.1`, `.2`, and you access the struct properties with `.a`, `.b`, `.c`. As you saw earlier in this chapter, you can add labels to tuples; for example, `(a:1, b:"Hello", c:2.2)` is a legal tuple:

```
let labeledTuple = (a:1, b:"Hello", c:2.2)
labeledTuple.1 // "Hello"
labeledTuple.b // "Hello"
```

When a tuple is defined using labels, you access the tuple both by order (`.0`, `.1`, `.2`) and name (`.a`, `.b`, `.c`). However, you cannot refer to a structure by field order. Swift doesn't offer a grand unified structure/tuple/class type. While these things seem more alike than different, people familiar with the language internals assure me that there are compelling reasons this has not happened yet.

You can access child properties in a limited way by using reflection. The following example shows how you can visualize each child of the structure or tuple:

```
let mirror1 = Mirror(reflecting: mystruct)
mirror1.children.count
mirror1.children.forEach{print("\($0.label): \($0.value)")}
let mirror2 = Mirror(reflecting: labeledTuple)
mirror2.children.count
mirror2.children.forEach{print("\($0.label): \($0.value)")}
```

You cannot, however, consume these `Any`-typed values in any meaningful way. At this time, mirroring is limited to debugging output.

When you run the previous example, the `mystruct` and `labeledTuple` mirrors reveal identical values but distinct labels:

```
Optional("a"): 1
Optional("b"): Hello
Optional("c"): 2.2
Optional(".0"): 1
Optional(".1"): Hello
Optional(".2"): 2.2
```

From Tuples to Structs

You cannot easily convert a struct to a tuple, but you can convert a tuple to a struct in a limited fashion:

```
let labeledTuple = (a:1, b:"Hello", c:2.2)
let mystruct = MyStruct(labeledTuple)
```

This compiles and runs, but you're not actually creating a struct from the tuple. You're using the tuple as arguments to the struct's initializer. Tuples can be passed to nearly any argument list—for initializers, functions, methods, closures, and so forth.

Because of the way structs create default initializers, you cannot build a MyStruct struct with an unlabeled tuple, such as (1, "Hello", 2.2). You must first add an initializer that doesn't require labels. The following example creates that second initializer:

```
struct MyStruct {
    var a: Int
    var b: String
    var c: Double
    init (a: Int, b: String, c: Double) {
        self.a = a; self.b = b; self.c = c
    }
    init (_ a: Int, _ b: String, _ c: Double) {
        self.init(a:a, b:b, c:c)
    }
}

let labeledTuple = (a:1, b:"Hello", c:2.2)
let mystruct = MyStruct(labeledTuple)

let unlabeledTuple = (1, "Hello", 2.2)
let mystruct2 = MyStruct(unlabeledTuple)
```

Once you add initializers that match both labeled and unlabeled elements, you can construct structs from either kind of tuple.

Tuple Return Types

Functions, methods, and closures may return tuples as well as any other return type. Tuples provide a convenient way to group related information together as an informal anonymous struct. In the following example, MyReturnTuple returns a labeled tuple:

```
func MyReturnTuple() -> (a:Int, b:String, c:Double) {
    return (1, "Hello", 2.2)
}
```

For a more meaningful example, a web service method might return an HTTP status code tuple such as (404, "Page not Found"):

```
func fetchWebStatus(url: NSURL) -> (Int, String) {
    // ...function code here...
    return (418, "I'm a Teapot (see RFC 2324)")
}
```

You decompose the tuple by assignment. A single assignment stores the entire tuple value. A tuple assignment extracts component elements by position:

```
let returnValues = fetchWebStatus() // returns tuple
let (statusCode, statusMessage) = returnValues // breaks tuple into components
```

When you're only interested in some of the tuple values, use the underscore _ "ignore" character to skip specific assignments. Instead of saying this, for example, to fetch the status message by position:

```
let statusMessage = returnValues.1
```

you can use this:

```
let (_, statusMessage) = returnValues
```

Variadic Parameters

Sometimes you don't know in advance how many parameters you'll need to pass to a function. As the name suggests, a variadic parameter *varies* with the number of items passed to it. For example, Recipe 4-4 prints a current tally as it creates a running sum from the values passed to it.

Recipe 4-4   **Using Variadic Parameters to Compute a Sum**

```
func RunningSum(numbers: Int...) {
    var sum = 0
    for eachNumber in numbers {
        sum += eachNumber
        print("\(eachNumber): \(sum)")
    }
    print("Sum: \(sum)")
}
```

The three periods after the Int type indicate that numbers is a variadic parameter. When you declare the parameter in this fashion, you can pass zero or more input values to it:

```
RunningSum()
RunningSum(1, 5, 3, 2, 8)
```

The function sees these parameters as a typed array—in this example, [Int]—even though the items are not passed using array notation. You can define one variadic parameter per function, and the variable argument can appear at any position, as in this example, where a list of items appears at the start of the method call:

```
func contextString(items: Any..., file: String = __FILE__,
    function: String = __FUNCTION__, line: Int = __LINE__) -> String {
    return "\(function):\(self.dynamicType):\(file):\(line) " +
        items.map({"\($0)"}).joinWithSeparator(", ")
}
```

Recipe 4-5 offers another example of using variadic assignments. This Array extension enables array lookups using multiple indices. You might create an array and want to index it with array[3, 5] or array[7, 9, 10, 4]. The extension adds subscripting for two or more indices on top of the single-index subscript already built into Array.

Recipe 4-5   Multi-index Array Subscripting

```
extension Array {
    typealias ArrayType = Element
    subscript(i1: Int, i2: Int, rest: Int...) -> [ArrayType] {
        var result = [self[i1], self[i2]]
        for index in rest {
            result += [self[index]]
        }
        return result
    }
}
```

This implementation uses three parameters to avoid conflict with the single-subscript implementation. Any implementation that accepts (Int, Int...) parameters is indistinguishable from (Int) at runtime if called with a single index. That's because variadic parameters accept zero or more values. To make this work, you need a signature that won't confuse Swift. The proper solution uses two nonvariadic arguments followed by a third variadic one: (Int, Int, Int...). Whenever at least two parameters are passed, Swift knows to call this function instead:

```
let foo = [1, 2, 3, 4, 5, 6, 7]
print(foo[2]) // prints 3, defaults to built-in implementation
print(foo[2, 4]) // prints [3, 5]
print(foo[2, 4, 1]) // prints [3, 5, 2]
print(foo[2, 4, 1, 5]) // prints [3, 5, 2, 6]
```

Capturing Values

Consider the following code snippet:

```
var item = 25
var closure = {print("Value is \(item)")}
item = 35
closure()
```

It creates a closure that prints out the value of the variable item. When it runs, should it print out 25, the value of the variable at the time the closure was created, or 35, the current contents of the memory pointed to by the variable reference?

If you run this in an app or a playground, you'll find that this code prints 35 rather than 25. Swift closures default to capturing references, not values. This behavior is distinct from Objective-C blocks, where you need to explicitly use the __block keyword to get this behavior. Whatever value is stored in item at the time of execution, and not at the time of declaration, is printed. To change this behavior and capture the value at the time the closure is defined, use a *capture list*, as in the following example:

```
var item = 25
var closure = {[item] in print(item)}
item = 35
closure()
```

The use of [i] enables you to capture the value of i at the time you create the closure instead of at a later runtime. Capture lists appear as the first item in a closure, before any parameter clauses or identifier lists, and require the in keyword to be used. Here's another example, which uses a class instance instead of an integer:

```
class MyClass {
    var value = "Initial Value"
}

var instance = MyClass() // original assignment
var closure2 = {[instance] in print(instance.value)}
instance = MyClass() // updated assignment
instance.value = "Updated Value"
closure2() // prints "Initial Value"
```

If you omit the [instance] from the capture list, this example prints out Updated Value, using the updated variable assignment stored in the referenced instance. With the capture list, it prints Initial Value. This is the value stored by the original assignment captured by the closure.

A capture list enables you to avoid reference cycles, where a closure owns a reference to the instance that owns the closure. Reference cycles commonly pop up when you're working with completion blocks, notification handlers, and Grand Central Dispatch blocks. In nearly every case, you'll want to use weak references to break reference cycles.

Add the `weak` keyword to the capture list and unwrap the value before using it. Here's an example of what that pattern looks like in real-world use:

```
class Bumpable {
    var weakBumpValueClosure: () -> Void = {}
    private var value = 0
    func showValue() {print("Value is now \(value)")}
    init() {
        self.weakBumpValueClosure = {
            [weak self] in
            if let strongSelf = self {
                strongSelf.value++
                strongSelf.showValue()
            }
        }
    }
}
```

This closure uses weak `self` capture; a weak reference may revert to `nil` when an instance is deallocated. Because of this, you must always treat them as optionals and unwrap them before use. This example uses an `if-let` statement to bind the optional. If the instance is still valid at the start of the binding, the binding ensures that it remains valid throughout the scope in which it is used. If the `self` reference is already invalidated, the captured value reverts to `nil`, and the `if-let` statement shortcuts. No harm, no foul.

There's a second, far more dangerous, approach you can use: `unowned` capture. This is equivalent to Objective-C's `unsafe-unretained`, and I cannot recommend using it. Apple writes that unowned references should be used when "the closure and the instance it captures will always refer to each other, and will always be deallocated at the same time." Unlike weak references that may revert to `nil` when an instance is deallocated, an unowned reference is not optional. It must stick around for as long as the closure exists. An unowned reference is roughly equivalent to and as desirable as using a weak value with forced unwrapping.

The advantage—if that's even the right word to use—is that an unowned reference is not an optional value and can be used directly without unwrapping. Consider the following example:

```
public func dispatch_after(delay: NSTimeInterval,
    queue:dispatch_queue_t = dispatch_get_main_queue(),
    block: dispatch_block_t) {
        let delay = Int64(delay * Double(NSEC_PER_SEC))
        dispatch_after(
            dispatch_time(DISPATCH_TIME_NOW, delay),
            queue, block)
}

class Bumpable {
    // If unownedBumpValueClosure was marked as private,
    // [unowned self] would be safe. The only ref would be to
    // the parent instance and they'd be deallocated together
```

```
        var unownedBumpValueClosure: () -> Void = {}
        private var value = 0
        func showValue() {print("Value is now \(value)")}
        init() {
            self.unownedBumpValueClosure= {
                [unowned self] in
                self.value++
                self.showValue()
            }
        }
    }
}

// Setting up for failure
var bumper = Bumpable()
dispatch_after(2.0, block: bumper.unownedBumpValueClosure)
bumper.showValue()
```

If the `bumper` instance deallocates at any time within the first two seconds before the dispatched block is called, the closure will crash during execution, as the co-deallocation guarantee cannot be maintained.

> **Note**
>
> Swift functions and closures are reference types. Apple writes, "Whenever you assign a function or a closure to a constant or a variable, you are actually setting that constant or variable to be a reference to the function or closure." Reference typing enables constant (`let`) closures to update as well as read the variables they've captured. It ensures that closures, no matter how assigned or passed, always refer to the same instance. Because of this, captured values don't depend on the context where the closure is executed.

Autoclosures

A Swift autoclosure creates an implicit closure for an expression passed as a parameter without explicit braces. That expression is automatically converted to a closure. Consider this example:

```
func wait(@autoclosure closure: () ->()) {
    print("Happens first");
    closure() // Executes now
    print("Happens last");
}
wait(print("This goes in the middle"))
```

Like any other closures, autoclosures enable you to delay statement evaluations until a later time but do not require you to enclose those calls in braces. This differentiates an autoclosure from simply passing the results of a normal expression as an argument, which would be executed immediately. Autoclosures cannot accept parameters (that is, the first part of their function type must be () or Void), although they can return any type desired.

Apple offers the following as its standard autoclosure example:

```
func simpleAssert(@autoclosure condition: () -> Bool, _ message: String) {
    if !condition() {print(message)}
}
```

This function produces less dramatic feedback than assert and precondition. Instead of stopping program execution, it prints out a warning when a condition is not met, creating a kinder, gentler in-code assertion mechanism.

For example, you might test whether a percentage falls between 0.0 and 1.0:

```
simpleAssert(0.0...1.0 ~= percent , "Percent is out of range")
```

Some developers use autoclosures in deployment to differentiate statements between phone and tablet targets—for example, idiom<T>(@autoclosure phone: () -> T, @autoclosure pad: () -> T). Others find them handy lazy multiway unwrappers—for example, when performing JSON parsing. At one point, I decided that UIView animations really needed auto-closures. I felt that an inline property assignment like this:

```
UIView.animate(2.0, view.backgroundColor = .blueColor())
```

was more aesthetically pleasing than the default syntax in the following examples, which can be written with or without trailing closures:

```
UIView.animateWithDuration(2.0, animations:{
    view.backgroundColor = .blueColor()})

UIView.animateWithDuration(2.0){
    view.backgroundColor = .blueColor()
}
```

So I built the following extension:

```
extension UIView {
    class func animate(duration: NSTimeInterval,
        @autoclosure _ animations: () -> Void) {
        UIView.animateWithDuration(duration, animations: animations) // error
    }
}
```

It didn't work but threw a compiler error. Specifically, the complier complained that I was attempting to use a non-escaping function (the autoclosure) in an escaping context (the animateWithDuration call). autoclosure defaults to noescape, an attribute which ensures that parameters are not stored for later execution and will not outlive the lifetime of the call.

You add no-escape implementation by marking closure parameters with the @noescape keyword, as in the following example:

```
typealias VoidBlockType = () -> Void
func callEscape(closure: VoidBlockType) {closure()}
func callNoEscape(@noescape closure: VoidBlockType) {closure()}

class MyClass {
    var value = 0
    func testNoEscape() {
        callNoEscape{print(value++)}
    }

    func testEscape() {
        // reference to property 'value' in closure requires
        // explicit 'self.' to make capture semantics explicit
        // callEscape{print(value++)} // error
        callEscape{print(self.value++)}
    }
}
```

Using `noescape` introduces performance optimizations and bypasses the need to annotate properties and methods with `self`. Normally, Swift can infer `self` in method bodies, so you don't need to include it with many property and method calls. In escaping closures, Swift requires that you add explicit `self` references. This signals and disambiguates capture semantics; it's clear that you're capturing `self` and may potentially create retain cycles.

Since `animateWithDuration` hasn't been updated to take no-escaping into account, the autoclosure parameter cannot be used in its default state. In Recipe 4-6, the escaping annotation overrides this limitation, solving the issue and enabling my custom `animate` method to work with an extended lifetime.

Recipe 4-6   **Adding Autoclosure to `UIView` Animation**

```
extension UIView {
    class func animate(duration: NSTimeInterval,
        @autoclosure(escaping) _ animations: () -> Void) {
        UIView.animateWithDuration(duration, animations: animations)
    }
}
```

When using no-escape closures, do not try to assign them to escaping variables, pass them to escaping contexts, use them as asynchronous blocks that may outlive the parent, or embed them in other, escaping closures. Here's a function that calls a `noescape` parameter:

```
func callNoEscape(@noescape closure: VoidBlockType) {

    // Using @noescape means closure ends its lifetime when its scope
    // ends its lifetime and closure will not be stored or used later
```

```
    // Invalid uses

    // Non-escaping function in escaping context
    // Cannot pass as escaping parameter
    // dispatch_async(dispatch_get_main_queue(), closure)
    // let observer = NSNotificationCenter.defaultCenter()
    //     .addObserverForName(nil, object: nil,
    //         queue: NSOperationQueue.mainQueue(), usingBlock: closure)

    // Non-escaping function in escaping context
    // Cannot store as escaping param
    // let holdClosure: VoidBlockType = closure

    // Closure use of @noescape parameter 'closure' may allow it to escape
    // Cannot use in normal escaping scope
    // let otherClosure = {closure()}

    closure() // call the no-escape closure
}
```

Adding Default Closures

Optional closures enable you to call functions both with and without trailing closures. For example, you might call a function with `myFunction()` *or* with `myFunction(){...}`, with the final closure an optional item. You achieve this by adding a default value to your closure, as in this example:

```
func doSomethingWithCompletion(completion: () -> Void = {}) {
    // ... do something ...
    completion()
}
```

The Swift compiler is smart enough to recognize that an omitted block argument, even a trailing one, should fall back to the default value, which in this case is a simple empty closure. That closure's type is automatically inferred through its declaration.

You can, of course, supply more complex defaults:

```
let defaultClosure: () -> Void = {print("Default")}
func doSomethingWithCompletion(completion: () -> Void = defaultClosure) {
    completion()
}
doSomethingWithCompletion() // "Default"
doSomethingWithCompletion(){print("Custom")} // "Custom"
```

The overhead for an empty default closure is minimal, especially with optimization enabled. Any time you add default arguments, there's a minor check involved. Method calls without default values run faster, which you can see if you run tens of millions of tests at once. For single calls, the difference is trivial.

Currying

Currying in Swift (and other programming languages) involves translating a function that accepts an argument tuple into a series of functions with single arguments. Wikipedia defines currying as follows:

> *In mathematics and computer science, currying refers to the technique of translating the evaluation of a function that takes multiple arguments (or a tuple of arguments) into evaluating a sequence of functions, each with a single argument (partial application). It was introduced by Moses Schönfinkel and later developed by Haskell Curry.*

In Swift, functions normally look like this:

```
public func convolve(var kernel: [Int16], image: UIImage) -> UIImage? {...}
```

This function, which I've elided here, uses the Accelerate framework to perform basic image processing. Specifically, it convolves a `UIImage` instance against an arbitrary kernel made up of weighted `Int16` values. This is a very handy way of creating special effects. It's also a perfect example of a function that benefits from currying.

> **Note**
>
> A convolution operation multiplies a matrix of number values (called a kernel) against the pixels of an image to create special effects such as blurring, sharpening, embossing, and so forth. The kernel passes over each image pixel (excluding areas at the very edge of the image where the kernel cannot fully fit within the image) and multiplies each of its values against the pixels that surround the center.

When curried, the preceding function's declaration looks like this:

```
public func convolve(var kernel: [Int16])(_ image: UIImage) -> UIImage? {...}
```

Notice the one major change? It's subtle. Instead of a single argument tuple, the declaration consists of a series of one-argument tuples before the return type. There's an extra set of parentheses in there between `[Int16]` and `image`.

Normally, you call this function with two arguments:

```
convolve(kernel, image)
```

With currying, you use two 1-tuples:

```
convolve(kernel)(image)
```

The extra parentheses are a dead giveaway that there's currying.

Why Curry?

Currying enables you to break up functions into partially specified components and then use and reuse those components however you like. And that's where this language feature becomes deeply powerful. You can decouple the `convolve(kernel)` portion of this call from `(image)`. Separating these enables you to delay setting an image argument until some indefinite time in the future. You can now perform assignments like this:

```
public var blur7Kernel: [Int16] = [Int16](count: 49, repeatedValue:1)
public let blur7 = convolve(blur7Kernel)
```

This snippet creates a reusable 7×7 blur effect. You can apply it to any image by calling this:

```
blur7(image)
```

Here's the best part: This isn't a throwaway. You establish a new function that can be used over and over by many programs in many circumstances: The customization is useful in and of itself, but the code that drives the customization is decoupled.

When you update the centralized convolution routine, every curried version updates as well. It's the same benefit as if you had written a full wrapper function, like the one that follows, but with significantly less overhead:

```
func blur7(image: UIImage)  -> UIImage? {
    var blur7Kernel: [Int16] = [Int16](count: 49, repeatedValue:1)
    return convolve(blur7Kernel, image)
}
```

Building Libraries

In fact, with currying, I can now build an entire suite of common image processing functions by passing various kernels, as you see in Recipe 4-7. Each definition raises the level of abstraction and prevents me from having to redevelop kernels (or even think about the math) when I want to emboss, blur, or sharpen an image.

Recipe 4-7   **Creating a Convolution Library with Currying**

```
// Embossing
public var embossKernel: [Int16] = [
    -2, -1, 0,
    -1, 1, 1,
    0, 1, 2]
public let emboss = convolve(embossKernel)

// Sharpening
public var sharpenKernel: [Int16] = [
```

```
    0,   -1,  0,
   -1,    8,  -1,
    0,   -1,  0
]
public let sharpen = convolve(sharpenKernel)

// Blurring
public var blur3Kernel: [Int16] = [Int16](count: 9, repeatedValue:1)
public let blur3 = convolve(blur3Kernel)
public var blur5Kernel: [Int16] = [Int16](count: 25, repeatedValue:1)
public let blur5 = convolve(blur5Kernel)
public var blur7Kernel: [Int16] = [Int16](count: 49, repeatedValue:1)
public let blur7 = convolve(blur7Kernel)
public var gauss5Kernel: [Int16] = [
    1,   4,   6,   4,  1,
    4,  16,  24,  16,  4,
    6,  24,  36,  24,  6,
    4,  16,  24,  16,  4,
    1,   4,   6,   4,  1
]
public let gauss5 = convolve(gauss5Kernel)
```

Everything here uses one central function. While each of these filters relies on distinct kernel presets, none of these assignments affects how convolution takes place.

Partial Application

What currying does and why it's particularly important in Swift and in other languages is that it lets you utilize partial application. According to Wikipedia, "In computer science, partial application (or partial function application) refers to the process of fixing a number of arguments to a function, producing another function of smaller arity."

Without built-in currying, you can still create partially applied functions in Swift. For this example, you could build wrapper closures around the convolve function by setting kernels like this:

```
public func createConvolveFunction(kernel: [Int16]) ->

    (UIImage -> UIImage?) {
    return { (image: UIImage) -> UIImage? in
        return convolve(kernel, image)}
}
```

This isn't too difficult to put together, but why bother? This kind of intermediate work isn't needed in Swift. Built-in currying gives you this feature for free: Just add parentheses.

Currying Costs

Currying does involve some costs, but for most purposes, they're pretty minor. Kevin Roebuck writes, in *Functional Programming Languages: High-Impact Strategies*, "Curried functions may be used in any language that supports closures; however, uncurried functions are generally preferred for efficiency reasons, since the overhead of partial application and closure creation can then be avoided for most function calls."

Reserve currying for highly parameterized functions. Currying enables you to specialize these to establish reusable already-primed-and-ready default configurations.

Currying and Callbacks

Many Cocoa and Cocoa Touch APIs use target action. In the following typical scenario, the `addTarget(_:, action:, forControlEvents:)` pattern enables you to assign a callback for when a user taps this button:

```
class Delegate: NSObject {
    func callback(sender: AnyObject) {
        // do something
    }
}
let delegate = Delegate()

let button = UIButton()
button.addTarget(delegate, action: "callback:",
    forControlEvents: .TouchUpInside)
```

In Swift, currying leverages this pattern in a new way for new types. It won't help you with the `UIButton`, which is stuck back in existing Cocoa Touch libraries, but it offers great possibility for new implementations. Instead of using a selector, store a reference to the method you wish to use:

```
let callbackMethod = Delegate.callback
```

Here's the fully qualified version of this assignment:

```
let callbackMethod: Delegate -> (AnyObject) -> Void = Delegate.callback
```

Using `Delegate.callback` points to the method without tying it to any particular instance. To associate it with an instance, add the target in parentheses:

```
let targetedCallback = callbackMethod(target)
```

You execute the callback by adding a parameter tuple:

```
targetedCallback(parameters)
```

The preceding call is equivalent to these direct (and more obviously curried) versions:

```
Delegate.callback(target)(parameters) // and
callbackMethod(target)(parameters)
```

When using currying with multiple parameters, you pass method parameters as a single *n*-ary tuple. Here's an example of a method that accepts three parameters:

```
class TestClass {
    func multiParameterMethod(arg1: Int, _ arg2: Int, _ arg3: Int) {
        print("\(arg1) \(arg2) \(arg3)")
    }
}
```

To call this method on an instance, pass the parameters after establishing the instance for the method to apply to:

```
let test = TestClass()
TestClass.multiParameterMethod(test)(1, 2, 3)
```

Practical Currying

It can help to think of curried functions in terms of staging. Add a tuple break to each point where a new client takes over. Consider the approach used in ProjectFunctionToCoordinate-System. This utility transforms a (CGFloat) -> CGFloat function into the coordinate system defined by two points, p0 and p1, and applies that function at a given x value. Unlike the image examples, Recipe 4-8 uses multiple currying points and differs in terms of how many parameters are supplied at each partial application. The middle set of parameters, which establishes the target coordinate system, accept two points.

Recipe 4-8 **Currying and Partial Application**

```
public typealias FunctionType = (CGFloat) -> CGFloat
public func projectFunctionToCoordinateSystem(
    function f: FunctionType)(p0: CGPoint, p1: CGPoint)
        (x: CGFloat) -> CGPoint {
    let dx = p1.x - p0.x
    let dy = p1.y - p0.y
    let magnitude = sqrt(dy * dy + dx * dx)
    let theta = atan2(dy, dx)

    var outPoint = CGPoint(x: x * magnitude, y: f(x) * magnitude)
    outPoint = CGPointApplyAffineTransform(outPoint,
        CGAffineTransformMakeRotation(theta))
    outPoint = CGPointApplyAffineTransform(outPoint,
        CGAffineTransformMakeTranslation(p0.x, p0.y))
    return CGPoint(x: outPoint.x, y: outPoint.y)
}
```

Currying enables you to establish reusable partially applied elements. In this `projectFunctionToCoordinateSystem` example, you might establish a projectable `Sin` function. The following `fSin` closure maps values from x to `sin(x * Pi)`. The `projectableSinFunction` created using this closure is typed `(p0: CGPoint, p1: CGPoint) -> (x: CGFloat) -> CGPoint`:

```
let fSin: FunctionType = {CGFloat(sin($0 * CGFloat(M_PI)))}
let projectableSinFunction = projectFunctionToCoordinateSystem(function: fSin)
```

Once this is established, you can use and reuse `projectableSinFunction` with any two points. This step applies the projectable function to a specific coordinate system. This next example creates a ready-to-use `(x: CGFloat) -> CGPoint` function by projecting to $x == y$:

```
let pA = CGPointZero; let pB = CGPoint(x:100, y:100)
let xequalySin = projectableSinFunction(p0: pA, p1: pB)
```

> **Note**
>
> Swift offers a `CGPoint.zero` alternative to `CGPointZero`. As a dinosaur, I tend to use the latter. As a rule, prefer the former if your fingers are not hardwired for old-style usage. Theoretically, inferencing enables you to drop the `CGPoint` prefix to use just `.zero` when the type is known in advance. There's a real point where the coolness of the compiler's capabilities starts interfering with general code readability, and this is probably that point or, more correctly, that `CGPoint`.

Once again, the result is a reusable component—in this case, the `xequalySin` function. `BuildPath` uses this function to create the Bezier path you see in Figure 4-1.

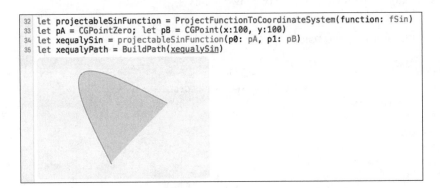

Figure 4-1   This example projects a `Sin` function to two arbitrary points.

As you see from this example, currying enables you to build reusable, decomposable functional components. Partially applied functions provide exceptionally easy-to-create and easy-to-maintain elements that unify multistage processes.

The sample code that accompanies this chapter uses this curried example to build SpriteKit animations that enable you to move sprites from one point to another along nonlinear paths. It's a great example of the synchronicity between Swift language features and decomposable mathematics. When running the samples, open the assistant editor to view the live animations.

Passing Closures as Function Parameters

Swift 2 enables you to pass closures to a parameter that expects a function pointer. I do a lot of work with Bezier paths, and until this feature was added to the Swift language, I literally had to write a custom description parser because I could not access the C-based CGPathApply function that iterates through path elements:

```
typealias CGPathApplierFunction = (UnsafeMutablePointer<Void>,
    UnsafePointer<CGPathElement>) -> Void

func CGPathApply(_ path: CGPath!, _ info: UnsafeMutablePointer<Void>,
    _ function: CGPathApplierFunction!)
```

Under the new system, you use a convention attribute to create a compatible closure type. The default convention is swift. It provides standard Swift-style calling for function values. To work with CGPathApply, use an Objective-C-compatible block. The block convention indicates an Objective-C-compatible block reference:

```
typealias CGPathApplierClosureType =
    @convention(block) (CGPathElement) -> Void
```

Apple explains in *The Swift Programming Language*, "The function value is represented as a reference to the block object, which is an id-compatible Objective-C object that embeds its invocation function within the object. The invocation function uses the C calling convention."

While this example uses the block convention, you can also use c—that is, @convention(c)— for C function types. Apple says, "The c argument is used to indicate a C function reference. The function value carries no context and uses the C calling convention."

You need not create type aliases. You can use the convention annotation inline, as in this example:

```
let myObjCCompatibleCallback: @convention(block) (CGPathElement) -> Void =
    {element in print(element)}
```

or as shown here:

```
let myCCompatibleCallback: @convention(c) (value: CGFloat) -> CGFloat =
    { (value: CGFloat) -> CGFloat in return value * 180.0 / CGFloat(M_PI)}
```

In Recipe 4-9, the new CGPathApplierClosureType type alias helps create a simple wrapper function to call the applier function. This little CGPathApplyWithSwiftClosure function is based on sample code provided by Apple on the Developer Forum. It's ugly; it's scary; it works.

Importantly, this code enables you to create the super-simple and Swift-friendly decomposePath implementation that follows it.

decomposePath iterates through CGPathElement source items to construct new Swift-based BezierElement enumerations. The odd numbering in this implementation (the destination point is variously at indices 0, 1, or 2) is based on how CGPathElement orders its point data.

Recipe 4-9   **Passing Closures to C Functions**

```
// Simple Swift enumeration to store path elements
public enum BezierElement {
    case CloseSubpath
    case MoveToPoint(point: CGPoint)
    case AddLineToPoint(point: CGPoint)
    case AddQuadCurveToPoint(point: CGPoint, controlPoint1: CGPoint)
    case AddCurveToPoint(point: CGPoint,
        controlPoint1: CGPoint, controlPoint2: CGPoint)
}

// Apply Swift closure to CGPath elements
// Thanks, Quinn the Eskimo
typealias CGPathApplierClosureType =
    @convention(block) (CGPathElement) -> Void
func CGPathApplyWithSwiftClosure(
    path: CGPath, closure: CGPathApplierClosureType) {
    CGPathApply(path,
        unsafeBitCast(closure, UnsafeMutablePointer<Void>.self)){
        info, element in
        let block = unsafeBitCast(info, CGPathApplierClosureType.self)
        block(element.memory)
    }
}

// Decompose a UIBezierPath into BezierElement components
func decomposePath(path: UIBezierPath) -> [BezierElement] {
    var points = [BezierElement]()
    CGPathApplyWithSwiftClosure(path.CGPath){
        element in
        switch element.type {
        case .CloseSubpath:
            points.append(.CloseSubpath)
        case .MoveToPoint:
            points.append(.MoveToPoint(point:element.points[0]))
        case .AddLineToPoint:
            points.append(.AddLineToPoint(point:element.points[0]))
```

```
    case .AddQuadCurveToPoint:
        points.append(.AddQuadCurveToPoint(point:element.points[1],
            controlPoint1: element.points[0]))
    case .AddCurveToPoint:
        points.append(.AddCurveToPoint(point:element.points[2],
            controlPoint1: element.points[0],
            controlPoint2: element.points[1]))
    }
  }
  return points
}
```

The best way to validate your decomposed path is to reconstruct and inspect it. This extension enables you to append an element to a Bezier path instance:

```
extension BezierElement {
    func appendToPath(path: UIBezierPath) {
        switch self {
        case .CloseSubpath: path.closePath()
        case .MoveToPoint(let point): path.moveToPoint(point)
        case .AddLineToPoint(let point): path.addLineToPoint(point)
        case .AddQuadCurveToPoint(let point, let controlPoint1):
            path.addQuadCurveToPoint(point, controlPoint: controlPoint1)
        case .AddCurveToPoint(let point, let controlPoint1, let controlPoint2):
            path.addCurveToPoint(point, controlPoint1: controlPoint1,
                controlPoint2: controlPoint2)
        }
    }
}
let path = UIBezierPath()
decomposePath(QPath()).forEach{$0.appendToPath(path)}
```

If your code has been done properly, the two paths should be visually identical, and the new path's deconstruction should be the same element-by-element—a comparison process that you can automate for testing. Misordering points is the most common reason that path deconstruction fails, which is why it's so vital to correctly position the points indices with your Swift representation.

Wrap-up

Swift transforms functionality into first-class objects. Its functions and closures enable you to build and deploy encapsulated behavior for both direct and indirect use. Whether you're currying, nesting, capturing values, or supplying blocks for deferred execution, Swift functions introduces flexible solutions that take your code to new and powerful places.

5

Generics and Protocols

Swift is a type-safe language. You cannot pass strings or colors or floats or double values to a function expecting Int. If you try to do so, the compiler errors. Type safety constrains parameters to those types declared as legal in the signature. For a more general implementation, look to Swift generics.

Generics help you build robust code that expands functionality beyond single types. A generic implementation services an entire group of types instead of just one specific version. This approach enables you to minimize code duplication while serving types that share common behaviors and characteristics.

The combination of generic types and behavior contracts (called *protocols*) establishes a powerful and flexible programming synergy. This chapter introduces these concepts and explores how you can navigate this often-confusing development arena.

Expanding to Generics

Consider the following function. It compares two Int instances and returns a truth value that expresses whether two integer parameters are equal. You cannot call testEquality using doubles, Booleans, or strings. This super-basic implementation is specific to integers:

```
func testEquality(x: Int, _ y: Int) -> Bool {
    return x == y
}
```

Now, contrast that functionality with the following version. This function updates test-Equality to accept a pair of generic parameters. Unlike the previous function, this version works with many types:

```
func testEquality<T where T:Equatable>(x: T, _ y: T) -> Bool {
    return x == y
}
```

In fact, this new version of `testEquality` works with any type that declares `Equatable` support. This updated version can compare strings, integers, doubles, Booleans, closed ranges, and so forth, all of which ship in standard Swift with that support built in, as well as any type for which you add that conformance. Since adding conformance is simply a matter of declaring protocol membership and implementing a single function, you can expand any type to be `Equatable` with a minimum of work. Once you do so, that type automatically works with `testEquality`.

The updated version of `testEquality` above uses a generic type declaration, which you see between angle brackets after the function name. Of course, both `x` and `y` must match each other's type—the same `T` type is used to declare both value parameters—but the function now offers a much wider set of possible use domains. The function uses this declaration to type its parameters to arbitrary types instead of being limited to `Int`. In this example, the type constraint's `where` clause mentions the `Equatable` protocol. This constraint limits types to items that can be compared for equality using `==`. Other than these edits, the function is identical to the original version.

Protocols

A Swift *protocol* is a contract that mandates how items behave and communicate. It provides a blueprint that sets out a list of requirements for a particular role or task. When a class, a structure, or an enumeration *adopts* a protocol, it agrees to implement all the requirements laid out in that protocol. Implementing these features is called *conforming* to the protocol. In the case of `Equatable`, the protocol specifies that a conforming type implements a `==` equality function. Here are some key ways protocols work:

- **Protocols act as gatekeepers.** When working with generics, protocols describe the minimum set of APIs required to power your functions. A protocol establishes compile-time checks which guarantee that all conforming types implement a certain base set of functionality. The `testEquality` example needs things that can be equated to each other. It doesn't care what those things are or how they're compared. It only matters that these items respond to a common function (`==`) and return a well-defined type, in this case Boolean.

- **Protocols act as mediators.** They enable you to solve the problem of both "I want to apply this same functionality to different kinds of things," as with `testEquality` and `Equatable`, and "I want to implement this same API interface in many different ways," which you might see in an `OutputDestination` or `IntegerConsumer` protocol. These latter two protocols are entirely hypothetical. They demonstrate how you can use a protocol to delegate required functionality without mandating any specific implementation details.

- **Protocols act as traits.** You can conform a type to multiple protocols and automatically receive any default implementations that have been established in protocol extensions. This *building-by-composition* approach introduces flexibility and power that you cannot gain from simple class inheritance. It limits duplicate code because it groups implementations by shared behaviors, not by object hierarchies. It flattens inheritance trees because you can build constructs using just the features you need for a given task.

Protocol Inheritance

Protocols offer multiple inheritance. That is, a protocol can inherit from one or more other protocols and add further requirements to that set of inherited requirements. In the following example, MyCustomProtocol inherits from Equatable and BooleanType:

```
protocol MyCustomProtocol: Equatable, BooleanType {
    // .. other requirements here ..
}
```

A conforming type, such as MyCustomStruct in the following example, must satisfy all the direct and inherited requirements of the protocols it adopts. In this example, Equatable is one of the inherited protocols, so any type that conforms to MyCustomProtocol must satisfy the requirements of Equatable:

```
struct MyCustomStruct: MyCustomProtocol { // declare conformance
    // implementation must satisfy Equatable, BooleanType,
    // plus any additional requirements introduced for MyCustomProtocol
}
```

MyCustomStruct conforms to MyCustomProtocol, and MyCustomProtocol inherits from Equatable. This means you can pass instances to any parameter that must conform to Equatable, so MyCustomStruct is ready to work with testEquality:

```
testEquality(MyCustomStruct(), MyCustomStruct()) // works
```

Protocols and Implementation

A protocol declaration doesn't include implementation. It just lists requirements that specify what implementation details you must include. The compiler will not let you add bodies to protocol declarations. You can add defaults for type alias declarations, but that's about it. Implementation is left up to conforming types (as with Equatable's == function) or to *protocol extensions* that add default protocol conformance implementations. Equatable's != functionality is implemented by the standard library and inherited for free by conforming types.

Tokens

The type used to describe both arguments in the updated testEquality function is T. There's nothing magical about the letter T. This descriptive *token* provides context about how a stand-in type is used. You might use any other letter or string, such as Item or Element or Stream, for example. Reserve T for the most generic of generic types. Arrays use Element, and dictionaries use Key and Value type stand-ins because those names make more sense. Tokens help distinguish the role each type will play:

```
Array<Element>
Dictionary<Key: Hashable, Value>
```

Using a single letter when there's no further semantic information about the type usage is conventional, or "what everyone else generally does." Additional type stand-ins within a single implementation are normally U, V, and so forth. I've seen people use R for return types, G for generator types, I for index types, and S for sequence types (also S1, S2, and so on for multiple sequences). There are no hard-and-fast rules beyond keeping your tokens unique and unambiguous in the context in which they're used.

That said, always prefer better semantics through words to single letters when possible. Element is superior to E, and Sequence is superior to S. I try to reserve single letters to T, U, and occasionally V—and only when truly working with the most generic types or when long names reduce the clarity of the declaration.

Type Constraints

The where clause between angle brackets is called a *type constraint*. It defines requirements for a generic type parameter. When you're building super-simple conditions like the Equatable conformance used in the following function, Swift offers a shorthand for the where clause. Drop the "T where T" phrase and simply declare the protocol after a colon, as you see here:

```
func testEquality<T: Equatable>(x: T, _ y: T) -> Bool {
    return x == y
}
```

The result is simpler, and you don't lose any clarity of intent. The Swift compiler knows how to parse this shorter form.

Type constraints can be as simple as a single protocol conformance, or they can establish complex relationships, as in the following example:

```
public init<C: CollectionType where C.Index: ForwardIndexType,
    C.Generator.Element == Element>(_ base: C)
```

This constraint allows a type to be initialized with collections that use an incrementable index. It also establishes a same-type constraint, specifying that the collection elements will match an element type used by this construct. Protocols add flexibility and power to development, but they, along with generics, can be intimidating, especially to developers new to the paradigm. Learning to create new type constraints and to understand constraints declared by the modules you use can be frustrating. I encourage you to persevere; you *will* be rewarded if you master these language features.

Adopting Protocols

The following snippet shows the standard library definition of the Equatable protocol. A protocol being declared does not directly implement the methods, properties, and other members it describes:

```
protocol Equatable {
    func ==(lhs: Self, rhs: Self) -> Bool
}
```

This declaration only says that to conform to `Equatable`, a type must implement the `==` operator. Protocols specify which elements must be included for classes, structures, and enumerations that adopt the protocol. Actual implementation details are left either to adopting types or to default implementations supplied by protocol extensions.

For example, here's a custom type. It's a new struct called `Point` that stores a pair of `Double` variables, an `x` and a `y`:

```
struct Point {
    var x: Double
    var y: Double
}
```

You create new instances by passing values for each member of the structure, as in the following examples:

```
var p1 = Point(x: 10, y: 30)
var p2 = Point(x: 10, y: 20)
var p3 = Point(x: 10, y: 20)
```

Although `Point` instances are clearly comparable in their design—they're just a pair of floating-point numbers after all—you cannot pass these variables to the `testEquality` function, even in its generic form. `Point` does not adopt `Equatable`. The constraining `where` clause remains unsatisfied. To remedy this, declare `Equatable` and implement the `==` operator, as in the following snippet:

```
extension Point: Equatable {}
func ==(lhs:Point, rhs:Point)->Bool {return lhs.x==rhs.x && lhs.y==rhs.y}
```

You declare the `==` function outside the struct declaration. That's because `==` is an operator, and Swift requires operators to be implemented at the global scope. After performing these changes, the generic `testEquality` function starts working with `Point` and can now be applied to instances created from this structure.

Declaring Protocols

Every protocol has a name that describes the type-specific qualities the protocol establishes. When establishing protocols, choose capitalized names that describe the role conforming types will fulfill. For example, the `Equatable` protocol mandates types that can be equated. The `Comparable` protocol that builds on `Equatable` adds ordering nuance to equivalence. `Comparable` types can describe binary relations like "greater than or equal to" and "strictly greater than" between ordered elements.

In a similar manner, convertible protocols like `CustomStringConvertible`, `FloatLiteralConvertible`, and `DictionaryLiteralConvertible` describe instances that can be converted and the manner in which they'll be used. For example, `FloatLiteralConvertible` can be used to create an instance from a floating-point literal:

```
/// Conforming types can be initialized with floating point literals.
protocol FloatLiteralConvertible {
    typealias FloatLiteralType

    /// Create an instance initialized to `value`.
    init(floatLiteral value: Self.FloatLiteralType)
}
```

Like `FloatLiteralConvertible`, most other protocol declarations are quite short. Their goal is to describe a crucial set of requirements so you can build behaviors that depend on those features.

You declare a protocol using the `protocol` keyword. A protocol can establish a new conformance set (for example, `Equatable`) or can build off inherited characteristics (for example, `Comparable`, which inherits requirements from `Equatable`):

```
protocol protocol-name: inherited-protocols {
    // protocol-member-declarations
}
```

The simplest possible protocol looks like this:

```
protocol SimplestProtocol {} // requires nothing
```

This is not very useful. You might theoretically use something like `SimplestProtocol` to mark types that you would associate together for some task. Adding a no-requirements protocol ensures that you don't have to implement any details, but that types can be tested by the compiler and at runtime for conformance.

What you don't generally do is this:

```
protocol DerivedProtocol: AncestorProtocol {}
```

I cannot think of meaningful circumstances in which you'd create a derived protocol without adding at least one new restriction.

Contrast that, however, with this next example, which creates a new protocol that blends the features of multiple parents but requires only a single point of conformance:

```
protocol UnionProtocol: AncestorProtocol1, AncestorProtocol2 {}
```

To be fair, this isn't a great choice to use, either. In its current form, it adds no new meaningful semantics and may hide details from clients; that is never a positive contribution. Protocol composition enables you to join protocols together into a single requirement. You add these between angle brackets after the `protocol` keyword, and you can list as many protocols as needed:

```
func doSomething(item: protocol<AncestorProtocol1, AncestorProtocol2>) {...}
```

A protocol composition does not define a new protocol type. It creates a temporary local protocol that combines the requirements of all the listed items.

Member Declarations

Protocol member declarations include *property, method, operator, initializer, subscript,* and *associated type* requirements. These components add state, behavior, initializer, lookup, and typing features to a protocol contract, describing the features a conforming construct must implement. The following protocol shows examples of what these members can look like:

```
protocol ComplexProtocol {

    // Establish associated types
    typealias Element // without constraint
    typealias Index: ForwardIndexType // type conformance

    // Readable and readwritable properties
    var readableProperty: Element {get}
    var readwritableProperty: Element {get set}
    static var staticProperty: Index {get}

    // Methods
    func method(foo: Self) -> Index
    static func staticMethod() -> Element

    // Initializers
    init(element: Element)
    init?(index: Index)

    // Subscripts
    subscript(index: Index) -> Element {get set}
}
```

Here are a few quick rules:

- Place `typealias` declarations at the top of your protocols to create *associated types.* These are used both by the protocol members that follow and as type stand-ins when you're creating generics. Moving them to the start of the protocol declaration ensures that they're easy to reference when you need to look up terms.

- Property *requirements* must be of variable type; that is prefixed with `var` and not `let`. Property *implementations* may substitute `let` for read-only `get` types, as in the following protocol and class:

  ```
  protocol HasAnIntConstant {var myInt: Int {get}}
  class IntSupplier: HasAnIntConstant {let myInt = 2}
  ```

- Protocols use the `static` keyword for property and method requirements. Implementations use `class` for classes and `static` for structures, although starting in Swift 1.2, classes also accept the `static` keyword.

Do not confuse `static`/`class` annotations with the `class` keyword that can be used to mark a protocol as class-only, as in the following declaration. Marking a protocol with `class` enables you to use `weak` properties typed as the protocol:

```
protocol MyClassOnlyProtocol: class, PossibleInheritedProtocol {}
```

- In protocols, the `mutating` keyword before `func` specifies a method that modifies its instance. Conforming classes don't need to use this keyword in implementations, but structs and enumerations do, as in the following examples:

```
protocol Mutable{mutating func mutate()}
class MutatingClass: Mutable {
    var x = 0
    func mutate(){self.x = 999}
}
struct MutatingStruct: Mutable {
    var x: Int
    mutating func mutate(){self.x = 999}
}
enum MutatingEnumeration: Mutable {
    case MyCase(Int)
    mutating func mutate() {self = MyCase(999)}
}
```

Mutating requirements can be satisfied by non-mutating implementations. (If the method actually mutates the struct or enum instance, the `mutating` keyword remains, of course, non-optional.) You cannot satisfy a *non-mutating* member requirement with a mutating implementation.

- When you add initializer members to a protocol, you must add the `required` keyword to your implementations *except* when the class is marked `final`:

```
protocol InitializableWithString {init(string: String)}
class StringInitializableClass1: InitializableWithString {
    required init(string: String ){} // required required
}
final class StringInitializableClass2: InitializableWithString {
    init(string: String ){} // required not required
}
```

- A protocol's failable initializer, such as `init?()`, can be satisfied with either a failable or a nonfailable implementation.

- A nonfailable initializer, such as `init()`, is satisfied with either a nonfailable initializer (preferred) or an implicitly unwrapped failable initializer. The latter approach is dangerous, for self-evident reasons.

- A `Self` requirement (that is, `Self`-with-an-uppercase-*S*) refers to the type that adopts a protocol. `Self` is a type placeholder for the conforming type. If that conforming type is `Double`, for example, then treat any references to `Self` in the protocol as `Double`.

Building a Basic Protocol

The `FloatLiteralConvertible` protocol mentioned earlier in this chapter describes types that can be initialized with floating-point instances. It's used to mark types that convert from floating-point literals. The following snippet turns that notion on its head by introducing a protocol for types that can be converted to doubles. It mandates a single `doubleValue` property, which expresses a conforming instance's value as a Swift `Double`:

```
// Declare DoubleRepresentable Protocol
public protocol DoubleRepresentable {
    var doubleValue: Double {get}
}
```

Here are conforming implementations for `Double`, `Int`, `CGFloat`, and `Float`:

```
// Requires Cocoa or UIKit for CGFloat support
extension Double: DoubleRepresentable {
    public var doubleValue: Double {return self}}
extension Int: DoubleRepresentable {
    public var doubleValue: Double {return Double(self)}}
extension CGFloat: DoubleRepresentable {
    public var doubleValue: Double {return Double(self)}}
extension Float: DoubleRepresentable {
    public var doubleValue: Double {return Double(self)}}
```

As you see, these implementations are identical except for the one for `Double`. This code is redundant but unavoidable. At this time, you cannot create a protocol requirement on another class. You can only state which properties, methods, and so on a conforming class itself implements.

If you *could* do otherwise, you might create a custom `DoubleInitializable` protocol with a requirement for `Double.init(Self)` and build a simple default implementation for `doubleValue`. By declaring `DoubleInitializable`, the `Int`, `CGFloat`, and `Float` types (along with any other types you might want to use) could declare conformance and inherit that identical implementation. This is not a reality and one I do not honestly anticipate ever being realized in Swift.

Once added to a project using the code you just saw, the `DoubleInitializable` protocol enables you to convert conforming instances to doubles by accessing a `doubleValue` property. Here's an example of how that would look for an integer-sourced example:

```
let intValue = 23 // 23
let d = intValue.doubleValue // 23.0
print(d.dynamicType) // Swift.Double
print(d) // 23.0
```

Adding Protocol Default Implementations

It may look redundant to include an implementation for `Double` that returns a double value property, but it's critical here, as with other protocol work, to consider how the contract will be consumed by other protocols and by generics. Protocols define the shape of the interface between structures, ensuring that they can be properly used for plug-and-play implementation. What follows is a real-world example of how a simple conformance detail propagates down to great utility.

The `ConvertibleNumberType` protocol in this snippet describes types that can be converted to common type destinations. Any compliant type can express itself in terms of these destinations:

```
public protocol ConvertibleNumberType: DoubleRepresentable {
    var doubleValue: Double { get }
    var floatValue: Float { get }
    var intValue: Int { get }
    var CGFloatValue: CGFloat { get }
}
```

I originally built this protocol to assist with Core Graphics development in Swift. Moving back and forth between `Double`, the Swift default, and `CGFloat` has proved to be a regular hassle. I decided that properties made my code more readable than endless back-and-forth casts. (Your opinion may, of course, vary from this viewpoint.) I implemented these type conversions using a protocol extension. All I had to do was declare type conformance:

```
extension Double: ConvertibleNumberType{}
extension Float: ConvertibleNumberType{}
extension Int: ConvertibleNumberType{}
extension CGFloat: ConvertibleNumberType{}
```

This works because Swift protocol extensions enable you to provide default implementations for method and property requirements. The following implementations automatically accrue to conforming types:

```
public extension ConvertibleNumberType {
    public var floatValue: Float {get {return Float(doubleValue)}}
    public var intValue: Int {get {return lrint(doubleValue)}} // rounds
    public var CGFloatValue: CGFloat {get {return CGFloat(doubleValue)}}
}
```

Each of the preceding property getters is built on top of `doubleValue`, which explains why it was so important to create that silly "return `self`" implementation. Without `Double`'s `DoubleRepresentable` conformance, it couldn't use this default implementation. With it, `Double` automatically offers a `CGFloatValue` property accessor, along with the `intValue` and `floatValue` created by the protocol extension.

Recipe 5-1 combines the `DoubleRepresentable` and `ConvertibleNumberType` protocols into a single implementation. It uses fewer moving parts than the examples shown so far in this section:

- Recipe 5-1 drops explicit `DoubleRepresentable` declarations; these are included in `ConvertibleNumberType`.

- Recipe 5-1 also drops the details of the `ConvertibleNumberType` members. The `doubleValue` requirement is covered in `DoubleRepresentable`. The other requirements are provided through the `ConvertibleNumberType` extension.

When a protocol offers its own implementations, you need not mention those properties or methods in the protocol declaration itself. You see this with `Equatable`. Its only publicly required method is `==`. Swift's standard library provides the `!=` variant implementation.

Recipe 5-1   Building Protocols with Default Implementations

```
//: Numbers that can be represented as Double instances
public protocol DoubleRepresentable {
    var doubleValue: Double {get}
}

//: Numbers that convert to other types
public protocol ConvertibleNumberType: DoubleRepresentable {}
public extension ConvertibleNumberType {
    public var floatValue: Float {get {return Float(doubleValue)}}
    public var intValue: Int {get {return lrint(doubleValue)}}
    public var CGFloatValue: CGFloat {get {return CGFloat(doubleValue)}}
}

//: Double Representable Conformance
extension Double: ConvertibleNumberType {
    public var doubleValue: Double {return self}}
extension Int: ConvertibleNumberType {
    public var doubleValue: Double {return Double(self)}}
extension CGFloat: ConvertibleNumberType {
    public var doubleValue: Double {return Double(self)}}
extension Float: ConvertibleNumberType {
    public var doubleValue: Double {return Double(self)}}
```

Optional Protocol Requirements

In Objective-C, a protocol establishes a communication contract between a client that adopts that protocol and a producer that sends callbacks to the client, using the protocol's declared methods. By default, all declared methods are required. Objective-C also enables you to specify *optional* requirements. Unlike standard requirements, these are implemented as needed.

Establishing an optional communication contract requires producers to check whether a client implements a selector (`respondsToSelector:`) before calling it. Swift-native protocols don't offer optional protocol requirements.

Objective-C interoperability means Swift supports optional protocol requirements on `@objc` protocols. When a protocol is annotated with `@objc`, you can prefix a requirement with an `optional` modifier. These `@objc` optional protocols are limited to classes and cannot be adopted by structures or enumerations. The `optional` modifier enables you to extend your protocols to use optional requirements even if your code won't ever be used with Objective-C. It's inelegant, but it's how Swift is currently designed. Once you add the `optional` modifier, you can use conditional chaining to shortcut execution when instances do not implement optional methods.

> **Note**
>
> While Objective-C allows you to declare `MyType<SomeProtocol> *instance`, you cannot declare a variable bound by both a class and a protocol in Swift.

Swift-Native Optional Protocol Requirements

It remains unclear whether optional method implementations are generally desirable in a value-typed world. That said, you could create a better equivalent Swift-native system without using the `@objc` keyword or limiting optional requirements to classes. In pure Swift, declare a method in a protocol and then implement a default version that method in a protocol extension:

```
protocol MyProtocol {
    func myOptionalMethod()
}
extension MyProtocol {
    func myOptionalMethod() {}
}
```

When working with delegate protocols, your extension implementation may need to return a default value. This approach enables adopting constructs to override default implementations. If they do not, they inherit the default behavior with only minor overhead. When they do, there's a well-grounded contract for communication with an adopting class.

Further, any construct that consumes this protocol needn't care whether an adopting type overrides this method or not. It can call it without checking in either case and with full safety. That is, of course, unless you go out of your way to ensure that an override is absolutely necessary, as in the following example:

```
extension MyProtocol {
    func myOptionalMethod() {fatalError("Implement this method!")}
}
```

Building Generic Types

A generic type is a class, a structure, or an enumeration that's built to manage, store, or process arbitrary types. Generics enable you to focus development efforts on shared behavior instead of specific type details. Rather than thinking about how a construct works with, for example, integers, strings, or coordinates, a generic implementation create semantics decoupled from the specific types your construct handles.

Swift's `Array`, `Set`, and `Dictionary` are all generic types. Generics enable them to store many kinds of instances, including numbers, strings, structures, and more. Their standard-library declarations underscore their generic implementation. Angle brackets follow the name of each type. Within these brackets, you find a list of one or more generic parameters:

```
struct Array<Element>
struct Set<Element: Hashable>
struct Dictionary<Key: Hashable, Value>
```

The number of parameters reflects the way types are used in the parent construct. Arrays and sets store collections of a single type such as `String` or `AnyObject`. In contrast, dictionaries span two types, one for keys and one for values. These types are unrelated in the generic parameter declaration. When used later for instances, they may be identical, as in `[Int: Int]` dictionaries, or distinct, as in `[String: AnyObject]` ones.

Type Parameters

Type parameters provide simple type stand-ins. Just as method parameters provide actors for values, type parameters offer ways to represent types. The type used for the following `storage` property is unknown until the construct is actually used in code:

```
public struct MyStruct <T> { // T is a type parameter
    let storage: T
}
```

You establish that type association by creating instances. The type parameter can either be inferred, as in the first of the following examples, or specified explicitly, as in the second.

```
MyStruct(storage: 15) // T is Int
MyStruct<String>(storage: "Test") // T is String
```

The fully qualified type includes the same angle brackets as the generic definition. Finalized type instances replace the generic stand-ins. A `[String: AnyObject]` dictionary is shorthand for `Dictionary<String, AnyObject>`. (As a rule, I use the former for declarations and the latter for generic type constraints.)

Recipe 5-2 creates a `Bunch` type. This is a simple generic type that stores an instance and a running count. You `push` new "copies" into the `Bunch`. You can also pop items off as long as sufficient versions remain in the count. When the count falls to zero, pops fail and return `nil` because there are no more copies to return.

Recipe 5-2   **Establishing a Generic Type**

```
//: A Bunch stores n instances of an arbitrary type
public struct Bunch<Element> {
    private let item: Element
    var count = 1

    // New instances always have one copy
    init(item: Element) {self.item = item}

    // Add items to the bunch
    mutating func push() {count++}

    // Copy items from the bunch
    mutating func pop() -> Element? {
        guard count > 0 else {return nil}
        count -= 1
        return item
    }
}
```

Because it is generic, Recipe 5-2 enables you to store bunches of any type. The implementation uses a type parameter called `Element`. This parameter establishes a stand-in type for `item`, is referenced in the construct initializer, and is used with the `pop` method that returns instances. The generic `Element` type is not known until the code is used by a client.

You can decorate generic type parameters just as you would with any Swift-supplied types. The `pop()` method adds a question mark because it returns an `Optional` instance. Since a bunch cannot return instances when its count hits zero, optionals enable this implementation to gracefully handle the no-more-copies-available case without error handling. When a bunch's supplies are replenished with pushes, clients can renew their requests and fetch further copies using `pop()`.

Generic Requirements

Set elements and dictionary keys conform to the `Hashable` protocol. This protocol ensures that elements can be converted to a unique identifier, preventing duplicate entries. The protocol is declared as a requirement. It acts as a *type constraint* on the generic parameter:

```
struct Dictionary<Key: Hashable, Value>
```

Generics use two kinds of type constraints: *conformance* constraints, as in this example, and *same-type* requirements, which equate two types. The following sections introduce these constraint styles.

Conformance Requirements

The first generic requirement type is *protocol conformance*, also called a *conformance requirement*. This requirement specifies that a type conforms to a specific protocol. The set and dictionary Hashable restrictions use this constraint type.

In the most succinct form, a protocol requirement follows a generic parameter, as in the following example. A colon appears between the type parameter and the protocol name:

```
public struct Thing<Item: Hashable> {
    private let thing: Item
}
```

This declaration is actually shorthand for the following snippet, which uses a fully qualified where clause instead of a type:protocol shorthand:

```
public struct Thing<Item where Item: Hashable> {
    private let thing: Item
}
```

Swift enables you to add multiple where clauses for compound conformance, as in the following example:

```
public struct Thing<Item where Item: Hashable, Item: Comparable> {
    private let thing: Item
}
```

But protocol composition offers a cleaner approach despite the extra angle brackets:

```
public struct Thing<Item: protocol<Hashable, Comparable>> {
    private let thing: Item
}
```

Since you must now construct Thing with items that conform to these protocols, the first of the following two examples succeeds, and the second fails. Strings are hashable and comparable, but CGPoints do not successfully meet these requirements:

```
Thing(thing: "Hello")
// Thing(thing: CGPoint(x: 5, y:10)) // error
```

Recipe: Same-Type Requirements

The second kind of requirement is a *same-type* restriction. This requirement equates two types. As you see in the following example, the second type (in this case, Int) need not be a type parameter:

```
public class Notion<C: CollectionType where C.Generator.Element == Int> {
    var collectionOfInts: C
    init(collection: C) {self.collectionOfInts = collection}
}
```

This example builds a class that stores a collection of integers. Type constraints ensure that the generic type is first a collection type (a conformance requirement) and then that its elements are `Int` (a same-type requirement):

```
let notion = Notion(collection: [1, 2, 3]) // works
// let notion = Notion(collection: ["a", "b", "c"]) // doesn't work
```

You cannot create a same-type restriction that creates two identically types parameters, as in the following example, because it results in a compiler error:

```
enum Pointed<T, U where T == U>{case X(T), Y(U)} // fail
```

You can, however, use same-type requirements to relate two generic types, such as `Element` and `C` in Recipe 5-3. The generic function in this recipe uses equality to test whether a collection contains a member, which is restricted to the same type.

Recipe 5-3   Adding Same-Type Requirements

```
func customMember<
    Element: Equatable, C: CollectionType
    where C.Generator.Element == Element>(
    collection: C, element: Element) -> Bool {

    return collection.map({$0 == element}).contains(true)
}
```

The compiler uses typing restrictions to ensure that you call `CustomMember` with matching arguments. You cannot, for example, pass an integer array and a string. These types do not pass the same-type requirement:

```
let memberArray = [1, 2, 3, 4, 5, 6]
CustomMember(memberArray, element: 2) // true
CustomMember(memberArray, element: 17) // false
// CustomMember(memberArray, element: "hello") // compiler error
```

Recipe 5-4 offers another take on type constraints. This function accepts a sequence of `Hashable` items and produces an array of unique elements. The `Hashable` constraint enables a Swift `Set<T>` to filter out unique elements. Since sets work only with hashable items, the same-type constraint ensures that the input sequence is constructed of those set-friendly elements.

Recipe 5-4   Using Type Constraints to Build Same-Type Results

```
// Normally it's better to use full words, like "unique" but this function
// calls back to historic uniq functions from other languages

func uniq<S: SequenceType, T: Hashable where
    S.Generator.Element == T>(source: S) -> [T] {
```

```
    // order not preserved
    return Array(Set(source))
}
```

The recipe's `T` type parameter token is referenced in the function's `[T]` array output and the `uniqueItems` declaration. You could replace these tokens at either or both points with the equivalent `S.Generator.Element`, as in the following example:

```
func uniq<S: SequenceType where S.Generator.Element:Hashable>
    (source: S) -> [S.Generator.Element] {
    return Array(Set(source))
}
```

Generic Beautification

Regardless of whether you use `T` or `S.Generator.Element`, the `uniq` function suffers from angle bracket overload. Too much constraint material is stuffed into and overflowing from this small function's type restrictions. By converting complex functions to protocol extensions, you introduce what Apple calls *generic beautification*.

Several of `uniq`'s restrictions serve to mention that this function is specific to sequence types. Expressing this behavior within a protocol extension using a method instead of a function creates a better and simpler implementation:

```
extension SequenceType where Generator.Element:Hashable {
    func uniq() -> [Generator.Element] {
        return Array(Set(self))
    }
}
```

The extension uses a `where` clause to establish that the `uniq` method applies solely to `Hashable` collections. This restriction allows `uniq` to build sets from sequence elements. The result is more readable and maintainable.

Collections don't *really* need another member function, in reality, but if they did, the same beautification process—constraining a protocol extension and converting to a method—could update Recipe 5-3 as well:

```
extension CollectionType where Generator.Element:Equatable {
    func customMember(element: Generator.Element) -> Bool {
        return self.map({$0 == element}).contains(true)
    }
}
```

Legal Tokens

You cannot refer to or mention Recipe 5-3's `Generator` and `Element` tokens until you first establish that `C` is a `CollectionType`. These tokens are valid only in the context of a collection type generic. Setting that conformance opens the door to the same-type restriction for integers. The tokens you use in type parameter declarations and within closure bodies represent a mix of items you declare and items you inherit.

Type Parameters

You list the custom generic types in angle brackets to the right of the type or function you're creating. These represent a base collection of custom tokens:

```
class Detail<A, B, C, D, E> {}
```

Protocols

Generic declarations can mention any protocol as a conformance requirement, whether custom or system supplied:

```
class Detail<A:ArrayLiteralConvertible, B:BooleanType> {}
```

Associated Types

A protocol's `typealias` declarations build associated types. These types provide placeholder names (also known as *aliases*) used in type declarations and constraints. The following example declares a protocol with a `CodeUnit` alias and implements a conforming class that establishes a value for that type, in this example `UInt32`:

```
protocol SampleProtocol{
    typealias CodeUnit
}

class Detail: SampleProtocol {
    typealias CodeUnit = UInt32
    var idx: CodeUnit = 0
}
```

Matching Aliases

The two following generic functions reference the `CodeUnit` associated type in their type constraints:

```
func sampleFunc1<T:SampleProtocol where T.CodeUnit == UInt16>(x: T) {}
func sampleFunc2<T:SampleProtocol where T.CodeUnit == UInt32>(x: T) {}
// sampleFunc1(Detail()) // does not compile
sampleFunc2(Detail()) // compiles
```

`Detail` sets its `CodeUnit` type alias to `UInt32`. Because of this, only the second of the two function calls compiles. The first fails because `Detail`'s `CodeUnit` alias does not match `SampleFunc1`'s same-type constraint.

Protocol Alias Defaults

A protocol may constrain associated types by specifying that they conform to a protocol or be members of a given class:

```
protocol-associated-type-declaration →
    typealias-headtype-inheritance-clause typealias-assignment
```

Here's a quick example that shows some of this in action. The following sample builds a protocol that defines an associated type with a default assignment:

```
// Protocol defines a default type, which is an array of
// the conforming type
protocol ArrayOfSelfProtocol {
    typealias ArrayOfSelf: SequenceType = Array<Self>
}
```

The `Self` keyword used in this example refers to the type that adopts this protocol. For integers, that type is `Int`, and `ArrayOfSelf` is `[Int]`. Once the protocol is declared, you can conform types to the protocol and then reference arrays of that type. The following snippet tests an array against `Int.ArrayOfSelf`, and it equates to true, using the default assignment:

```
extension Int: ArrayOfSelfProtocol {}
[1, 2, 3] is Int.ArrayOfSelf // true
```

You can also use the default with functions:

```
// This generic function references the type alias default
func ConvertToArray<T: ArrayOfSelfProtocol>(x: T) -> T.ArrayOfSelf {
    return [x] as! T.ArrayOfSelf // works
}
```

```
// Example of calling the function
let result = ConvertToArray(23)
print(result) // [23]
print(result.dynamicType) // Swift.Array<Swift.Int>
```

If you want to push the limit on this example, try changing the default in the protocol from `Array<Self>` so the forced cast to `T.ArrayOfSelf` throws a fatal error.

While this example is fairly contrived, the utility of default values is not. In the Swift standard library, `CollectionType` provides a default value for the `Generator` associated type with `IndexingGenerator<Self>`. This default enables all collections to automatically `generate()` themselves.

Collating Associated Types

Valid associated types are both listed directly within a protocol and inherited from other protocols. This means that tokens listed in the standard library in a protocol declaration may not be exhaustive. For example, the `SequenceType` protocol lists one typealias, `Generator`:

```
protocol SequenceType {
    /// A type that provides the *sequence*'s iteration interface and
    /// encapsulates its iteration state.
    typealias Generator: GeneratorType

    ...
}
```

Then `GeneratorType` itself lists an `Element`. It's extremely common to constrain a generic sequence function on the type of its `Generator.Element`. You will not see these other associated types unless you get down and dirty in the standard library and explore them further through their references.

To collect types, you must ascend the conformance tree to find protocol ancestors. You should also search items mentioned in associated type declarations as these add further possible tokens that you may need in generic constraints.

I've posted source code for automating token collection at GitHub, at https://gist.github.com/erica/c50f8f213db1be3e6390. The output of this code should help you track down available vocabulary that you can use for building protocol-based type references.

Extending Generic Types

When extending a generic type, you can reference any and all type parameters declared in the initial type. You do not specify a new type parameter list or add new parameter names. For example, this `Array` extension references `Element`, which was defined in the original type definition:

```
extension Array {
    var random: Element? {
        return self.count > 0 ?
            self[Int(arc4random_uniform(UInt32(self.count)))] : nil
    }
}
```

You cannot add specific typing because doing so converts generic types into non-generic versions. The following example produces a compiler error:

```
extension Array where Element == Int {} // not allowed
```

You can, however, use protocols to narrow an extension's range of application. Protocols limit extensions to conforming types. For example, this next snippet works only with arrays composed of `Hashable` elements:

```
extension Array where Element: Hashable {
    func toHashString() -> String {
        var accumulator = ""
        for item in self {accumulator += "\(item.hashValue) "}
```

```
        return accumulator
    }
}
```

You can use this extension with arrays of Double but not CGPoint:

```
[1.0, 2.5, 6.2].toHashString() // works
// [CGPointMake(2, 3)].toHashString() // error
```

Using Protocols as Types

Protocols can often be used in place of Swift types, including as method parameters and return types and as the types of constants, variables, and properties. In the following snippet, the play() function accepts a single DeckType parameter:

```
protocol DeckType {
    func shuffle()
    func deal()
}

func play(deck: DeckType) {
    deck.shuffle()
    deck.deal()
}
```

No further typing information is provided in the function beyond the protocol. The compiler knows that protocol conformance is sufficient to ensure that the function code (first shuffling and then dealing) can be executed properly by the passed parameter.

Protocol-Based Collections

You can use protocol types to create collections. Protocol-based collections are heterogeneous by default as they limit membership based on protocol conformance and not type. For example, you might create an Array<DeckType> instance that would store any kind of object that adopted the DeckType protocol:

```
var heterogeneousArray = Array<DeckType>() // or [DeckType]()
heterogeneousArray.append(someConformingDeck)
heterogeneousArray.append(anotherDeckWithADifferentType)
```

To build a homogeneous DeckType array, replace DeckType with a specific type such as MyTypeThatConformsToDeckType. This is the default behavior for creating arrays, namely Array<Type> versus Array<Protocol>.

`Self` Requirements

In protocol declarations, `Self` requirements are placeholders for the specific type that conforms to that protocol. These enable you to differentiate between homogeneous (same type) and heterogeneous (same protocol but possibly different type) elements. Consider the following two alternative protocol members:

```
func matchesDeckOrder(deck: DeckType) -> Bool
func matchesDeckOrder(deck: Self) -> Bool
```

The first uses a `DeckType` parameter. This function can compare a deck against any other type that conforms to the protocol. The second uses `Self`. The comparison in this case is limited to decks of the same type, which is probably a much easier, consistent, and efficient function to implement but isn't always what you want or need.

When you must compare heterogeneous elements, protocol extensions enable you to use uppercase-`Self` to restrict implementation and compare types. The following protocol extension implements a heterogeneous version of `matchesDeck`. This implementation is restricted to cases where `Self` is a collection and will only try to match if the other deck is of the same type:

```
extension DeckType where Self: CollectionType,
    Self.Generator.Element: Equatable {

    func matchesDeck(deck: DeckType) -> Bool {
        if let deck = deck as? Self { // test for same type
            if self.count != deck.count {return false} // same count
            return !zip(self, deck).contains({$0 != $1}) // same items
        }
        return false
    }
}
```

You can see this behavior in action by extending `Array` to conform to `DeckType`:

```
extension Array: DeckType {...}
```

The `Self`-powered default implementation enables you to compare decks by checking types, member count, and member equality even when the decks are of different types:

```
// Build some decks
let x = [1, 2, 3, 4] // reference deck
let y = [1, 2, 3, 4] // matches
let z = [1, 2, 3, 5] // doesn't
let w = ["a", "b", "c", "d"] // different type

x.matchesDeck(y) // true
x.matchesDeck(z) // false
x.matchesDeck(w) // false
```

Protocol Objects and `Self` Requirements

A protocol object refers to an object typed by a protocol. For example, this snippet creates an array of `Basic`-typed objects:

```
protocol Basic {}
var basicArray = Array<Basic>()
```

You can add an integer to this array by extending `Int` to conform to `Basic`:

```
extension Int: Basic {}
basicArray.append(5)
```

However, you cannot use protocol objects with any protocol that enforces `Self` or associated type requirements. For example, consider the following snippet:

```
protocol TypeAliasRequired {
    typealias Foo
}
// var typeAliasRequiredArray = Array<TypeAliasRequired>() // fail
// error: protocol 'TypeAliasRequired' can only be used as a generic
// constraint because it has Self or associated type requirements

protocol SelfRequired {
    func something(x: Self)
}
// var selfRequiredArray = Array<SelfRequired>() // fail
// error: protocol 'SelfRequired' can only be used as a generic
// constraint because it has Self or associated type requirements
```

The problem encountered is this: When you ask Swift to create a protocol object, you're saying "build a heterogeneous collection of items, all of which conform to this protocol." At the same time, the `Self` requirement says "members have to be able to refer to this specific type." That works with a homogenous collection (all the same type) but not a heterogeneous one (all the same protocol but potentially different types). The same issue arises with any other type restriction, so you see it also with associated type requirements. You most commonly run into this issue when working with common protocols like `Hashable` and `Equatable`, both of which enforce `Self` requirements.

To fix this, either avoid `Self` and associated type requirements entirely or build generic constraint implementations that enforce homogeneity. The following example creates a homogenous typed array, whose members all belong to a single type that in turn conforms to `Hashable`:

```
// func f(array: [Hashable]) {} // fail, has Self requirements
func f<T:Hashable>(array: [T]) {} // works
```

Leveraging Protocols

Here are a few points to keep in mind when considering protocols:

- **Prefer functionality to implementation.** Protocols tell you what a construct *does* and not how it does it. To create generics-friendly projects, focus your code on the connections between data creation and data consumption instead of the particulars of specific types.

- **Watch out for repeated code across different types.** Redundant code segments with just a few type-specific changes hint at patterns that lend themselves to generic and protocol implementations. Focus on the commonalities of design to find your targets of opportunity.

- **One protocol does not rule them all.** Keep your protocols short, sweet, and meaningful. Each one should be a noun (often ending with `Type`) or an adjective (ending with `ible` or `able`; see http://ericasadun.com/2015/08/21/swift-protocol-names-a-vital-lesson-in-able-vs-ible-swiftlang/ for details). Think of protocols as defining either "this is a specific kind of thing" or "this is able to do this kind of work." Avoid overloading protocols with too many semantics that distract from a protocol's one true calling.

- **Refactor functions with extensive angle bracket clauses to use protocol extensions and methods.** Swift's protocol extensions use `where` clauses to constrain where methods apply, enabling you to move clauses away from overloaded angle brackets and into a more meaningful context.

- **Conform at the highest possible level.** When adding protocol conformance and default implementations, do so at the highest possible abstraction that still makes sense. Instead of adding separate adoptions for, for example, `Int` and `String`, check whether there is a unifying concept at a common protocol they both already adopt. If doing so becomes too general, create a new protocol, conform the types that apply, and maybe even add an extension to implement the generic behavior you're looking for.

- **Design with collections in mind.** Differentiate whether you will work with heterogeneous (same-protocol) or homogeneous (same-type) functions and design your protocols correspondingly. `Self` requirements enable you to add same-type constraints. Protocol names support common conformance.

- **It's never too late to refactor.** While it's great to write generics and protocols right out of the box, it's extremely common to develop code and then later consider how to retrofit.

Wrap-up

Protocols and generics are some of Swift's most exciting features. Protocols define the shapes and behaviors of the types that adopt them, enabling you to create more generic implementations. Together, protocols and generics reduce code, raise the level of abstraction, introduce reuse, and generally make the world a better and happier place.

6

Errors

In Swift, as in any other programming language, things fail. In daily development tasks, you encounter both logical errors—that is, things that compile but don't work the way you expect them to—and runtime errors—errors that arise from real-world conditions such as missing resources or inaccessible services. Swift 2's redesigned error-handling system enables you to respond to both kinds of error conditions. Its response mechanisms range from assertions that fail fatally to error types that support recovery, enabling you to track what went wrong and offer runtime workarounds.

The updated error system takes into account Apple's vast Cocoa/Cocoa Touch ecosystem. Cocoa has a particular way of working. APIs return a usable value or some fail sentinel, such as `false` or `nil`. There's often an error parameter that's simultaneously populated. At each step, you check whether a call has failed. If so, you print an error message and return early from the method or function.

Objective-C and its flexible type system support this traditional Cocoa paradigm where code follows a smooth linear path of calls, tests, and returns. Swift, in contrast, offers a poor fit to this approach because of its higher safety standards. Type safety doesn't marry easily into return polymorphism and side effects. The Swift 2 language update addressed these issues, offering greater safety and reliability in its redesigned error-handling system.

Failing Hard

When your app recognizes programmer errors, your code should fail loudly, forcibly, and noticeably. These errors include conditions that should never happen and reflect serious flaws in overall logic. Swift offers several ways to prematurely terminate an application. Its constructs help assure overall program correctness, test for outlier cases, and mandate conditions that must be true for your application to perform properly.

Fatal Errors

When you need your app to terminate, look no further than `fatalError`. The `fatalError` function unconditionally prints a message and stops execution. Use this function to exit your application after printing a note about why the app has stopped working. For example, you might encounter an inconsistent state:

```
fatalError("Flag value is zero. This should never happen. Goodbye!")
```

Or you might meet a requirement from an abstract superclass:

```
fatalError("Subclasses must override this method")
```

The failure reason is optional but strongly recommended, especially for any app that will ever be used by another human being—or even future-you. The compiler allows you to omit the error, like this, but common sense suggests that this isn't such a good plan:

```
fatalError()
```

"It just quit" isn't likely to improve anyone's day, including yours.

Assertions

Use the `assert` function to establish a traditional C-style assertion with an optional message. Your assertions test assumptions and help locate design errors during development. As with `fatalError`, an explanatory message is optional but recommended:

```
assert(index < self.count)
assert(index < self.count, "Index is out of bounds")
```

The details of the compiler flags used to control evaluation are specified in the standard library module interface. False assertions stop execution to a debuggable state on debug builds (typically -Onone). For release builds, an assertion is entirely ignored, and the assertion's condition clause is not executed.

To use checks in release builds, substitute the related `precondition` function, which is described in the following section. A `precondition`'s condition clause won't execute in -Ounchecked builds.

As a rule, the simpler the assertion, the more valuable it tends to be. An assertion should mandate conditions you know to be true and necessary for proper execution. Assertions simplify debugging by ruling out conditions you know to be true, ensuring that failures occur for more exotic reasons. Here's a trivial example of checking for valid values:

```
assert(1...20 ~= value, "Power level out of range. (Must be between 1 and 20.)")
```

Or you might test that a string contains some text:

```
assert(!string.isEmpty, "Empty string is invalid")
```

The `assertionFailure` variation does not use a predicate test; it always triggers as a false assertion. `assertionFailure` marks code that should never be reached and forces applications to terminate immediately:

```
assertionFailure()
assertionFailure("Not implemented")
assertionFailure("Switch state should never reach default case")
```

The `assertionFailure` function follows the same evaluation pattern as `assert`. It is ignored in release builds and enters a debuggable state for debug builds.

You can easily build a non-terminating version of `assert` that mimics its predicate testing and reporting behavior with less drastic outcomes than an application exit:

```
public func simpleAssert(
    @autoclosure condition:  () -> Bool,
    _ message: String) {
    if !condition() {print(message)}
}
```

To differentiate between debug and release builds, add the `#if DEBUG` trick described in Chapter 2, "Printing and Mirroring." Since Swift does not automatically support a check for debug/release conditions, you must add a custom `-D DEBUG` compiler flag to your debug build settings, as described in that chapter. You might use this check, for example, to stop an application when debugging and throw errors in release builds.

> **Note**
>
> Avoid using conditions for side effects.

Preconditions

There's no great philosophical benefit in allowing code to execute in production builds that you would not permit in debug ones. Unlike assertions, `precondition` and `precondition-Failure` calls are checked and will stop an app in release mode except when compiled with `-Ounchecked`. Of course, you try not to ship flawed code in the first place, but an out-of-bounds index will not magically fix itself in either situation. Weigh early termination against possible loss and corruption of user data.

For somewhat obvious reasons, use preconditions sparingly. With great failure comes great responsibility—and not-so-great one-star reviews. Also, with unexpected app termination comes another opportunity for your iTunes Connect App Store reviewer to spin the Wheel of Rejection. Here are several examples of how you'd use precondition calls with and without feedback messages:

```
precondition(index < self.count)
precondition(index < self.count, "Index is out of bounds")
preconditionFailure()
preconditionFailure("Switch state should never reach default case")
```

Precondition fails stop to a debuggable state in debug builds. They simply end execution in release builds.

> **Note**
>
> When compiling without optimization, `preconditionFailure()` emits the same code as `fatalError()`. Under optimization, `fatalError()` emits the same call, but `preconditionFailure()` ends up as a trap instruction.

Aborting and Exiting

Part of the Darwin library and most commonly used for command-line apps, `abort` produces simple abnormal process termination:

```
@noreturn func abort()
```

Use `exit` for traditional exit code support, which can then be tested in shell scripts for success and fail conditions:

```
@noreturn func exit(_: Int32)
```

`exit` causes normal process termination. The status value passed to the `exit` function returns to the parent, where it can then be evaluated. The C standard uses `EXIT_SUCCESS` and `EXIT_FAILURE` constants, both of which are available through Darwin.

Failing Gracefully

Applications often encounter runtime conditions that arise from conditions such as bad user input, network outage, or a file no longer existing. Despite errors, you'll want ways to recover and continue normal execution rather than crash. To address this, Swift offers support for constructing, throwing, catching, and propagating errors at runtime.

Unlike many other programming languages, Swift does not use exceptions. Although Swift errors may resemble exception handlers (with its `try`, `catch`, and `throw` keywords), Swift does not unwind the call stack. Its errors are computationally efficient. A Swift `throw` statement resembles a `return` statement in terms of overhead.

These keywords may superficially remind you of exceptions, but they represent a distinct technology. As developer guru Mike Ash puts it, "Swift looks just enough like other languages (outside of Rust or Haskell or other hipster languages) to make you think you can get a head start but it's different enough that little of your prior knowledge actually applies." Swift may quack like an exception-producing duck, but don't hold your breath waiting for eggs and a down vest.

The `ErrorType` Protocol

An error describes the conditions under which an operation failed. The traditional Cocoa error class is NSError. Its properties include a string-based error domain, a numeric code, and a localized dictionary of information to support issue reporting. Although the original design intended errors to be presented directly to users, developers are the primary consumer of NSError instances and their Swift descendants. Swift strips down error features to provide NSError interoperation support at the most minimal level.

A Swift error conforms to the ErrorType protocol. Although this is a public protocol, the standard library reveals nothing publicly about how the protocol works or is implemented. These are the official module declarations for this protocol:

```
public protocol ErrorType {
}

extension ErrorType {
}
```

Any Swift type—enumeration, class, or structure—supports ErrorType by declaring protocol conformance, as you see in the following examples. Internally, ErrorType implements two key NSError features: the string domain (_domain) and the numeric code (_code). These features provide compatibility with NSError. This quick peek at private implementation details is not intended for use in any App Store product:

```
class ErrorClass: ErrorType{}
ErrorClass()._code // 1
ErrorClass()._domain // "ErrorClass", the type name

struct ErrorStruct: ErrorType{}
ErrorStruct()._code // 1
ErrorStruct()._domain // "ErrorStruct"

enum ErrorEnum: ErrorType {case First, Second, Third}
ErrorEnum.First._code // 0, the enum descriminant
ErrorEnum.Second._code // 1
ErrorEnum.Third._code // 2
ErrorEnum.First._domain // "ErrorEnum"
```

Conforming to ErrorType enables any Swift construct to be NSError compatible. This applies regardless of whether the construct is a class. For example, you can cast a structure with ErrorStruct() as NSError to produce a minimal error populated with a code and domain:

```
print(ErrorStruct() as NSError)
    // Error Domain=ErrorStruct Code=1 "(null)"
```

The resulting error discards all custom state information you have added.

The "(null)" description usually describes material in the NSError's userInfo dictionary, but at this time there is no way to populate that dictionary via casting. Apple's Joe Groff wrote on Twittter, "It isn't possible yet to control the userInfo or localized messages of a bridged NSError."

Choosing Between Optionals and Error Handling

Many current APIs, especially those based on Core Foundation calls, have yet to be audited and transitioned to the new error-handling system. In such cases, you're stuck using the old design. Make sure to always check your result for nil, 0, NULL or another signal *before* attempting to access an NSError instance.

When crafting new methods, consider how their results are used and whether you're communicating an error or returning a true some-or-none situation. Not all nil-returning methods equate to errors. For example, consider optional chaining. Chaining ideally creates a parsimonious and readable set of operations that flow smoothly from one call to the next. Using optionals enables that chain to naturally break, albeit at the cost of not knowing *why* that break happened. When a method doesn't require explicit error conditions, you can enable chaining by choosing optionals over errors.

Use optionals whenever your code explicitly handles a nil case. If the nil case is never of interest to the client code, error handling means you never have to unwrap.

As a rule, avoid using nil as a signal to indicate error states. Don't pass-and-populate intermediate error structures as side effects. Throwing an error enables a caller to implement a recovery scheme that works around a failure scenario. Errors also enable you to represent and differentiate between distinct conditions and to better handle situations where you'd normally leave a scope and report an error.

Don't forget that returning optionals and throwing errors are not mutually exclusive. An API can use optionals and errors to report three states: "request succeeded and returned value," "request succeeded without returning value," and "request had an error."

> **Note**
>
> Swift's try? command bridges between error handling and optionals, enabling API consumers to convert throwing calls into optional chaining. This approach discards error details, establishing try? as the ugly offspring of error:nil calls.

Swift Error Rules

Swift error handling offers ways to respond to and recover from application error conditions. You need only follow a few simple rules to be a good citizen under the current system. This section overviews those rules and discusses how to best follow them in your applications.

Rule 1: Move Away from `nil` Sentinels

Until Swift 2, failable methods would take an `in-out` error parameter or error pointer and return an optional value. Here's an example from `NSAttributedString`, pre-Swift 2:

```
func dataFromRange(range: NSRange,
    documentAttributes dict: [NSObject : AnyObject],
    error: NSErrorPointer) -> NSData?
```

In this older approach, you tested the returned optional value. If the method didn't succeed and would return `nil`, the method populated its error, which in turn might then be passed back through successive calls to some originating function. At each stage, a calling function might report an error, discard an error, or create and populate an error. The following example shows a fairly common approach for `nil`-sentinel use:

```
if let resultOfOptionalType = failableOperation(params, &error) {
    // use result
} else {
    // report error
}
```

Until now, there were best practices but no fixed rules on how this was implemented or even if this was done properly. You might be a confident, reliable coder, but could you place equal trust in the coders of the APIs you called?

Worse, this approach encouraged repetitive error-prone code that lent itself to duplicated logic, excessive nesting, and late return. `nil`-sentinel calls that used error-populating side effects allowed you to bypass or ignore returned errors and didn't offer a sufficiently reliable pathway from the source of a failed operation to the consumer of that issue. Swift 2 was designed to avoid these issues.

The updated error system offers a new pathway for errors. In the revised system, errors are considered at the point where they're generated and at the point where they're consumed. You no longer pass errors directly, avoiding those situations where you might have erroneously substituted the wrong error parameter or accidentally passed `nil`. Instead, you `throw` an error to the runtime system and `try` and/or `catch` it where you'll use it. The `throws` keyword annotates any method that supports the new system.

Consider the updated API for the `NSAttributedString` function that started this section. This function gains the `throws` keyword, the `NSData?` return value is no longer optional, and the `NSError` argument has entirely disappeared:

```
// New
func dataFromRange(range: NSRange,
    documentAttributes dict: [String : AnyObject]) throws -> NSData
```

Where possible, your failable functions should adopt this standard and replace optionals-as-sentinels in favor of throwing functions that return non-optional values. This migration involves nontrivial work, as you see in the following steps, which describe the tasks you must perform:

1. Add the `throws` keyword after the argument list.

2. If the return type was used as a sentinel, change the return type from optional to non-optional by removing the question mark.

3. If needed, create an error type that represents the possible error states your type may encounter.

4. Replace any `return nil` call that was meant to report errors with `throw` statements, using your custom error types.

5. Audit your calling points:

   - If you do not care about error information, add `try?` to your calls. This approach enables you to largely retain your preconversion consumer code as `try?` calls hook into the new error mechanism but return optionals. Of course, ignoring errors isn't generally a good idea; APIs report errors for good reasons.

   - If you're guaranteed to return successful results without thrown errors, use `try!` and remove your optional-handling code like `guard` and `if-let`. This approach is dangerous. Any thrown errors result in application crashes.

   - If you want to handle the error, replace `guard`, `if-let`, and other optional-handling constructs with `try` and embed those calls in `do-catch`. This preferred approach enables you to differentiate errors and provide runtime mitigation. It also requires the most refactoring work.

Rule 2: Use `throw` to Raise Errors

When your app cannot continue its normal flow of execution, `throw` an error at the point where the issue occurs:

```
if some-task-has-failed {throw error-instance}
```

Throwing an error leaves the current scope (after executing all pending `defer` blocks) and invokes Swift's error-handling system. That system enables API consumers to down the line to report the error, to handle it (using `do-catch` or as an optional with `try?`), and to attempt workarounds.

An error conforms to the `ErrorType` protocol, but there are essentially no other restrictions with regard to what that error looks like or how you implement it. While you are more than welcome to construct `NSError` instances, many Swift developers prefer to use Swift-native `ErrorType` constructs that better represent and communicate issues. For example, Swift enumerations provide a great way to group related errors together:

```
enum MyErrorEnumeration: ErrorType {case FirstError, SecondError, ...}
```

You might create an error enumeration related to authentication. In the following example, one of the cases uses an associated value to indicate a minimum retry period:

```
enum AuthenticationError : ErrorType {
    case InvalidUserCredentials
    case LoginPortalNotEnabled
    case PortalTimeOut(Int)
}
```

All standard Swift features from associated values to type methods to protocols are available to your errors. You're not sending abstract signals; you're throwing concrete type instances. Swift does not limit you to just printing your errors and returning prematurely from method calls, although you are certainly able to do that if your app does not need more complex functionality. Context-rich features enable you to catch and consume error instances that help you recover from failure and offer workarounds to your users.

> ### Note
> Internally, Swift implements any function that `throws` with an extra parameter. That parameter points to an error-storage slot that the caller places on the stack. On return, after calling with `try`, the caller checks whether a value has been placed in that slot.

Rule 3: Use Error Types with Visible Access

The error types you use can be declared anywhere, as long as they are visible to the points where they're thrown and caught. If your errors are class specific, you can incorporate them as nested types directly into the class they support. Use access control modifiers to ensure appropriate visibility.

In the following example, the `AuthenticationError` type is nested within `AuthenticationClass`. Its `public` modifier ensures that the error can be seen, consumed, and used by any client of the parent class, even items external to the current module:

```
public class AuthenticationClass {
    public enum AuthenticationError : ErrorType {
        case InvalidUserCredentials
        case LoginPortalNotEnabled
        case PortalTimeOut(Int)
    }

    public func performAuthentication() throws {
        // ... execute authentication tasks ...
        // ... now something has gone wrong ...
        throw AuthenticationError.InvalidUserCredentials
    }
}
```

Rule 4: Mark All Error-Participating Methods with `throws`

Annotate throwing methods with the `throws` keyword. You place the keyword just after the parameter list and before any return type:

```
func myFailableMethod() throws -> ReturnType {...}
```

Mark any method that directly throws an error. You might not initially consider that you must also mark methods that use `try` but do not themselves consume errors. So, for example, if your method does not catch or otherwise handle the error, *it must use the* `throws` *keyword*:

```
func myMethodThatCallsTry() throws {
    try someFailableMethod()
}
```

When your method uses `do-catch`, `try!`, or `try?`, each of which can provide an endpoint for an error, you do not use `throws` unless, of course, the method itself throws further errors or does not consume all possible errors. The following method does not need a `throws` annotation:

```
func myMethodThatCatches() {
    do {
        try someFailableMethod()
    } catch {
        // handle error
    }
}
```

but this one does:

```
func myMethodThatCatches() throws {
    do {
        try someFailableMethod()
    } catch MyErrorType.OnlyOneKindOfError {
        // handle just this kind of error
        // but other errors may fall through
    }
}
```

Rule 5: Use `rethrows` Consistently

The `rethrows` keyword refers to a method that executes a closure that can itself throw. When you call that closure with `try`, the closure `throws` and the parent `rethrows` any errors:

```
func myRethrowingMethod(closure: () throws -> Void) rethrows {
    try closure()
}
```

When working with protocols, a `throws` method cannot override a `rethrows` member (although you can satisfy a throwing member with a rethrowing one). Use `rethrows` to consistently indicate a two-stage error-handling process and avoid potential compiler errors. If your function takes a closure as an argument and you want to allow the argument closure to throw (but your function does not itself actually throw anything or call any APIs that throw besides the argument closure), use `rethrows`.

Rule 6: Consume Errors Where They Matter

At some point along the error chain, a method may sufficiently care about a potentially failable task to take responsibility for an error. In such circumstances, your code has lots of flexibility. It can consume the error entirely. It may perform partial mitigation before turning around and continuing the error chain. It may wrap the error into a higher-level error rather than leak the error from underlying APIs. If continuing the chain, mark the method with `throws`. Even when a method consumes an error, it can throw one as well:

```
func myPartiallyMitigatingMethod() throws {
    do {
        try someFailableMethod()
    } catch {
        // perform mitigation tasks ...
        // then continue error chain
        throw error
    }
}
```

Rule 7: Terminate Threaded Error Chains

When working with asynchronous code, provide a natural endpoint for any throwing methods. Many asynchronous Cocoa calls use completion handlers. You place a request, and the completion block executes when the request completes, regardless of whether that request succeeded or failed.

You don't `try` these asynchronous calls. There's no point as you're usually passing a handler that understands and manages error states. Instead, you work with returned values in the handler, which is already designed for this. A typical handler provides a data and error argument parameter tuple, as in this Social framework example:

```
slrequest.performRequestWithHandler {
    (NSData!, NSHTTPURLResponse!, NSError!) -> Void in
    // code handling
}
```

You test the data argument, and if its value is set to a `nil` sentinel of some kind, you handle error mitigation. Otherwise, you process the data. This offers a natural fit for `if-let` handling.

Swift's redesigned error system doesn't affect the externals of this call. There's nothing to catch from this request. You do not have to call it with `try`. Inside the handler is another matter.

The following example places an asynchronous request. It converts returned data to a string and saves that string to a file:

```
slrequest.performRequestWithHandler {
    (data: NSData!, response: NSHTTPURLResponse!, error: NSError!) -> Void in
    if let string = String(data: data, encoding: NSUTF8StringEncoding) {
        try string.writeToFile("/tmp/test.txt",
            atomically: true,
            encoding: NSUTF8StringEncoding)
    }
}
```

Because the `writeToFile:atomically:encoding:` function `throws`, you call it using some variant of `try`. This sets up an error-handling microenvironment within the handler closure.

At this point, you encounter an issue. The compiler complains about an error, specifically:

```
invalid conversion from throwing function of type '(NSData!, NSHTTPURLResponse!,
NSError!) throws -> Void' to non-throwing function type '@convention(block) (NSData!,
NSHTTPURLResponse!, NSError!) -> Void'
```

Adding `try` to the handler closure converts that closure to a throwing type. There's no exhaustive `catch` or `try?` or `try!`, so it's possible that an unhandled error could propagate further. The `performRequestWithHandler` parameter doesn't accept throwing closures. To mitigate this issue, return the closure to a non-throwing version.

You do this by consuming thrown errors within the block. Use any of the myriad of Swift solutions, such as `do-catch` or `if-let-try?`. Exhaustively consuming errors converts the throwing closure to a non-throwing version and enables it to be passed as the handler parameter. By providing a full pathway for the errors to follow, you ensure that each potential error reaches an endpoint.

You see a similar issue when working with Grand Central Dispatch (GCD). Like the Social request, GCD executes a closure asynchronously. It is not set up to accept one whose signature includes throwing. In the following example, an outer function dispatches a block that throws:

```
public func dispatch_after(delay: NSTimeInterval, block: () throws -> Void) {
    // Construct error-handling equivalent dispatch
    dispatch_after(

        // build time offset
        dispatch_time(DISPATCH_TIME_NOW,
            Int64(delay * NSTimeInterval(NSEC_PER_SEC))),

        // "It is recommended to use quality of service class values to
        // identify the well-known global concurrent queues."
        dispatch_get_global_queue(QOS_CLASS_DEFAULT, 0),
```

```
        // Integrate error-throwing block into self-contained
        // do-catch error-handling structure
        {
            do {
                try block()
            }
            catch {
                print("Error during async execution")
                print(error)
            }
        }
    )
}
```

To succeed, this example must try the block and catch any errors. An exhaustive catch prevents those errors from propagating further and transforms the inner closure into one without a throws signature.

Without this overhead, the internal `dispatch_after` call won't compile. It expects a non-throwing `dispatch_block_t` argument that cannot be provided if the closure contains any remaining error pathways.

> **Note**
>
> You can easily adapt this code to accept an error handler and/or completion handler to extend the functionality and flexibility of this approach.

Building Errors

To raise an error, throw any instance that conforms to `ErrorType`. In the simplest case, create a struct and throw it, as in the following example:

```
public struct SomethingWentWrong : ErrorType {}
...something happens...
throw SomethingWentWrong()
```

In the best of all possible worlds, your diagnostics should read less like random fortune cookie paper slips and more like constructive pointers that explain your failure. For example, avoid:

```
public enum SomethingWentWrongError: ErrorType {
    case YouWillFindNewLove
    case AClosedMouthGathersNoFeet
    case CynicsAreFrustratedOptimists
    case WhenEverythingIsComingYourWayYouAreInTheWrongLane
}
```

Good Errors

Errors exist at the intersection of information and flow control. Good errors should be written for human consumption in a professional environment. The following points discuss how you might best create error content for developer consumption:

- **Be clear.** A good error message should establish what the issue is, the cause of the issue, the source of the issue, and how to resolve the issue. Take inspiration from Foundation and offer both failure reasons and recovery suggestions in your error feedback.

- **Be precise.** The more your error traces back to a specific fail point, the better able an end programmer will be able to use it to fix the code or respond with runtime workarounds.

- **Incorporate details.** Swift errors enable you to create structures, associate values, and provide vital context about where and why things went wrong. Create more informative errors with details.

- **Prefer clarity to concision.** Don't eliminate words just for the sake of short error messages. Yes: "Unable to access uninitialized data store." No: "Uninitialized." At the same time, limit your explanations to the issue your error is dealing with. Avoid unneeded extras.

- **Add support.** When you incorporate API and documentation references, you further help explain the condition and support recovery. Links are good. Snippets can be good. Full documentation is unnecessary. Allow features like Quick Help to properly fill their role without attempting to usurp them.

- **Avoid jargon.** Avoiding jargon is especially important if your error may be consumed outside the context of your immediate working environment. When in doubt, prefer simpler and more common words to project-specific names and acronyms.

- **Be polite.** Use phrasing that does not insult your cubical mate, your manager, or the persons who developed the API you're struggling with. Minimize humor as humor travels poorly. An error message that's meant to be self-deprecating may misfire at some future point.

> **Note**
>
> Communicating error conditions to end users lies outside the scope of this chapter.

Naming Your Errors

I don't use a lot of rules for error naming tasks, but I do want to offer a few recommendations in this space:

- When dealing with trivial applications, feel free to use trivial names, especially in playgrounds, sample code, and test apps:

```
enum Error: ErrorType {case WrongFile, ItsMonday, IFeelCranky}
```

- Use the word `Error` in type names. Yes: `FileProcessingError`. No: `FileProcessing`.

- Clearly describe the error circumstances in enumeration cases and structure names. Yes: `FileNotFound` (enumeration case) or `FileNotFoundError` (struct). No: `Missing`.

- Support enumeration cases with labeled associated values:

  `case FileNotFound(fileName: String)`

Adding String Descriptions

`ErrorType` was first introduced solely for enumerations, and it was later extended to classes and structures. There's a tendency for Swift developers to create enumerations to represent errors, but unless your code represents true enumerated conditions, there's no real advantage in, for example, using `ParseError.UnexpectedQuoteToken` over `ParseError("Encountered unexpected quote token")`. When there *are* true enumerated conditions, the former example enables error consumers to know what the exact parsing error is. This allows you to implement specific workarounds on a per-type basis. Using string-typed errors limits the consumer to knowing the error type (a parse error) without establishing the kind of parse error it was.

Prefer enumerations whenever doing so makes sense, as when there's a distinct syntactic set of possible error conditions. For example, use enumerations when you expect the consumer to use a `switch` statement to differentiate actions depending on the error that was thrown. Prefer structs for non-enumerated conditions where the focus lies with error information and all errors will be treated equally. In this latter case, where the focus lies more with developer communication than programmatic action selection, it helps to incorporate string descriptions to document why errors arose.

Adding Reasons

Supplying clear informative errors is simplified with strings. They provide the opportunity to pass information about errors without adhering to a predetermined domain of error conditions. The following snippet builds an `ErrorType`-conforming structure that accepts an arbitrary string description:

```
struct MyErrorType: ErrorType {
    let reason : String
}
```

The default initializer establishes the `reason` property, which travels with the error struct when it is thrown:

```
throw MyErrorType(reason: "Numeric input was out of range")
```

This custom error prints as follows:

```
MyErrorType(reason: "Numeric input was out of range")
```

Simplifying Output

To remove the structure overhead you see in the preceding example, conform to `CustomStringConvertible` or `CustomDebugStringConvertible`, as in the following snippet:

```
struct MyErrorType: ErrorType, CustomDebugStringConvertible {
    let reason : String
    var debugDescription: String {
        return "\(self.dynamicType): \(reason)"
    }
}
```

This updated error prints more simply, presenting only the type and the reason, as in the following example:

```
MyErrorType: Numeric input was out of range
```

You can bundle this behavior into a protocol, as in Recipe 6-1, and then conform error types to the new protocol instead of `ErrorType`.

Recipe 6-1   **Self-Describing Error Types**

```
public protocol ExplanatoryErrorType: ErrorType, CustomDebugStringConvertible {
    var reason: String {get}
    var debugDescription: String {get}
}

public extension ExplanatoryErrorType {
    public var debugDescription: String {
        // Adjust for however you want the error to print
        return "\(self.dynamicType): \(reason)"
    }
}
```

In the following example, instances of `CustomErrorType` use the default print behavior provided by the protocol extension:

```
public struct CustomErrorType: ExplanatoryErrorType {
    public let reason: String
}
```

Extending String

`ErrorType` actually enables you to extend `String` so you can throw string instances as errors. The following example throws, catches, and prints `"Numeric input was out of range"` but without the `MyErrorType` overhead:

```
extension String : ErrorType {}
do {throw "Numeric input was out of range"} catch {print(error)}
```

While this is a handy solution for simple applications, there are drawbacks. This approach requires that you universally conform `String` to `ErrorType` with a single point of conformance. Redundant conformances raise compile-time errors. If you use the trick in one file, and then use the same trick in a module, you'll run into issues.

Type-Specific Errors

Use type-specific public errors to ensure that `ErrorType` definitions are local to the types that `throw` them. Don't feel that repetitive code like this:

```
public struct FileInitializationError: ErrorType {let reason: String}
```

and this detracts from your development work:

```
public struct ServiceError: ErrorType {let reason: String}
```

On the contrary, context-specific type names add utility in describing error sources. Their minimal implementations add little overhead to your projects, even though their code looks nearly identical. Adding errors to the type that utilizes them means they travel with the code where they're relevant. This way, you avoid cross-file definitions and limit redundant definitions across project source files. Nest error types wherever possible into a parent construct for even stronger ties between the types that utilize the errors and the errors themselves.

Retrieving Context

Knowing where an error comes from adds context to understanding and utilizing it. In Recipe 6-2, a simple extension to `ErrorType` produces a string that describes the source of an error. This extension implements its `contextString` method by leveraging built-in Swift keywords (`__FILE__`, `__FUNCTION__`, `__LINE__`). These keywords describe the context of a calling scope. Used as default values, they automatically populate parameters for function name, filename, and line number.

Recipe 6-2   **Adding Context to Errors**

```
extension ErrorType {
    public func contextString(
        file : String = __FILE__,
        function : String = __FUNCTION__,
        line : Int = __LINE__) -> String {
            return "\(function):\(file):\(line)"
    }
}
```

Because this is an `ErrorType` extension, the `contextString()` method is available to all conforming types. You can use this approach to modify an error before throwing it, normally by assigning the context to a property from the throwing context. If you try to use `contextString()` from the initializer instead, the context string will report the initializer file, line, and function, which is not what you want. Here's an example of how you can use this approach:

```
struct CustomError: ErrorType {
    let reason: String
    var context: String = ""
    init(reason: String) {
        self.reason = reason
    }
}

class MyClass {
    static func throwError() throws {
        var err = CustomError(reason: "Something went wrong")
        err.context = err.contextString()
        throw err
    }
}
```

You can use this approach to add context to logging as well as to customize your errors.

> **Note**
>
> You can also build context-grabbing features into `ErrorType` initializers. The write-up at
> http://ericasadun.com/2015/06/22/swift-dancing-the-error-mambo/ offers an example of
> how you might use this approach. This post was written before Swift 2 extended error types to
> structures and classes; you no longer need to manually build _domain and _code properties.

Contextualizing Strings

The following variation on Recipe 6-2 enables you to grab context using a standalone function:

```
func fetchContextString(file : String = __FILE__,
    function : String = __FUNCTION__,
    line : Int = __LINE__) -> String {
        return "\(function):\(file):\(line) "
}
```

This approach enables you to grab context wherever you construct strings. For example, you can use the function to construct a `reason` property for a thrown error:

```
struct MyError: ErrorType {let reason: String}
do {
    throw MyError(reason: fetchContextString() + "Something went wrong")
} catch { print(error) }
```

Or, if you're already working with string errors, you can directly prepend a string with its context:

```
extension String: ErrorType {}
do {
    throw fetchContextString() + "Numeric input was out of range"
} catch {print(error)}
```

In this scenario, strings are, themselves, error types. While this is a convenient solution for simple apps, it inherits the problematic issues with using String as an error type.

Contextualizing Throwing Types

Recipe 6-3 offers another slightly more complicated take on contextualization. In this approach, the context task is redirected to the type that implements the failable method—in this example, MyStruct. In this recipe, any type that conforms to Contextualizable can use a default constructContextError method to build and throw a ContextualizedErrorType. The constructor accepts an arbitrary number of arguments, offering more flexibility in error reporting. Unlike Recipe 6-2, Recipe 6-3's protocol implementation enables you to refer to the throwing context's dynamic type.

Recipe 6-3   **Using a Contextualizable Protocol to Build Errors**

```
// Contextual error protocol
public protocol ContextualizedErrorType : ErrorType {
    var source: String {get set}
    var reason: String {get set}
    init(source: String, reason: String)
}

// Enable classes to contextualize their errors
public protocol Contextualizable {}
public extension Contextualizable {
    // This constructor accepts an arbitrary number of items
    public func constructContextError <T:ContextualizedErrorType>(
        errorType: T.Type,
        _ items: Any...,
        file : String = __FILE__,
        function : String = __FUNCTION__,
        line : Int = __LINE__) -> T {
        return T(
            source:"\(function):\(self.dynamicType):\(file):\(line) ",
            reason:items.map({"\($0)"}).joinWithSeparator(", "))
    }
}
```

```
// This custom error type conforms to ContextualizedErrorType and can
// be constructed and thrown by types that conform to Contextualizable
public struct CustomErrorType: ContextualizedErrorType {
    public var reason: String
    public var source: String
    public init(source: String, reason: String) {
        self.source = source
        self.reason = reason
    }
}

// The conforming type can build and throw a contextualized error
public struct MyStruct: Contextualizable {
    func myFunction() throws {
        throw constructContextError(
            CustomErrorType.self, "Some good reason", 2, 3)
    }
}
```

As you can see from this recipe, setup involves more steps, but the actual error construction and throwing portion is quite simple. Normally I'd want to prepend the constructContextError method with self for clarity. You cannot do that in this case, though, since it is implemented in a protocol extension.

Simplifying Contexts

Recipe 6-4 offers one last context approach, a simplified version of Recipe 6-3. This recipe retains detail-gathering features but limits thrown errors to a single Error type. Since the source context is included in the error's source member, this implementation offers a realistic trade-off.

Recipe 6-4 **Simpler Context Errors**

```
public struct Error: ErrorType {
    let source: String; let reason: String
    public init(_ source: String = __FILE__, _ reason: String) {
        self.reason = reason; self.source = source
    }
}

protocol Contextualizable {}
extension Contextualizable {
    func contextError(
        items: Any...,
        file : String = __FILE__,
        function : String = __FUNCTION__,
```

```
            line : Int = __LINE__) -> Error {
            return Error(
                "\(function):\(self.dynamicType):\(file):\(line) ",
                items.map({"\($0)"}).joinWithSeparator(", "))
    }
}

public struct Parent: Contextualizable {
    func myFunction() throws {
        throw contextError("Some good reason", 2, 3)
    }
}
```

Calling Throwing Functions

As Yoda may not have put it, "try or try not, there is no do." In Swift, there is `try`. There is also `do`. Knowing how these features work enables you to hook your methods into the new error-handling system.

Mark any throwing method with `throws` or `rethrows` and call these throwing items using `try`, `try?`, or `try!`. The undecorated `try` operator provides core error-handling behavior. The `try?` operator (known to its closest friends as `try`-with-a-question-mark) acts as a bridge between error-handling methods and optional-handling consumers. The exclamation point `try!` represents the forced-`try` expression. It enables you to skip the `do-catch` tango.

A few facts:

- The `throws` keyword is automatically part of a function's type (and the same goes for `rethrows`). Non-throwing functions are subtypes of throwing functions. So you can use the `try` operator with non-throwing functions.

- When currying, the `throws` applies only to the innermost function.

- You can't override non-throwing methods with throwing ones, but you can override a throwing method with a non-throwing method.

- Throwing functions cannot satisfy protocol requirements for non-throwing functions, but you can satisfy a throwing requirement with a non-throwing implementation.

Using `try`

Unlike with optionals, whose fail case is limited to `nil` sentinels, error handling enables you to determine what went wrong and offer runtime mechanisms to respond to those conditions. Swift offers flexible errors that you can build to encapsulate any relevant information needed to report and recover from failure. You participate in this system by calling failable throwing methods with `try`. Place the `try` keyword before any call to a throwing method or function:

```
try myFailableCall()
```

To respond to thrown errors, wrap the `try` call in a `do-catch` construct:

```
do {
    try myFailableCall()
} catch {
    // handle error here
}
```

The preceding snippet uses a single `catch` clause that matches all errors. `do-catch` is also designed to support multiple clauses using both pattern matching and `where` clauses, as in the following example:

```
enum StateError : ErrorType {
    case GeneralError // simple enumeration case
    case UnsupportedState(code: Int, reason: String) // associated values
}


// Throw an error with associated values
func myFailableCall() throws {
    if !testForSuccess() {
        throw StateError.UnsupportedState(code: 418, reason: "I'm a teapot")}
}


do {
    try myFailableCall()
} catch StateError.GeneralError {
    print("General Error")
} catch StateError.UnsupportedState(
    let code, let reason) where code == 418 {
    print("Unsupported Coffee state: reason \(reason)")
} catch {
    print("Error is \(error) of some kind")
}
```

The final `catch` clause is exhaustive in the preceding example. It matches all thrown errors. Although this clause does not use any `let` or `var` assignments, by default it has access to a local constant named `error`, which stores the newly caught error. This `error` constant is not available to pattern-matching clauses.

Error Propagation

When a do statement is not exhaustive, its error propagates to the surrounding scope, as in the following example:

```
func partiallyHandle() throws -> String {
    do {
        try myFailableCall()
    } catch StateError.UnsupportedState(let code, _) where code == 0 {
        // this will never happen because code is never 0
        return("Error Condition")
    }
    return "Success Condition"
}
```

In this contrived example, the catch statement is rigged to never succeed. This function requires the throws keyword as errors are not fully handled within its scope. The preceding code is functionally equivalent to the following:

```
func partiallyHandle() throws -> String {
    try myFailableCall()
    return "Success Condition"
}
```

If the catch were, instead, exhaustive, the function could be converted to the following non-throwing version:

```
func handle()-> String {
    do {
        try myFailableCall()
    } catch {
        return("Error Condition")
    }
    return "Success Condition"
}
```

In this case, the function loses the throws keyword, and the error-handling chain ends. The function returns a valid String value, even when its try statement fails.

> **Note**
>
> In the real world, partial handling might occur when dealing with the special case of NSUserCancelledError or, when deleting a file, NSFileNoSuchFileError. Both cases are sometimes rerouted into the success path because they represent a positive match to user expectations and desires. For example, consider a function that removes cached files, such as func removeMyCachedFile() throws, which internally handles NSFileNoSuchFileError but reports all other errors to the caller.

Using `try!`

Forced `try` (`try!`) wraps your calls in a runtime assertion made with the highest-quality assertions lovingly crafted through the magic of artisan compilation to disable error propagation:

```
try! myFailableCall() // may succeed, may crash
```

When they fail, they fail loudly, throwing runtime errors instead of passing errors to handlers for in-app resolution. Your app crashes, and your users begin writing your gluten-free, all-natural, one-star reviews.

So why would you use this command? `try!` is meant for calls that throw but that you pretty much know a priori will never fail, such as when they're documented to never throw for the parameters you're calling them with. Normally you test for those fail conditions first, and only then do you force your `try`. As a rule, don't `try!` unless you're sure a throwing function won't throw. A forced `try` basically says, "Just go ahead and perform this throwing operation, and if it fails, so be it." `Try!` is particularly handy for quick playground hits where you just want something to run, and you don't really care if it fails and crashes.

Using `try?`

The `try?` operator offers a bridge between Swift's error-handling system and optionals. It returns an optional value that wraps successful results and "catches" errors by returning `nil`. Use it with standard optional handlers, as in the following examples:

```
guard let result = try? somethingThatMayThrow() else {
    // handle error condition and leave scope
}
if let result = try? somethingThatMayThrow() {}
let result = (try? somethingThatMayThrow()) ?? myFallbackValue
```

In each of these examples, the code conditionally binds a non-optional to a result, and the error is discarded. Instead of this pre-Swift 2 approach:

```
if let value = request(arguments, error:&error) {
    ...success..
} else {
    ...print error and return/die...
}
```

or this non-optional Swift 2 error-handling implementation:

```
do {
    let value = try request(arguments)
} catch {... print error and return/die ...}
```

you work in a system where error conditions are transformed automatically into `nil` values. This approach offers these benefits:

- Interoperability between Swift's nullable optionals and its error system. For example, you can write throwing functions and consume them with `if-let`. `try?` bridges these paradigms.

- A focus on success/failure where the calling context solely assumes responsibility for reporting error conditions. "I tried to do some task and it failed somewhere." Traditionally errors describe what went wrong. Now you describe what you were trying to do.

What you lose is this:

- Cocoa-style error handling. Any errors that are generated are eaten away, and you won't see them or know about them.

- Error source information such as the file and routine that generated the issue. All you know is that the calling chain failed somewhere, but you don't know why or how.

- Railway/freight-train-style development, where you combine functions with a binding operator to propagate errors through the end of the chain.

So, when do you want to use this error-to-optional bridging? Here are a couple of scenarios you might consider this:

- When you're focused more on success/failure than on why things failed

- When you're working with well-tested API chains, so if you can't construct a URL or save to a file or whatever, you just want to note it and move on with your recovery code for a "did not succeed" scenario

Implementing Alternatives to `try`?

The nice thing about `try?` is that you don't have to encapsulate calls within a `do-catch` block. Your result returns as an optional: `.Some` for success, `.None` for failure. You can use `try?` both in `if-let` statements and with `guard`. The bad thing about `try?` is that it discards errors, leaving you unable to figure out what when wrong when things go wrong. That's never a great thing.

You can roll your own alternative by implementing a simple result enumeration, as in Recipe 6-5. This enumeration represents both success and failure cases in a single type.

Recipe 6-5   **Bypassing `try?` with a Custom Result Enumeration**

```
enum Result<T> {
    case Value(T)
    case Error(ErrorType)

    func unwrap() throws -> T {
        switch self {
```

```
        case .Value(let value): return value
        case .Error(let error): throw error
        }
    }

    // Value property
    var value: T? {
        if case .Value(let value) = self { return value }
        return nil
    }

    // Error property
    var error: ErrorType? {
        if case .Error(let error) = self { return error }
        return nil
    }

    init(_ block: () throws -> T) {
        do {
            let value = try block()
            self = Result.Value(value)
        } catch {
            self = Result.Error(error)
        }
    }
}
```

With Recipe 6-5, instead of using the `try` operator directly, as in this example:

```
let result = try myFailableCoinToss()
```

you call the `Result` constructor:

```
let result = Result(myFailableCoinToss)
```

To unwrap your result outside of `if-let` and `guard`, use switches and pattern matching:

```
switch result {
case .Value(let value): print("Success:", value)
case .Error(let error): print("Failure:", error)
}
if case .Value(let value) = result {
    print("Success:", value)
} else if case .Error(let error) = result {
    print("Failure:", error)
}
```

Guarding Results

Recipe 6-5's implementation enables you to use the `value` and `error` properties with a standard `guard` statement. Unlike with `try?`, the error is ready for use and propagation. This example uses `fatalError` because it's demonstrated in a sample playground. In real-world code, you'd throw, wrap, or handle the error. You'd also want to work around the forced-unwrapping used here:

```
// guard the result value, otherwise handling the error with forced unwrap.
guard let unwrappedResult = result.value else {
    fatalError("\(result.error!)")
    // leave scope
}

// result is now usable at top level scope
print("Result is \(unwrappedResult)")
```

Building a Printing Version of `try?`

Recipe 6-6 offers another approach that more closely mimics `try?` while printing any errors that are raised. This `attempt` function performs the same tasks as `try?` with a custom implementation.

Recipe 6-6   **Mimicking `try?` with Printing**

```
func attempt<T>(block: () throws -> T) -> Optional<T>{
    do {
        return try block()
    } catch {
        print(error)
        return nil
    }
}
```

This recipe's approach earns you the `if-let` and `guard` behavior of `try?` but ensures a measure of respect to returned errors. You call it as follows:

```
let result = attempt(myFailableCoinToss)
```

In this approach, you can't base error-recovery strategies on the error type and its details, but it's not completely throwing away that information either.

Working with `guard` and `defer`

When working in Swift's updated error-handling system, rely on `guard` and `defer` to ensure robust execution. These constructs enable you to control whether code is permitted to proceed through the current scope and add mandatory clean-up tasks that run when control leaves that scope. Recipe 6-7 shows the practical interaction of these three elements in a function that executes a system call using popen.

Recipe 6-7   **Optimizing guard and defer**

```
public struct ProcessError : ErrorType {let reason: String}

// Execute a system command return the results as a string
public func performSystemCommand(command: String) throws -> String {

    // Open a new process
    guard let fp: UnsafeMutablePointer<FILE> = popen(command, "r") else {
        throw ProcessError(reason: "Unable to open process")
    }; defer{fclose(fp)}

    // Read the process stream
    let buffer: UnsafeMutablePointer<UInt8> =
        UnsafeMutablePointer.alloc(1024); defer {buffer.dealloc(1024)}
    var bytes: [UInt8] = []
    repeat {
        let count: Int = fread(buffer, 1, 1024, fp)
        guard ferror(fp) != 0 else {
            throw ProcessError(reason: "Encountered error while reading stream")
        }
        if count > 0 {
            bytes.appendContentsOf(
                Array(UnsafeBufferPointer(start:buffer, count:count)))
        }
    } while feof(fp) == 0

    guard let string =
        String(bytes: bytes, encoding: NSUTF8StringEncoding) else {
        throw ProcessError(reason:"Process returned unreadable data")
    }
    return string
}
```

I chose this example because it provides a pleasantly diverse set of defer and guard statements. The recipe showcases these two commands at multiple points.

A guard statement introduces one or more prerequisites. If met, it allows execution to continue in the current scope. If not, the guard's mandatory else clause executes and must exit the current scope. guard is most commonly used in tandem with conditional binding, as in the string initialization step at the end of Recipe 6-7. If the string cannot be created, the binding fails, and the `else` clause throws an unreadable-data error. If it succeeds, it makes the string variable available in the outer scope, unlike other cases of optional binding.

`guard` isn't limited to working with optionals, as you see in the `ferror` test that checks the process stream's error indicator. This is a simple Boolean test that returns `true` or `false`. Since execution should not continue on a stream error, a `guard` statement ensures that a thrown error exits the function scope.

You cascade `guard` statements with comma-separated clauses as you do with `if-let`. This creates a simple way to establish variables at the start of your methods and functions, with a single error-handling block to handle any failed condition statements.

`defer` adds commands whose execution is delayed until the current code block prepares to exit. You can close files, deallocate resources, and perform any other clean-up that might otherwise need to be handled from early exit fail conditions in a single call. I like to add my `defer` statement right next to the setup calls that require their execution. Recipe 6-7's `defer` calls close streams and free memory.

Each `defer` block executes at the end of a scope whether or not errors were encountered. This ensures that they run whether the function returns a value or throws an error. Swift stores its `defer` blocks in a stack. They execute in reverse order of their declarations. In this example, the deallocation always precedes `fclose`.

Wrap-up

Swift's error system introduces a positive way to respond to and mitigate errors without having to test sentinels and unwrap values before use. Error propagation ensures that you work with errors only when failure conditions are of interest to your code, enabling you to avoid repetitive and error-prone middleman implementations. Swift's new approach simplifies error handling and returns optionals to their original purpose, for when `nil`s are of actual interest to their callers instead of just stand-ins for "something went wrong."

7

Types

When it comes to types, Swift offers three distinct families. Its type system includes classes, which provide reference types, and enumerations and structures, which are both algebraic value types. Each provides unique strengths and features to support your development. This chapter surveys some of the key concepts used in the Swift language and explores how its types work in your applications.

Language Concepts

Before diving into type specifics, this section offers a quick review of some key concepts that Swift uses in its language design. The following terms support your understanding of Swift's type system and enable you to better understand what each type brings to your programs.

Reference and Value Types

When selecting types, it's critical to understand the distinction between value types and reference types. The big difference between the two is this: A reference type is not copied when assigned to a variable or passed as a parameter, but the data in a value type is.

Instead of copying the value, reference types keep track of a single data location in memory. The *reference* to that value is copied instead of the value itself. Two references that track the same location can access and modify that memory using different names. This is known as *aliasing*. A modification to one reference affects the contents of the other and vice versa. In contrast, two values initialized with the same semantic contents will not affect each other no matter how their data is updated.

This is best seen by example. In Swift, classes are reference types, and structures are value types. The following code establishes two constructs with identical member properties:

```
class MyClass {
    var name: String = "Tom"
    var age: Int = 35
}

struct MyStruct {
    var name: String = "Tom"
    var age: Int = 35
}
```

The following statements create an instance of each type and perform an assignment to this instance:

```
let classInstance1 = MyClass()
let classInstance2 = classInstance1
var structInstance1 = MyStruct()
var structInstance2 = structInstance1
```

In this example, the class instances are constants (using `let`), and the struct instances are variables (using `var`).

When working with reference types, you modify the data the reference points to, not the reference itself. Changes to the shared reference affect both variables:

```
classInstance1.age = 88
print(classInstance2.age) // 88
classInstance2.age = 55
print(classInstance1.age) // 55
```

In contrast, structs are value types. Because data is copied, updates to one leave the other instance unchanged and vice versa:

```
structInstance1.age = 88
print(structInstance2.age) // 35
structInstance2.age = 55
print(structInstance1.age) // 88
```

> **Note**
>
> Swift closures and functions are reference types.

Copy-and-Write-Back

Swift does not use pointers. When you call a method using an `inout` parameter, it uses a *copy-and-write-back* mechanism that avoids using references to an outer variable from inside a function. This approach means you need not dereference pointers, the way you would in C or Objective-C. The following code updates the value stored in `myString` using its `inout` string parameter:

```
func myFunction(inout myParameter: String) {
    myParameter = "Hello"
}


var myString = "My String"
myFunction(&myString)
print(myString) // "Hello"
```

Although the call uses an ampersand to indicate `inout`, it is not applying an address function or directly modifying the instance. You see this best by calling the same function using a computed property. This structure establishes a gettable/settable property that isn't actually affected by assignment:

```
struct MyTest {
    var property: String {
        get {print("getting property"); return "Precomputed"}
        set {print("setting property")}
    }
}
```

When you construct a new instance, the property value remains unaffected by assignment:

```
var myTestInstance = MyTest()
myTestInstance.property // "Precomputed"
myTestInstance.property = "Try to update but can't"
print(myTestInstance.property) // It is still "Precomputed"
```

Copy-and-write-back means this structure works with the `myFunction` implementation in a way that it could not if you were using Objective-C and using direct memory updates. The following snippet calls the getter to populate `myParameter`, executes the code in `myFunction`, and then attempts to copy back the value using the setter:

```
myFunction(&myTestInstance.property) // calls getter and then setter
print(myTestInstance.property) // "Precomputed"
```

Chris Lattner writes on the old Apple DevForums, "An important design point of [S]wift is that we want it to provide strong support for long-term API evolution....[Y]ou can replace a stored property with a computed property without breaking clients. Being able to run getters and setters in the face of `inout` is a key part of this."

Algebraic Data Types

An *algebraic data type* is a composite type formed from other types. That is, it's a data type that can be constructed using primitive data types like strings, doubles, and so forth, and from other composite types, like `CGPoint`, `GLKVector3`, and `CLLocationCoordinate2D`. These come in two forms, which you may already be familiar with under the C-style names *struct* and *union*. Swift-specific algebraic data types are structures, which are *product types*, and enumerations, which are *sum types*:

- A product type is a *record*. Its components consist of members that can be accessed by label. It retains a fixed order of its member properties no matter how the type is used. For example, a `person` struct might be composed of a string-type `name` and an integer-type `age`.

- A sum type is a *tagged union* (also called a *variant record*). Its storage can be configured using several layouts, called *cases*. Only one case applies at any time, and that case defines a fixed order of member properties. An enumeration might have several cases, one of which, the `person` case, stores a string and an integer, a `pet` case that stores a species enumeration, and a `rock` case that stores no further data. Each case uses the same memory footprint, but the layout specifics vary depending on which case is active.

Other Terminology

As Swift uses several kinds of types, it's hard to discuss the entire language using legacy concepts like "classes" and "objects." Not all Swift types are classes, and not all Swift instances are objects. You can instantiate an enumeration and extend a struct. To address this, Swift offers new unifying terms to express the things you're working with more concretely:

- Classes, structures, and enumerations are *constructs*. You use these programmatic building blocks to build your code. *Declarations* establish new constructs. You create new *instances* by calling a *constructor*.

- Constructs include *members*. These include stored and computed *properties*, *initializers* (and *deinitializers*), *methods*, and *subscripts*. When you work with protocols, they too refer to required members and use the same member terminology as the constructs that conform to and implement those requirements.

- A *static* member maintains just one version for the entire type. You can create static methods and properties for all constructs, not just classes, even though many people think of them as "class methods" and "class properties."

- A construct uses *initializers* to set up an instance's starting state and optional *deinitializers* to prepare an instance for deallocation. A *convenience* initialializer adds a simple entry point for creating constructs without requiring you to provide initial values for all properties or to derive properties from a related type. When working with classes, a *designated* initializer provides a primary initialization point; it is guaranteed to fully initialize all subclass and inherited properties. A *required* initializer must be added to subclasses or provided for protocol conformance for any type.

- In Swift, a global function is a *function*. Within a type, it's a *method*. A special class of functions called *operators* enables you to use symbols and phrases to apply behavior outside the standard method name and parenthesized argument list grammar.

- You extend construct behavior by implementing *extensions*. Constructs also extend behavior by conforming to protocols with default implementations. This is called *traits* or *mix-ins* in other programming languages, although the phrases are not standard for Swift. Classes (and only classes) *inherit* behavior by subclassing. Conformance-based behaviors are *included*, not inherited.

- Swift's *access control* establishes the degree to which code is visible relative to the source file and modules they're defined in. You declare an *access level* for constructs that participate in this system. *Public* access ensures that entities can be universally seen and used and specifies a *public interface* for your code. Using *internal* access creates module-wide visibility that's not seen by any source files external to that module. You limit access on a source file-by-source file basis with a *private* access level, which hides implementation details beyond the scope of its source file. Marking a module as *testable* enables unit tests to bypass access levels and access any construct.

Enumerations

Enumerations contain sets of named distinct elements. A finger enumeration might include Thumb, Index, Middle, Ring, and Pinkie. A level enumeration could establish Low, Medium, and High values. Enumerations need not make sense or be conceptually complete in any way. The set of Shinbone, Sneeze, PixieDust, and Penguin is as valid as the enumeration Hearts, Moons, Stars, and Clovers. (To be technically accurate, I should note that over the years, Lucky Charms also included diamonds, horseshoes, balloons, trees, rainbows, and pots of gold, among other charms; the "default" charm set is non-canonical.) Enumerations need only be syntactically complete as some Swift features like switch statements rely on exhaustive cases.

Swift offers three styles of enumeration, with one extra variation that doesn't quite meet the standard of a distinct style. These include basic enumerations, raw value enumerations, enumerations with associated values, and enumerations with indirect values. The following discussion introduces these styles and describe their roles in Swift development.

Basic Enumerations

A basic enumeration consists of a list of cases. The enum keyword declares the construct. The case declarations follow within braces. You can break each enumeration into individual case declarations or combine them together, as in this example:

```
enum Finger {case Thumb, Index, Middle, Ring, Pinkie}
```

Supply one case keyword per line and separate colinear cases with commas. Use uppercase type (Finger) and case (Thumb, Index, and so on) names.

Basic enumerations automatically implement Equatable, enabling you to use them with ==. Each case has an associated hash value. These values are not guaranteed to follow any particular algorithm, although you can pretty easily guess how they're being generated. You cannot construct instances from those hash values:

```
Finger.Thumb.hashValue // 0
Finger.Middle.hashValue // 2
```

An enumeration does not report how many cases it has (in this example, five). A basic enumeration without associated or raw values does not provide constructors. You create new instances simply by listing the type name followed by the case (for example, `Finger.Ring`).

Swift's type inference system enables you to skip the type name prefix in situations where the type itself is unambiguous. In such cases, you begin the enumeration with a raw period—for example, passing `[.Index, .Ring, .Pinkie]` to a parameter marked as an array of `Finger`.

Using Hash Values to Support Ranges

You can list several fingers in a single `switch` case, as in the following example:

```
let finger: Finger = .Index
switch finger {
case .Thumb, .Index, .Middle, .Ring: print("Not pinkie")
default: print("Pinkie")
}
```

You cannot, at least in raw Swift, apply ranges to your basic enumeration cases even though basic enumerations provide hash values that are intrinsically numeric and ordered; these are implementation details that can change in future Swift updates. The following code won't compile in its current state:

```
switch finger {
case .Thumb...(.Ring): print("Not pinkie")
default: print("Pinkie")
}
```

The compiler complains that the range operator (. . .) cannot be applied to these arguments. While there are many solutions to this problem, the simplest involves conforming to the `Comparable` protocol, as pointed out by developer Davide De Franceschi. Add the conformance declaration operator implementation in Recipe 7-1, and the `switch` case begins to work.

Recipe 7-1 **Adding `Comparable` Support to Basic Enumerations**

```
extension Finger: Comparable {}
func <(lhs: Finger, rhs: Finger)-> Bool {
    return lhs.hashValue < rhs.hashValue }
```

In this approach, the minimum hash value is always 0, and the maximum hash value is unknown. It assumes that a semantic ordering of the values is reflected by the underlying hash value.

It's always dangerous to reference language implementation details because they may change at a future date, but it's compelling to understand how basic enumerations work, which is why I included this section. A basic enumeration that holds between 2 and 255 cases is just a byte with a name for each value. Longer enumerations require additional storage.

Using this knowledge, you can theoretically create a protocol that allows you to construct instances from hash values and enumerate members. (Don't do this for production code.) The following snippet provides a few great wins for throw-away utilities that can save you some time:

```
protocol HashableEnumerable {}
extension HashableEnumerable {
    // Construct a byte and cast to the enumeration
    init?(fromHashValue hash: Int) {
        let byte = UInt8(hash)
        // "Warning: Breaks the guarantees of Swift's type system;
        // use with extreme care.  There's almost always a better way
        // to do anything." -- unsafeBitCast docs
        // Also, if you pass this an out-of-range value, it returns garbage
        self = unsafeBitCast(byte, Self.self)
    }

    // Enumerate members
    static func sequence() -> AnySequence<Self> {
        var index = 0
        return AnySequence {
            return anyGenerator {
                return Self(fromHashValue: index++)
            }
        }
    }
}
```

Reserve this approach for "fun" implementations; it isn't suitable for App Store code. If you really need this behavior, use raw value enumerations instead, which are described in the following section.

To use the preceding approach, just declare conformance. Here are some examples of how you might conform and call the default implementations:

```
extension Finger: HashableEnumerable {}
Finger(fromHashValue: 2) // Middle
Finger(fromHashValue: 8) // nil
for item in Finger.sequence() { print(item) } // prints members
```

You might use this approach to create an array of random fingers:

```
extension Array {
    var randomItem: Element {
        return self[Int(arc4random_uniform(UInt32(count)))]
    }
}
var allFingers = Array(Finger.sequence())
let myFingers = (1...10).map({_ in allFingers.randomItem})
print("My random fingers array is \(myFingers)")
```

And then iterate through the sequence, counting how many times each enumeration case appears in that array:

```
for eachFinger in Finger.sequence() {
    let count = myFingers.filter({$0 == eachFinger}).count
    print(eachFinger, count, separator: "  \t")
}
```

As you can see, if you're using enumerations to mark cases in any collection, this is an interesting way to explore them. As things stand in the current state of Swift, however, I recommend that you avoid this `hashValue` solution and use raw value enumerations, described next.

Raw Value Enumerations

You establish a raw value enumeration by appending a type name after the initial declaration. For example, you might use strings to create a greetings enumeration:

```
enum Greetings: String {
    case Hello = "Hello, Nurse!"
    case Goodbye = "Hasta la vista"
}
```

Each case uses the *same* type but offers a *unique* value, which you access through the `rawValue` member:

```
Greetings.Hello.rawValue // Hello, Nurse!
Greetings.Hello.hashValue // 0
Greetings.Goodbye.rawValue // Hasta la vista
Greetings.Goodbye.hashValue // 1
```

Unlike with basic enumerations, you can construct instances from raw values. Swift offers default initializers that take a `rawValue` argument:

```
Greetings(rawValue: "Hasta la vista")?.hashValue // 1
Greetings(rawValue: "No-op") // nil
```

The initializers are failable and return `nil` when you pass an invalid raw value.

In many programming languages, enumerated values are based on numbers. Swift supports numeric enumerations and can automatically populate its members. Here's a simple example:

```
enum Dwarf: Int {
    case Bashful = 1, Doc, Dopey, Grumpy, Happy, Sleepy, Sneezy
}
```

Order matters. Only `Bashful` uses an explicit assignment. Swift infers the remaining values, starting with 2 and continuing from there. Although `Dwarf` uses 1 as its first value, the default count starts at 0, as you see in the following example:

```
enum Level: Int {case Low, Medium, High}
Level.High.rawValue // 2
```

However, you can set any value you like. This example offers some meaningless (but necessarily non-overlapping) values for each case:

```
enum Charm: Int {case Heart = 5, Moon = 30,
    Star = 15, Clover = 20}
Charm.Star.rawValue // 15
```

Raw Value Members and Sequences

Raw value enumerations use failable initializers, which means if you know the starting value for the first enumeration member and the raw value sequence pattern from one member to the next, there's a predictable mechanism for creating generators, counting members, and so forth. Recipe 7-2 adds both a computed members property and a computed sequence. This recipe works only because `Dwarf` uses consecutive raw values, and the loop breaks at the first gap.

Recipe 7-2   **Creating Sequences from Raw Value Enumerations**

```
extension Dwarf {
    // The computed members property constructs an array on each call
    static var members: [Dwarf] {
        var items : [Dwarf] = []
        var index = 1 // initial value
        while let dwarf = Dwarf(rawValue: index++) {
            items.append(dwarf)
        }
        return items
    }

    // The simpler sequence implementation offers a better solution
    // for most iteration and member queries
    static func sequence() -> AnySequence<Dwarf> {
        return AnySequence {
            _ -> AnyGenerator<Dwarf> in
            var index = 1
```

```
        return anyGenerator {
            return Dwarf(rawValue: index++)
        }
    }
  }
}
```

Recipe 7-2's approach is a lot safer than the private-implementation-specific `hashValue` initializer you read about earlier in this chapter. You *must* still account for individual enumeration quirks. Recall that the `Dwarf` enumeration started with an initial value of 1, which is why `index` starts at 1 for these methods. The declaration of `index` is internal to the `AnySequence` scope, ensuring that multiple calls to `generate()` don't share an index.

This approach is most suited for raw value enumerations with a well-defined underlying sequence. With this understanding, you can then use this solution for any number of situations where you store members in collections, such as when you create and sort a deck of cards or iteratively roll members of a dice enumeration and want to evaluate their statistics.

Associated Values

Associated values enable you to create variable structures whose fields vary by enumeration case. With a true sum type or disjoint union, the storage in each enumeration instance changes based on the case in use. This approach allows the enumeration to use variable data layout while sharing the same memory footprint for each case.

In the following example, `Clue.NextClue` stores an integer and a string. `Clue.End` uses no additional storage:

```
enum Clue {
    case End
    case NextClue(Int, String)
}
```

You construct new instances either by direct reference (for no-value cases, `Clue.End`) or by passing a tuple of values (`Clue.NextClue(5, "Go North 5 paces")`). You access their associated values by using pattern matching, as in the following example:

```
let nextClue = Clue.NextClue(5, "Go North 5 paces")
if case Clue.NextClue(let step, let directions) = nextClue where step > 2 {
    print("You're almost there!. Next clue: \(directions)")
}
```

Pattern matching enables you to reach within the enumeration to perform conditional assignments based on the case while accessing constituent associated values.

Although the preceding example does not use labels, labels can add helpful context to your cases. In the following example, labeled enumerated values help build stages for a turtle graphics interface:

```
enum TurtleAction {
    case PenUp
    case PenDown
    case Goto(x: Double, y: Double)
    case Turn(degrees: Double)
    case Forward(distance: Double)
}
```

```
var actions: Array<TurtleAction> = [.Goto(x:200.0, y:200.0), .PenDown,
    .Turn(degrees:90.0), .Forward(distance:100.0), .PenUp]
```

You can ignore labels when performing variable binding, as in the following example:

```
let action = actions[0]; var x = 0.0; var y = 0.0
if case let .Goto(xx, yy) = action { (x, y) = (xx, yy) }
```

If you want to perform the assignment in a single line and are willing to leave the scope for case other than .Goto, you can use guard as in the following example:

```
// Unwrap and use in primary scope, else return
guard case let .Goto(x, y) = action else {return}
```

This approach enables you to convert x and y to constants and use them directly in the primary scope.

Enums with associated values do not provide either hash values or raw values. They cannot and should not provide the sequence semantics that were discussed with respect to basic and raw value enumerations.

Indirect Values

Indirect enumerations enable you to create recursive data structures by storing associated values indirectly. You can declare a single case indirect or the enumeration as a whole. For example, you might create a linked list as in Recipe 7-3. This recipe creates a generic enumeration type with two cases. A Nil list offers a natural termination point. A Cons constructor adds a new value to the head of a list and points to a tail with the rest of the list. It's a standard Intro to Data Structures implementation that adds a Swift flair with its indirect enumeration implementation.

Recipe 7-3 **Using Indirect Values to Create a Recursive Linked List**

```
enum List<T> {
    case Nil
    indirect case Cons(head: T, tail: List<T>)
    func dumpIt() {
        switch self {
            // This case uses Lisp-style notation
            // You can read more about Lisp's car, cdr, and cons
```

```
            // at https://en.wikipedia.org/wiki/CAR_and_CDR
            case .Cons(head: let car, tail: let cdr):
                print(car); cdr.dumpIt()
            default: break
        }
    }
}

// Construct a list and dump it
// Always adds the new value to the head
// so the constructed list is 5.4.3.2.1.Nil
var node = List<Int>.Nil
for value in [1, 2, 3, 4, 5] { node = List.Cons(head: value, tail: node) }
node.dumpIt()
    // As each value is appended to head, this implementation
    // prints its output in reverse numeric order
```

Switches

As in other languages, Swift's `switch` statements enable you to branch code. Their code orga-
nization joins run-on conditionals into well-organized flows. Starting with a single value, you
test that value against any number of conditions. When the condition succeeds, the `switch`
construct executes associated statements.

The simplest `switch` statement is this:

```
switch value {
default: break
}
```

Unlike in Objective-C, you do not add parentheses around the value unless the value is actually
a tuple and requires parentheses for syntax. The cases are unfortunately left-aligned, which is
admittedly not visually appealing.

When you add a body to this `default` case, the `switch` executes that behavior, regardless
of any value that is passed. A `switch` without `case` requests means "ignore the value and do
whatever the default case says to do." The body can appear to the right of the `case`, as in the
following example, or indented beneath it:

```
switch value {
default: print("Always prints")
}
```

Branching

You branch a `switch` statement by adding `case` bodies. Follow each `case` keyword with one or
more values, a colon, and then one or more statements, either on the same line or on following

lines. When the `case` matches, the associated statements (and only those statements) execute. For example, the following statement adds two `cases` in addition to its `default`. When the integer value is 2 or 5, it prints messages specific to those values:

```
switch intValue {
case 2: print("The value is 2")
case 5: print("The value is 5")
default: print("The value is not 2 or 5")
}
```

`switch` statements must be exhaustive. If a value can pass through each `case` without matching, you must add a `default` clause, the catchall `else` branch of switches. The wildcard expression _ (that's an underscore) adds another way to provide exhaustive coverage. It matches anything and everything. The following statement is functionally equivalent to the `default`-only example you saw at the start of this `switch` discussion:

```
switch value {
case _: print("Always prints")
}
```

Breaks

Use the `break` statement to create do-nothing cases or to short-circuit ongoing evaluation. This next code snippet showcases `break`, and it ignores any value except 4 and 6:

```
switch (intValue) {
case 1...3: break
case 4...6:
    if intValue == 5 {break}
    print("4 or 6")
default: break
}
```

Fallthroughs

Unlike in Objective-C, Swift `switch-cases` do not normally fall through. In Objective-C, the `break` keyword ends `case` evaluation and prevents other `cases` from executing—a common point for programming errors when you forget to add that critical "stop here" directive. Swift supports `break`, but it is not required for the most part. After matching, `switch` normally completes its execution at the start of the next `case` statement.

> ### Note
> The only place you really need `break` in `switch` statements is for no-op default cases, although in the current Swift (but please don't do this), you can substitute () for the `break` keyword.

In the following example, the second `case 2` never gets executed:

```
switch intValue {
case 2: print("The value is 2")
case 2: print("The value is still 2, by heavens!")
default: print("The value is not 2")
}
```

It is legal, however, to put it there, and this code will compile without erroring. The takeaway is that the *first* matching case is executed. This is especially important when you're working with ranges and other complex cases that may include members with special handling requirements.

A `fallthrough` keyword continues execution into the next `case`, regardless of whether that next `case` is satisfied or not. When you pass a value of 5, this next `switch` statement prints out first 5 and then 5 or 6:

```
switch intValue {
case 5: print("5"); fallthrough
case 6: print("5 or 6")
case 7: print("7")
default: print("not 5, 6, or 7")
}
```

It's an odd feature that I don't use much except in one circumstance. When dealing with behavior that applies to a subset of `case` members as in the following, `fallthrough` enables special-handling cases to continue to more general cases:

```
switch myVariable {
    case needsSpecialHandling1, needsSpecialHandling2:
        // code specific to these cases
        fallthrough // handling continues in the following case
    case generalCases1, generalCases2, etc:
        // code that applies to both the general cases and
        // the code that needed special handling
    other cases and default: // blah blah
}
```

In such cases, call out the `fallthrough` behavior with commenting or consider alternative approaches. For example, you might use two successive `switch` statements or an `if` statement followed by the `switch`. Although you may be fully trained in the nuances of `fallthrough`, the people reading your code in the future might fail to recognize the oddities of this particular flow. Comment copiously regardless.

> **Note**
>
> `fallthrough` cannot be used when the following `case` binds any values in its pattern.

Complex Cases

It's simple to combine cases by adding comma-delimited and range values to a case. switch uses the pattern match operator ~= to test case elements against the passed argument. This approach enables you to test against ranges as well as single values, as in the following example:

```
switch intValue {
case 5, 6: print("5 or 6")
case 7...12: print("7 - 12")
case 13...15, 17, 19...23:
    print("13, 14, 15, 17, or 19-23")
default: print("Not 5-15, nor 17, nor 19-23")
}
```

Tuples

switch matches tuples as well as individual values. This example tests a 2-ary tuple to check whether 3s appear within the tuple. The wildcard expressions in the second case match a single 3 to either position:

```
switch tup {
    case (3, 3): print("Two threes")
    case (_, 3), (3, _):
        print("At least one three")
    case _: print("No threes")
}
```

Swift enables you to use ranges inside tuple arguments, offering even more flexibility for your cases:

```
switch tup {
case (0...5, 0...5):
    print("Small positive numbers")
case (0...5, _), (_, 0...5):
    print("At least one small positive number")
default:
    print("No small positive numbers")
}
```

Pattern Matching with Value Bindings

The let and var keywords bind values to temporary variables. This is where switch statements move beyond simple if replacements and showcase their true power. This next example shows how binding and coercion can be combined with cases for a powerful effect:

```
enum Result<T> {
    case Error(ErrorType)
    case Value(Any)
    init (_ t: T) {
        switch t {
        case let error as ErrorType: self = .Error(error)
        default: self = .Value(t)
        }
    }
}
```

```
struct CustomError: ErrorType {let reason: String}
print(Result("Hello")) // Value("Hello")
print(Result(CustomError(reason: "Something went wrong")))
    // Error(CustomError(reason: "Something went wrong"))
```

The initializer tests its parameter t against the coerced ErrorType to try to construct an enumeration instance. If that assignment succeeds, the case continues to its body. If the cast fails, the result is wrapped in a general Value.

Although the var keyword is available, it's rarely needed. Here's a pointless example that uses var instead of let:

```
switch intValue {
case var value: print(++value)
}
```

where Clauses

Using where adds logic to case conditions beyond pattern matching. This example tests for membership in a range and tests whether the number is even or odd:

```
switch intValue {
case 0...20 where intValue % 2 == 0: print("Even number between 0 and 20")
case 0...20: print("Odd number between 0 and 20")
default: print("Some other number")
}
```

The where clause offers flexible logic. It lets you compare members of a tuple or test values against ranges or add any other condition your application demands:

```
switch tuple {
case (let x, let y) where x == y:
    print("tuple items are equal")
case (0, let y) where 0...6 ~= y:
    print("x is 0 and y is between 0 and 6")
default: break
}
```

You can also use `where` clauses in for loops, guards, and `if-let` statements. The following example prints out just the even numbers:

```
for num in 0...10 where num % 2 == 0 {print(num, "is even")}
```

Unwrapping Optional Enumerations

`switch` statements are amazing when you work with associated types. Here's an example that I used until I replaced my implementation with a superior solution based on enumerations. Forgive me. It's a poor example of how to represent Bezier elements but a good one on how to use optional members:

```
public struct BezierElement {
    public var elementType: CGPathElementType =
        CGPathElementType.CloseSubpath
    public var point: CGPoint?
    public var controlPoint1: CGPoint?
    public var controlPoint2: CGPoint?
}
```

The `point`, `controlPoint1`, and `controlPoint2` fields are all optional. Not every element type requires every field. For example, a quadratic curve doesn't use `controlPoint2`. The following `switch` statement emits Swift code by matching elements against a field tuple:

```
extension BezierElement {
    public var codeValue: String {
        switch (elementType, point, controlPoint1, controlPoint2) {
        case (CGPathElementType.CloseSubpath, _, _, _):
            return "path.closePath()"
        case (CGPathElementType.MoveToPoint, let point?, _, _):
            return "path.moveToPoint(CGPoint(x:\(point.x), y:\(point.y)))"
        case (CGPathElementType.AddLineToPoint, let point?, _, _):
            return "path.addLineToPoint(CGPoint(x:\(point.x), y:\(point.y)))"
        case (CGPathElementType.AddQuadCurveToPoint, let point?,
            let controlPoint1?, _):
            return "path.addQuadCurveToPoint(" +
                "CGPoint(x:\(point.x), y:\(point.y)), " +
                "controlPoint:" +
                "CGPoint(x:\(controlPoint1.x), y:\(controlPoint1.y)))"
        case (CGPathElementType.AddCurveToPoint, let point?,
            let controlPoint1?, let controlPoint2?):
            return "path.addCurveToPoint(" +
                "CGPoint(x:\(point.x), y:\(point.y)), " +
                "controlPoint1:" +
                "CGPoint(x:\(controlPoint1.x), y:\(controlPoint1.y)), " +
                "controlPoint2:" +
                "CGPoint(x:\(controlPoint2.x), y:\(controlPoint2.y)))"
```

```
            default: break
            }
            return "Malformed element"
        }
    }
```

The `let x?` constructs are equivalent to `let .Some(x)` and unwrap optional fields. Not only does this `switch` statement match element type, all relevant field data is prepared for use in the `case` body. Best of all, each `case` won't execute if the element is malformed and does not provide the required fields. Although you can use compound `if-let` statements to achieve the same result, using `switch` statements enables you to pattern match and add tests (using `where`) at the same time.

As this discussion showcases, `switch` statements are ridiculously powerful and remarkably useful. They are simply one of the best Swift language features available and a perfect companion to enumerations, both with and without associated types.

Embedding Values by Type

It's common to use enumerations to handle type-specific heterogeneous storage, like the kinds you run into with JSON. This next example doesn't use generics at all. It creates a container that stores an integer, a string, or a double or that indicates `nil`:

```
enum Container {
    case NilContainer
    case IntContainer(Int)
    case StringContainer(String)
    case DoubleContainer(Double)
}
```

This next example creates several `Container` instances and prints them out. This initial implementation is both long and wordy:

```
for c in [.NilContainer,
    .IntContainer(42),
    .StringContainer("Hello!"),
    .DoubleContainer(M_PI)] as [Container] {
        switch c {
        case .NilContainer: print("nil")
        case .DoubleContainer (let d): print("Double: \(d)")
        case .StringContainer (let s): print("String: \(s)")
        case .IntContainer (let i): print("Int: \(i)")
        }
}
```

Raw values simplify this printing task. This next extension returns raw values extracted from the associated types. The return instances are typed Any?. This accommodates the heterogeneous mix-and-match nature of the extracted values:

```
extension Container {
    var rawValue: Any? {
        switch self {
        case .NilContainer: return nil
        case .DoubleContainer (let d): return d
        case .StringContainer (let s): return s
        case .IntContainer (let i): return i
        }
    }
}
```

Now, you can just print the contained value for each item. Since they're returned as optionals, use nil coalescing to extract values and print a string for the nil case:

```
for c in [.NilContainer,
    .IntContainer(42),
    .StringContainer("Hello!"),
    .DoubleContainer(M_PI)] as [Container] {
        print(c.rawValue ?? "nil")
}
```

Despite improvements, the constructors remain cumbersome. Contrast with how you create an optional by passing a value:

```
Optional(23)
```

So why not extend Container to perform the same kind of inferred typing for construction? Here's an extension that uses type casting and conditional binding to test for type matches to establish new instances:

```
extension Container {
    init() {self = .NilContainer}
    init<T>(_ t: T){
        switch t {
        case let value as Int: self = .IntContainer(value)
        case let value as Double: self = .DoubleContainer(value)
        case let value as String: self = .StringContainer(value)
        default: self = .NilContainer
        }
    }
}
```

Now creating each type is super simple. Just pass a value of any type and let the `Container` type build enumeration instances for you:

```
for c in [Container(), Container(63),
    Container("Sailor"), Container(M_PI_4)] {
        print(c.rawValue ?? "nil")}
```

There is still room to improve. If you extend the `Container` enumeration for `CustomStringConvertible` conformance, you can skip the awkward `c.rawValue` implementation:

```
extension Container: CustomStringConvertible {
    var description: String {let v = rawValue ?? "nil"; return "\(v)"}
}
for c in [Container(), Container(63),
    Container("Sailor"), Container(M_PI_4)] {
        print(c)
}
```

The result is a really simple set of constructors and an even simpler way to print the values they produce.

Here's one last trick before moving on. Using `for-case` iteration enables you to pluck out single enumeration members, as you see in the following example:

```
let items: [Any] = [1, 20, "Hello", 3.5, "Narf", 6, "Weasels"]
let containedItems = items.map({Container($0)})
for case .StringContainer(let value) in containedItems {print("String:", value)}
for case .IntContainer(let value) in containedItems {print("Int:", value)}
for case .DoubleContainer(let value) in containedItems {print("Double:", value)}
```

This approach offers a convenient way to operate on heterogeneous enumeration collections, selecting just the `case` you are interested in.

Option Sets

Option sets are lightweight sets of Boolean values. This feature received a welcome facelift in Swift 2. Option sets enable you to store and query independent flags, which Swift treats as a collection of orthogonal settable switches. Now, you just build sets using simple, readable constructs and then add and remove and test members as needed. Option sets are easier to use than before, and the code you work with is more readable and maintainable than ever.

Revisiting NS_OPTIONS

To understand `OptionSetType`, it helps to step back and look at Objective-C's bit fields. In iOS 6 and OS X Mountain Lion, Apple introduced `NS_OPTIONS` along with its sibling `NS_ENUM` to replace `typedef enum` statements. These macros created a consistent way to build bit flags and enumerations, allowing the compiler to test for completeness in `switch` statements and ensuring that all `cases` were covered. They specify both the type and size of option and enumeration members.

Many Objective-C constructs use `NS_OPTIONS` to create bit flag sets. For example, you might want to specify the edges along which a view controller might extend:

```
typedef NS_OPTIONS(NSUInteger, UIRectEdge) {
    UIRectEdgeNone   = 0,
    UIRectEdgeTop    = 1 << 0,
    UIRectEdgeLeft   = 1 << 1,
    UIRectEdgeBottom = 1 << 2,
    UIRectEdgeRight  = 1 << 3,
    UIRectEdgeAll    = UIRectEdgeTop | UIRectEdgeLeft |
        UIRectEdgeBottom | UIRectEdgeRight
} NS_ENUM_AVAILABLE_IOS(7_0);
```

In Objective-C, you *or* together, for example, the `UIRectEdgeTop` and `UIRectEdgeLeft` values provided by `UIRectEdge`. In addition to individual edges, this option set also offers both `UIRectEdgeNone` and a `UIRectEdgeAll` option that combines all edges into a single value. Swift imports `NS_OPTIONS` to conform to the `OptionSetType` protocol, which in Swift 2 provides simple easy-to-use construction and testing.

Building Enumerations

Until Swift 2, you tested options using low-level bitwise math. For example, you might have written the following test to determine whether the `.Left` flag was set in a `UIRectEdge` value:

```
if edgeOptions & .Left == .Left {...}
```

Now, in Swift 2, you replace that test with a membership function:

```
if edgeOptions.contains(.Left) {...}
```

The syntax looks and feels like you're working with standard sets. You use square brackets and apply functions like `contains`, `union`, `intersection`, `exclusive-or`, and so forth. Instead of a no-flags raw value of `0`, use an empty set `[]`. Here's what option membership looks like in Swift 2:

```
 // Create empty option set
var options : UIRectEdge = []
options.insert(.Left)
options.contains(.Left) // true
options.contains(.Right) // false

// Create another set and union
var otherOptions : UIRectEdge = [.Right, .Bottom]
options.unionInPlace(otherOptions)
options.contains(.Right) // true
```

The following call uses the options just built to set a view controller's extended layout edges with respect to its parent's navigation container:

```
UIViewController().edgesForExtendedLayout = options
```

Building Option Sets

Default protocol implementations are another powerful Swift 2 feature. These enable option sets to create fully working bit flag implementations requiring almost no work on your part. Consider Recipe 7-4, which builds a new option set. The Features struct declares OptionSetType conformance, adds a rawValue field, and then declares a simple list of static flags.

Recipe 7-4   **Creating an Option Set**

```
struct Features : OptionSetType {
    let rawValue : Int
    static let AlarmSystem = Features(rawValue: 1 << 0)
    static let CDStereo = Features(rawValue: 1 << 1)
    static let ChromeWheels = Features(rawValue: 1 << 2)
    static let PinStripes = Features(rawValue: 1 << 3)
    static let LeatherInterior = Features(rawValue: 1 << 4)
    static let Undercoating = Features(rawValue: 1 << 5)
    static let WindowTint = Features(rawValue: 1 << 6)
}
```

Unlike enumerations, which can self-populate with integers, option sets require you to code each raw value by hand, as you see in this example. This may change in future Swift updates, as this approach is vulnerable to typos. Start with a value of 1 (1 << 0) and increase from there with single bit-shift increments.

Every other feature is already built in. The default option set implementations mean you inherit initialization, set operations (union, intersect, exclusive or), membership management (contains, insert, remove), bitwise operations (unionInPlace, intersectIn-Place, exclusiveOrInPlace), and more. In fact, all you need to do is define your flags, and you're immediately ready to use them, as in the following examples:

```
var carOptions : Features = [.AlarmSystem, .Undercoating, .WindowTint]
carOptions.contains(.LeatherInterior) // false
carOptions.contains(.Undercoating) // true
```

Viewing Options

Although Swift 2's mirroring automatically converts enumeration representations to printable descriptions, this convenience does not yet extend to OptionSetType instances. For example, this enumeration prints each member in a human-consumable fashion:

```
enum Colors {
    case Red, Orange, Yellow, Green, Blue, Indigo, Violet
}
print(Colors.Red) // prints Colors.Red
```

When you print the option sets created earlier in this section, they look something like this instead:

```
C.UIRectEdge(rawValue: 14)
Features(rawValue: 194)
```

Raw values are both ugly and not particularly helpful. I doubt this lack of print support will continue for long as the developer community files its bug reports with Apple. Until a fix appears, you can create custom representations by using the CustomStringConvertible protocol and adhering to successive-bit declarations.

The extension in Recipe 7-5 applies the new Swift 2 for-in-where construct to gather just those flags contained in the active set and returns a string representation of those members. It works by enumerating the static featureStrings array and testing each offset against the option set. This implementation assumes that your flags start at 1 << 0 and monotonically increase bit by bit from there.

Recipe 7-5 **Printable Option Sets**

```
extension Features : CustomStringConvertible {
    static var featureStrings = ["Alarm System", "CD Stereo",
        "Chrome Wheels", "Pin Stripes", "Leather Interior",
        "Undercoating", "Window Tint"]
    var description : String {
        return Features.featureStrings.enumerate().lazy
            .filter({(flag, _) in //test membership
                self.contains(Features(rawValue:1<<flag))})
            .map({$0.1}) // extract strings
            .joinWithSeparator(", ") // comma-delineated
    }
}
print(carOptions) // Alarm System, Undercoating, Window Tint
```

If you want the output to look more set-like, you can easily add square brackets around the comma-delineated string returned by the property extension.

Classes

In Swift, nearly all advantages that many developers mentally attribute to classes are available for both structures and enumerations. You can add methods and computed properties, implement type extensions, and conform to protocols. With all these improvements and added compiler efficiency for value types, why use classes? The answer boils down to reference semantics, Objective-C interoperability (Objective-C limits its type-level methods to classes), and the ability to subclass.

Reference semantics ensure that each instance occupies a unique location in memory and that the assignment always points to the same object. You use reference semantics for any item that might be used and modified by multiple owners. If it doesn't make sense to create an entirely new instance on assignment (think views, data stores, resource managers, and so on), use classes to implement them. There is no other way to achieve this outside of classes.

Subclassing offers another important reason to prefer classes in Swift, although perhaps it is the weakest reason, especially when you distance yourself from Objective-C interoperability and view/view-controller specialization. With generics, protocols, enumerations, and extensions, many of the traditional reasons to use subclasses no longer apply to Swift.

Unlike subclassing, Swift's newer technologies enable you to differentiate behavior based in the types in play (generics and protocols) or differentiate stored structure based on roles (enumerations and variable unions). Although there are still compelling reasons to create root classes and differentiate them through inheritance, the need for this particular pattern is diluted by the availability of other elegant approaches.

Optimization

Swift offers a way to combine reference semantics with computational efficiency. You achieve this by limiting subclassing behaviors for class types. The `final` keyword prevents a method, property, subscript, or even an entire class from being overridden by a subclass. Marking items with `final` enables the compiler to introduce performance improvements. These improvements depend on moving away from dynamic dispatch indirection, which requires a runtime decision to select which implementations to call. Removing indirect calls for methods and property access greatly improves your code performance.

Swift's new whole-module optimization can automatically infer many `final` declarations by scanning and compiling an entire module at once. Its inference capabilities apply only to constructs and members marked as `internal` (it's the default access modifier) and `private`. Class members that use `public` access must explicitly declare `final` to participate in this optimization.

> **Note**
>
> In classes, `static` is equivalent to `class final`.

Initializers

In development, initializers prepare language elements for use. They establish default values for stored properties and perform basic setup tasks. Swift enables you to initialize instances of classes, structures, and enumerations, but it is the initializers in classes that prove the trickiest to work with. That's because classes adopt inheritance, enabling subclasses to inherit the features and initializers of their superclass.

When you build a subclass and add stored properties, that storage must be set up either with a default value or by using an initializer. A class that declares default values for each property does not need initializers beyond those it inherits. The following `UIViewController` subclass compiles without errors:

```
class MyControllerSubclass: UIViewController {
    var newVar: String = "Default"
}
```

Without that default assignment, the compiler complains that the subclass has no initializers. It's up to you to build one or, typically in the case of view controllers, more.

Initialization Steps

A normal Swift instance initializer follows three basic steps:

1. You initialize any instance variables created by your class to a default starting state.

2. You call the superclass (if one exists) to initialize its instance variables. Yes, in Swift, you perform this action after you set up locally declared variables. This ordering ensures that the class storage is consistent at all hierarchical levels. You'll have a chance to update these values after this primary initialization.

3. Perform any other setup duties required by your instance. Here is where you can override or tweak any inherited properties and call instance methods, and freely refer to `self` as a value.

Designated and Convenience Initializers

Swift (and Objective-C, and many other modern languages for that matter) uses two distinct initializer patterns. A *designated initializer* follows the three steps you just read through. It exhaustively establishes default values for all storage introduced by the class declaration. When you introduce a subclass, the subclass's designated initializer sets its new properties first and then calls an initializer that walks up the superclass chain.

A *convenience initializer* provides a secondary construction utility. Although designated initializers should be few and functionally complete, a convenience initializer enables you to piggyback on designated initializers. They provide constructors that are shorter to call or provide an indirect initialization mechanism.

Initialization Rules

Swift's documentation officially defines three base initializer rules:

1. Designated initializers in subclasses must call designated initializers in superclasses and must never call convenience ones.

2. Convenience initializers must call other initializers (designated or convenience) defined in the same class. Convenience initializers always delegate sideways and may not walk up the chain to a superclass.

3. Convenience initializers must end up redirecting to a designated initializer in the same class. Eventually the initializer chain from Rule 2 must end, and it must do so by calling a designated initializer declared in the same class as itself.

No matter how much you keep delegating sideways, eventually you end up at a designated initializer that walks up the chain. And because designated initializers cannot call convenience initializers, that chain stops wandering as soon as you hit the designated one. By Rule 1, you walk up the class tree in a straight path of designated initializers.

There are two more rules for automatic initializer inheritance that go like this:

4. If you provide default values for all new properties (or simply do not add new properties) and your subclasses don't define designated initializers, the subclasses automatically inherit designated initializers from the superclass.

5. Any class that inherits or overrides all its superclass's designated initializers inherits its convenience initializers.

Rules 4 and 5 work because the convenience initializers defined in the superclass always have a local designated initializer to end up at. Rule 2 ensures that the inherited initializers hop sideways through the child class. Because the possible initializer endpoints from Rules 1 and 3 are well defined, the inherited initializers are guaranteed to end up at a designated initializer in the child class.

Custom iOS view controllers inherit two designated initializers:

```
public init(nibName nibNameOrNil: String?, bundle nibBundleOrNil: NSBundle?)
public init?(coder aDecoder: NSCoder)
```

If you want to create a more convenient way to construct instances in code, you default to working through these initializers. Fortunately, the nib version accepts nils for both parameters, enabling you to establish fully code-based view controller creation:

```
class MyControllerSubclass: UIViewController {
    var newVar: String

    convenience init(newVar: String) {
        self.init(nibName: nil, bundle: nil)
        self.newVar = newVar
    }
}
```

Unfortunately, view controllers and let properties don't blend well, especially if you want to share code between your initializers. You cannot call a shared setup routine because you're not allowed to call methods and use self until after the preliminary tasks. The easiest solution is to use variables instead of constants. You might also consider using a custom structure to store constant properties, which allows you to use a common constructor. It's ugly, but it does work. It's generally easier to stick to variables with default values over constants to lower your initialization task overhead.

Building Convenience Initializers

Convenience initializers are, as their name suggests, convenient or handy. For example, you might pass a string that holds the path to a `nib` for a view class or provide an offset relative to the current time (`timeIntervalSinceNow`) in place of a canonical reference time (`timeIntervalSinceReferenceDate`) that an `NSDate` instance normally uses to set itself up. Convenience initializers provide entry points built around the typical API needs of a client rather than the internal structure of the class. They offer a developer-friendly way to create shortcut patterns for instance construction.

The `convenience` keyword marks initializers that provide these entry points. Rule 4 enables you to simplify the `MyControllerSubclass` implementation by providing a default value for `newVar`. In the following streamlined implementation, supplying defaults for all new stored properties means the subclass inherits its superclass's initializers. The convenience initializer need only call a designated version and then perform any work based on the parameters supplied to it:

```
class MyControllerSubclass: UIViewController {
    var newVar: String = ""

    convenience init(newVar: String) {
        self.init(nibName: nil, bundle: nil)
        self.newVar = newVar
    }
}
```

Failable and Throwing Initializers

A failable initializer may produce a fully initialized instance, or it may return `nil`. This approach enables an initialization task to fail when it cannot establish a valid instance. A failable initializer is marked with a question mark (`init?`) and returns an optional value:

```
class MyFailableClass {
    init?() {
        // This initializer fails half the time
        if arc4random_uniform(2) > 0 {return nil}
    }
}

guard let test = MyFailableClass() else {return} // test is MyFailableClass?
```

The `return nil` command for failed construction is a bit of a semantic oddity. Initializers set up values; they don't return them. You don't return anything when the construction succeeds. At the time this book was being written, you needed to satisfy the `init` rules and initialize all properties before returning `nil`. Hopefully this issue will be addressed in a future Swift update.

Initializers can also throw, as you see in the following convenience initializer:

```
class MyThrowingClass {
    var value: String
    init() {
        value = "Initial value"
    }
    convenience init(string: String) throws {
        if string.isEmpty {throw Error()}
        self.init()
        value = string
    }
}
```

When working with throwing initializers, you must try to create them, just as you would with any other throwing functionality:

```
instance = try MyThrowingClass(string: "Initial StringValue")
```

Initializers fail because of missing resources (such as `UIImage`/`NSImage` initializers), because required services are not available, because of invalid parameter values, and for any other reason that prevents the class from setting up an instance properly. Prefer throwing initializers in cases where an instance cannot be properly constructed and use failable initializers in situations that don't represent errors.

For example, choose `init?` when mapping a value to one of several enumeration variants and `init throws` for situations that should explain *why* an initialization failed. Cocoa provides numerous examples of the latter. For example, the following `NSAttributedString` constructor throws on failure:

```
init(URL url: NSURL,
    options options: [String : AnyObject],
    documentAttributes dict:
        AutoreleasingUnsafeMutablePointer<NSDictionary?>) throws
```

This is a Swift 2 redesign of a failable initializer call that previously populated an error when the initialization failed:

```
init?(
    fileURL url: NSURL!,
    options options: [NSObject : AnyObject]!,
    documentAttributes dict:
        AutoreleasingUnsafeMutablePointer<NSDictionary?>,
    error error: NSErrorPointer)
```

As a rule, combine strategies like `guard` or `nil` coalescing (that is, using the `??` operator) with failable `init?` initializers and `try`/`throws` with throwing ones. This enables you to ensure that only valid values move forward either with default backup values or through early exit.

> **Note**
>
> Each initializer signature must be unique. You cannot offer both a failable and a non-failable initializer using the same parameter labels and types.

Deinitializers

Use `deinit` to perform cleanup tasks before a class instance is deallocated. (Chapter 6, "Errors," includes a discussion on using `defer`, which enables you to run similar tasks as you leave a scope.) Swift's `deinit` support makes it simple to observe deallocation. You can throw a `print` statement into the implementation and watch when items go away:

```
deinit {
    print("Deallocating instance")
}
```

When you're going to watch object life cycles, it helps to track which object you're dealing with. Swift value types don't have identifiers. There's no "notion of identity" for structs, enums, functions, and tuples, since you create new items on each assignment. For classes, which are reference types rather than value types, you can use `ObjectIdentifier` to fetch a unique representation of each instance:

```
class MyClass {
    init () {
        print("Creating instance",
            ObjectIdentifier(self).uintValue)
    }

    deinit {
        print("Deallocating instance",
            ObjectIdentifier(self).uintValue)
    }
}
```

This approach is handy for tracking when items are instantiated and deallocated. Here's an example that jumps through hoops to force an item past its natural life:

```
class MyClass {
    let message = "Got here"

    func test() {
        let ptr = unsafeBitCast(self, UnsafeMutablePointer<Void>.self)
        let handler = HandlerStruct(ptr: ptr)
```

```
            let numberOfSeconds = 2.0
            let delayTime = dispatch_time(
                DISPATCH_TIME_NOW,
                Int64(numberOfSeconds * Double(NSEC_PER_SEC)))

            dispatch_after(delayTime,
                dispatch_get_main_queue()) {
                    [self] // capture self
                    handler.unsafeFunc()
            }
        }

    init () {
        print("Creating instance",
            ObjectIdentifier(self).uintValue)
    }

    deinit {
        print("Deallocating instance",
            ObjectIdentifier(self).uintValue)
        CFRunLoopStop(CFRunLoopGetCurrent())
    }
}

MyClass().test()
CFRunLoopRun()
print("Done")
```

When you run this example, you see the instance's lifetime from start to end.

Property Observers

You monitor changes and add failsafe behavior to properties by implementing observers in your Swift types. Swift offers two variations of these: willSet, which is called just before a property updates, and didSet, which is called just after.

You use willSet to prepare for the new assignment, often cleaning things up. For example, you might remove gesture recognizers before assigning a new view property:

```
var view: UIView {
    willSet {
            if let view = view {
                view.removeGestureRecognizer(myTapGestureRecognizer)
            }
        }
    ...
}
```

In a similar vein, you might add a recognizer after a `view` is assigned:

```
didSet {
  if let view = view {
      view.addGestureRecognizer(myTapGestureRecognizer)
  }
}
```

`didSet` offers the opportunity to check for boundary conditions and to clamp values to appropriate settings:

```
public class ImageTiler : NSObject {
    public var hcount : Int = 1 {didSet {if hcount < 1 {hcount = 1}}}
    public var vcount : Int = 1 {didSet {if vcount < 1 {vcount = 1}}}
    ...
}
```

This example potentially updates the values of both properties. When you assign a property in its own observer, the new value replaces the one that was just set, but you do not trigger another round of observations.

> **Note**
>
> `willSet` and `didSet`, respectively, provide `newValue` and `oldValue` constant parameters. You can override these parameter names, although I cannot imagine why you'd want to.

Getters/Setters and Access-Level Modifiers

By default, a getter or a setter is established at the same access level as its parent property. Typically if you can read a property publicly, you can also write it publicly. You override this default behavior by adding `private` and `internal` keywords specific to `get` and `set`. Here's an example of a public structure with two public properties. These level modifiers create nuanced read-only access. The `status` property uses a `private` access level modifier. It can be updated only within the same source code file. The `result` property's `set` modifier is `internal`, so it can be modified within a module but not by external clients:

```
public enum Status {case Okay, Error}
public struct Attempt {
    public private(set) var status: Status = .Okay
    public internal(set) var result: String = "Nothing"
    public init() {}
    mutating public func execute() {
        let succeeded = arc4random_uniform(2) > 0
        switch succeeded {
        case true:
            status = .Okay
            result = "Attempt Succeeded"
```

```
        case false:
            status = .Error
            result = "Attempt Failed"
        }
    }
}
```

> **Note**
>
> Jared Sinclair wrote an excellent overview of Swift and the protected extension design pattern, which enforces overrides by subclasses. See http://blog.jaredsinclair.com/post/93992930295/for-subclass-eyes-only-swift.

Extensions and Overrides

Swift's ability to extend types and, in the case of classes, override methods established by super-classes, introduces enormous development flexibility and power. Use the `override` keyword to mark any method that replaces a parent implementation. A compiler check for the keyword prevents you from replacing parent behavior by accident. Extensions add methods, initializers, subscripts, and computed properties to an existing type, letting you extend behavior beyond the original.

For example, consider Recipe 7-6. It extends `CGRect`, a workhorse structure for UIKit views. This implementation adds initializers for Swift doubles and integers, allows rectangles to be zeroed or centered around points, and provides a way to center one rectangle in another. These kinds of instant wins are emblematic of how joyful working with Swift can be.

Recipe 7-6   **Extending `CGRect`**

```
public extension CGRect {
    // Init with size
    public init(_ size: CGSize) {
        self.init(origin:CGPoint.zero, size:size)
    }

    // Init with origin
    public init(_ origin: CGPoint) {
        self.init(origin:origin, size:CGSize.zero)
    }

    // Init with x, y, w, h
    public init(_ x: CGFloat, _ y: CGFloat, _ width: CGFloat, _ height: CGFloat) {
        self.init(x:x, y:y, width:width, height:height)
    }
```

```
// Init with doubles
public init(_ x: Double, _ y: Double, _ width: Double, _ height: Double) {
    self.init(x:x, y:y, width:width, height:height)
}

// Init with integers
public init(_ x: Int, _ y: Int, _ width: Int, _ height: Int) {
    self.init(x:x, y:y, width:width, height:height)
}

// Move origin to zero
public var zeroedRect: CGRect {return CGRect(size)}

// Move to center around new origin
public func aroundCenter(center: CGPoint) -> CGRect {
    let origin = CGPoint(x: center.x - size.width / 2.0,
        y: center.y - size.height / 2)
    return CGRect(origin:origin, size:size)
}
}
```

Lazy Evaluation

I had a hard time deciding where to put a discussion of lazy in this book and eventually ended up placing it into this types chapter. Lazy evaluation means deferring computation until a value is actually needed. Its opposite is *eager*, which is not a keyword or an official Swift term.

Lazy Sequences

In Swift, several things can be lazy. Sequences can be lazy, for example, when the work to create each value in a generator is performed only when a consumer requests a new value. You can use the lazy collection property to convert a collection to a lazy sequence. The following example prints Fetching Word each time its mapped functionality runs, enabling you to see when each stage executes:

```
let words = "Lorem ipsum dolor sit amet".characters.split(
    isSeparator:{$0 == " "}).lazy.map{
    characters -> String in print("Fetching Word"); return String(characters)}
    // words is now a lazy map collection
```

If this is the entire bit of code, nothing prints. The lazy evaluation ensures that the map does not execute until needed. If you add a single request, Fetching Word prints once:

```
words.first // prints Fetching Word once
```

When you iterate through the entire collection, the `print` request executes before each value is returned:

```
for word in words {
    print(word) // prints Fetching Word before each word
}
```

Lazy Properties

Stored properties can be lazy. Their initial evaluation can be deferred until their first use, enabling you to bypass that computation entirely if the property is never used. A lazy property must be a variable; constants must be assigned a value *before* initialization completes.

Consider Recipe 7-7. In this example, the `lazy` keyword ensures that `item` is not constructed until after at least three seconds have passed. If you remove the `lazy` keyword, the value stored in `item`'s string drops to near zero.

Recipe 7-7   **Deferring Initialization with `lazy`**

```
var initialTime = NSDate()
struct MyStruct {
    lazy var item: String = "\(-initialTime.timeIntervalSinceNow)"
}

var instance = MyStruct()
sleep(3)
print(instance.item) // for example, 3.01083701848984
```

> **Note**
>
> Stored static type properties are lazily initialized, just like global variables.

Wrap-up

From terminology to practicalities, this chapter has explored many of Swift's type features. You read about structures, classes, and enumerations, as well as some of the mechanisms that support them and the trade-offs in functionality. Swift is inherently a safe, flexible, and extensible language, and its multifaceted type system helps support those goals.

8

Miscellany

Swift is a vibrant and evolving language with many features that don't fit tidily under a single umbrella. This chapter introduces an assortment of topics that did not otherwise have proper homes elsewhere in this book but that still deserve your attention.

Statement Labels

In various languages, commands like `break`, `continue`, `return`, and `goto` address program flow, enabling you to conditionally redirect execution from loops, switches, and other scopes. Swift offers control flow features including `continue` and `break` for loops, `break` and `fallthrough` for switches, and so forth. Here's an example that uses `continue` to skip a `print` statement whenever an `index` is odd:

```
for index in 0...5 {
    if index % 2 != 0 {continue}
    print(index) // prints 0, 2, 4
}
```

Less widely known is that Swift also offers *statement labels*. These mark points at which execution continues outside the default nearest scope. You see an example of this in the following snippet, which marks the outer `for` loop with an `outerloop` label:

```
outerloop: for outer in 0...3 {
    for inner in 0...3 {
        if (outer == inner) {continue outerloop}
        print(outer, inner)
        // (1, 0), (2, 0), (2, 1), (3, 0), (3, 1), (3, 2)
    }
}
```

Statement labels let you `continue` not just to the next iteration of the innermost loop but to any level. Whenever the values of `inner` and `outer` equate to each other in this example, control redirects to the outer loop and continues to the next value. In this example, the printed value of `inner` never matches or exceeds that of `outer`. These labels, which may look familiar to D and Rust developers, control which flow a `continue` or `break` statement applies to.

Swift allows you to mark loop statements, conditionals, and `do` statements with labels. (In fact, you cannot break out of a `do` or `if` block without a label.) Each label is an arbitrary developer-selected identifier, such as `outerloop`. You place the label on the same line as the keyword that starts the statement, followed by a colon. This next snippet demonstrates `do`-statement control flow and includes a statement label redirection using `break`:

```
print("Starting")
labelpoint: do {
    // Waits to execute until the scope ends
    defer{print("Leaving do scope")}

    // This will always print
    print("Always prints")

    // Toss a coin and optionally leave the scope
    let coin = Int(arc4random_uniform(2))
    print("Coin toss: " + (coin == 0 ? "Heads" : "Tails"))
    if coin == 0 {break labelpoint}

    // Prints if scope execution continues
    print("Tails are lucky")
}
print("Ending")
```

In this example, the `do` scope executes synchronously in code. This code prints `Starting`, executes the do statement, and then prints `Ending`. When the coin toss is *heads*, the `break` statement redirects to the label at the start of the do scope and continues execution to the next statement. The `Tails are lucky` line isn't printed.

Unlike with `goto` statements, you cannot `break` to any label in your app, just to associated ones. The advantage of this flow is that it allows you to shortcut local scopes and continue execution on demand. The `break` provides a kind of "return" statement, like you'd use in closures.

In this example, as with all other scopes, a `defer` statement executes at the end of its parent scope, regardless of the circumstances of its ending. This behavior includes labeled redirects. You can `return`, `break`, throw an error, and so on. If you leave the scope, the `defer` runs upon exit.

Custom Operators

Operators enable you to break out of the function-name-followed-by-parentheses-and-arguments mold to use more natural mathematical relationships between arguments. Swift operators behave like functions but differ in syntax. An operator is usually placed just before or after the item it works on (prefix and postfix form) or between two operands (infix form), where it combines those values into some result. Swift's built-in operators include mathematical operations like ++, +, and - and logical ones like && and ||, among many others.

Swift also offers operator customization, which provides two significant features. First, you can extend existing operators to your custom types. You can, for example, add instances together using a plus sign by applying code that adds their properties. In this example, a custom operator implementation extends the semantics of what + means. Second, you can declare new operators such as dot products and cross products using a wide range of primarily Unicode-sourced characters. This allows you to introduce custom operator syntax to your code.

Declaring Operators

You declare custom operators at the global level. Use the `operator` keyword and mark your declaration with `prefix`, `infix`, or `postfix`, depending on the style of operator you're defining. The following operator prints and returns a value, allowing the printing to occur as a side effect in normal evaluation:

```
postfix operator *** {}
postfix func ***<T>(item: T) -> T {print(item); return item}
```

You can also write an infix custom operator to mesh a format string with arguments:

```
infix operator %%% {}
func %%%(lhs: String, rhs: [CVarArgType]) -> String {
    return String(format: lhs, arguments: rhs)
}
```

You'd call the %%% operator like this:

```
print("%zd & %@" %%% [59, "Bananas" as NSString]) // "59 & Bananas"
```

This next example performs a case-insensitive regular expression match on a string using Foundation calls:

```
// Regex match. Requires Foundation.
infix operator ~== {
    associativity none
    precedence 90
}

func ~==(lhs: String, rhs: String) -> Range<String.Index>? {
    return lhs.rangeOfString(rhs,
        options: [.RegularExpressionSearch, .CaseInsensitiveSearch],
        range: lhs.startIndex..<lhs.endIndex,
        locale: nil)
}
```

The braces that follow an infix operator declaration can include information about associativity (`left`, `right`, or `none`) and precedence, which defaults to a level of 100. A precedence level increases operator priority as the value rises and decreases as it falls. Associativity defines how operators of the same precedence group together in the absence of explicit parentheses. With left-associative operators, operations are grouped from the left; with right-associative operators, they are grouped from the right. A non-associative operator prevents chaining.

Conforming with Operators

If an operator is already defined, you don't redeclare it when implementing it for custom types. For example, the `Equatable` protocol requires the `==` operator. To conform, you declare the protocol and implement `==` at the global level:

```
struct MyStruct {let item: Int}
extension MyStruct: Equatable {}
func ==(lhs: MyStruct, rhs: MyStruct)-> Bool {return lhs.item == rhs.item}
```

The preceding example uses a trivial structure with a single integer property. In Swift, it's common to work with generic types, as in the following snippet:

```
struct MyGenericStruct<T: Equatable> {let item: T}
extension MyGenericStruct: Equatable {}
func ==<T>(lhs: MyGenericStruct<T>, rhs: MyGenericStruct<T>)-> Bool {
    return lhs.item == rhs.item
}
```

Here you see a more real-world use case where the generic struct is composed of a property that is itself equatable. To conform the entire structure, the `==` implementation must be itself genericized to limit the application to same-type structs.

Evaluating Operator Trade-offs

Custom operators enable you to move code away from their function forms using a more natural expressions, such as A $\in$ B vs. $\in$(A, B), but they do so with a non-trivial cost:

- You are limited to the characters you can use for operators: /, =, -, +, !, *, %, <, >, &, |, ^, ?, or ~ plus the limited set of legal Unicode that is detailed in Apple's documentation.

- You cannot override already-reserved uses such as =, ->, //, /*, and */.

- You cannot confuse the compiler, which is looking for optional-handling operators ending with ! and ?, even if the grammar suggests that your operators are otherwise legal. For example, if you want to write a factorial operator (normally !) and a choose operator (normally parentheses with one number placed above the other), how would you select operator characters, given the limitations of the Swift grammar?

- You want to select operators whose meaning is easily recognized and whose use is easily recalled. Further, to construct Unicode operators in code, you may need to use copy/paste from reference sheets or complex keyboard entry.

As these limitations suggest, you should use novel operators sparingly and meaningfully. Overloading the meaning of existing operators may be more generally productive than introducing new operators.

Array Indexing

Array lookups can fail, and when they do, it's usually loudly and uncomfortably. Attempt to access an out-of-range index and get ready to experience an application crash. This is not a feature you can guard against or conditionally try with an error handler. You must deal with the natural fallout, which is this:

```
fatal error: Array index out of range
```

Fortunately, you can implement a safe custom workaround, as you see in Recipe 8-1. Swift's support of custom subscripts and subscript labels, such as myArray[safe: index], makes it safer to check arbitrary indices than to look up myArray[index] directly. This recipe creates a labeled subscript extension. It checks index validity before returning an optional result.

Recipe 8-1 **Adding Index Safety to Arrays**

```
extension Array {
    subscript (safe index: Int) -> Element? {
        return (0..<count).contains(index) ? self[index] : nil
    }
}
```

This implementation returns nil for out-of-bounds indices and wrapped .Some(x) values otherwise. To use this approach, your code must expect optional return values and adapt to unwrap them before use. In the following example, Swift's guard statement assigns unwrapped versions of these lookups to local variables, skipping processing in the case of a failed index:

```
let tests: [UInt] = [1, 50, 2, 6, 0]
for indexTest in tests {
    guard let value = alphabet[safe: indexTest] else {continue}
    print("\(indexTest): \(value) is valid")
}
```

When using safe indexing, consider how to react to out-of-bounds conditions. You can throw an error, continue on by ignoring the failure, or exit the current scope. Sometimes the best way to fail is to allow your application to terminate, in which case you can discover and re-architect around logical errors that led to the failure in the first place. Limit use of safe lookups to situations in which you do not have control over potentially bad data and when you wish to provide a robust and recoverable mechanism for handling data–index mismatches.

In theory, you can extend safe lookups to any collection type. The following snippet creates a generic implementation that works with any collection type with a comparable index:

```
extension CollectionType where Index: Comparable {
    subscript (safe index: Index) -> Generator.Element? {
        guard startIndex <= index && index < endIndex else {
            return nil
        }
        return self[index]
    }
}
```

In practice, there are few collections outside of arrays where using this approach makes any sense.

Multi-indexed Array Access

Swift enables you to use subscripting with multiple indices. For example, you might create an array and want to index it with myArray[3, 5] or myArray[7, 9, 16]. Implementing a general solution involves some trickery. While you can easily build a custom subscript when you know a priori the number of elements you're aiming for, extending behavior to an arbitrary argument count is less straightforward.

The following extension returns two items at a time:

```
// Two at a time
extension Array {
    subscript(i1: Int, i2:Int) -> [Element] {
        return [self[i1], self[i2]]
    }
}
```

This is easy to implement, and Swift can easily use parameter matching to figure out the overloaded results you're aiming for.

You must take care when extending this behavior for an arbitrary number of arguments. The following approach won't work but will lead to infinite loops and failed execution. Swift cannot distinguish this parameter declaration from an override of the standard single-item indexing. Variadic parameters accept zero or more values of a specified type, so [2], [2, 4], [2, 4, 6], and [2, 4, 6, 8] all match this declaration:

```
subscript(i1: Int, i2:Int...)
```

To Swift, (Int, Int...) is virtually identical to (Int) at runtime, and the compiler chooses your override in preference to the original implementation for single-parameter lookups. That's where the infinite loops arise. The single-index requests that are needed to gather result components inadvertently self-reference. You need a subscript signature that won't confuse Swift in this way. A proper solution uses two non-variadic arguments followed by a third variadic one, creating a "use this implementation only for two or more parameters" scenario.

Recipe 8-2 provides a working solution. When you provide at least two subscript arguments to this Array extension, Swift knows to use the right subscripting implementation.

Recipe 8-2   **Multiple-Array Subscripting**

```
extension Array {
    // specifying two initial parameters differentiates
    // this implementation from the default subscript
    subscript(i1: Int, i2: Int, rest: Int...) -> [Element] {
        get {
            var result: [Element] = [self[i1], self[i2]]
            for index in rest {
                result.append(self[index])
            }
            return result
        }

        set (values) {
            for (index, value) in zip([i1, i2] + rest, values) {
                self[index] = value
            }
        }
    }
}
```

Wrapped Indices

One way to avoid out-of-bounds conditions is to wrap indices so overflows and underflows still map into legal ranges. For example, for an array consisting of five items, the sixth item would wrap around to the first element, and the minus-first element (-1) would wrap around to the last. Recipe 8-3 implements a simple modulo approach which ensures that an integer always maps to a valid index.

Recipe 8-3   **Using Subscript Wrapping**

```
extension Array {
    subscript (wrap index: Int) -> Element? {
        if count == 0 {return nil}
        return self[(index % count + count) % count]
    }
}

myArray[wrap:-1] // last element
```

Array Slices

In Swift, a slice points into an existing array without creating a new copy. Slices describe rather than duplicate. You encounter them when performing lookups, as in the following example. This snippet builds a new array and then creates a slice by indexing:

```
var myArray = "abcdefgh".characters.map({String($0)}) // Array<String>
let slice = myArray[2...3] // ArraySlice<String>
```

You can mostly treat the slice as if it were a standard array. If you count the new slice, it reports two members. You can index it as well, although the indices retain their original numbering. You can look up `slice[2]` (which is c) but not `slice[0]`. The latter will error even though `myArray[0]` is valid.

A few more points:

- Arrays are value types. If you mutate `myArray` after creating a slice, that updated value does not propagate to the already-created slice.

- You can reference the `startIndex` and `endIndex` of the slice as well as the complete range (`indices`).

- Enumerated array slices (`slice.enumerate()`) lose their indices. The count starts at 0 because all sequence counts start at zero. It's a sequence thing, not a slice thing.

You work around the enumeration issue by zipping together the slice with its indices. The following function creates an enumeration that preserves the slice ordering:

```
extension ArraySlice {
    func enumerateWithIndices() -> AnySequence<(Index, Generator.Element)> {
        return AnySequence(zip(indices, self))
    }
}
```

General Subscripting

Swift subscripts extend beyond collections. If you can imagine a way to index an object internally, you can build a custom subscript to access it. Supply an argument (and, optionally, an external label, as Swift supports subscript labels) and calculate a logical value based on that argument. Recipe 8-4 demonstrates custom subscripting by accessing a UIColor instance by RGBA channel. As not all UIColor instances provide RGBA values, this implementation returns 0.0 for unfetchable channels.

Recipe 8-4   **Subscripting Colors**

```
public typealias RGBColorTuple =
    (red: CGFloat, green: CGFloat, blue: CGFloat, alpha: CGFloat)
public extension UIColor {
    public var channels: RGBColorTuple? {
        var (r, g, b, a): RGBColorTuple = (0.0, 0.0, 0.0, 0.0)
        let gettableColor = self.getRed(&r, green: &g, blue: &b, alpha: &a)
        return gettableColor ? (red: r, green: g, blue: b, alpha: a) : nil
    }
```

```
public enum RGBAChannel {case Red, Green, Blue, Alpha}

public subscript (channel: RGBAChannel) -> CGFloat {
    switch channel {
    case .Red:    return channels?.red ?? 0.0
    case .Green:  return channels?.green ?? 0.0
    case .Blue:   return channels?.blue ?? 0.0
    case .Alpha:  return channels?.alpha ?? 0.0
    }
  }
}
```

In this color example, you can use the public `Channel` enumeration to individually access each channel using standard subscripting:

```
let color = UIColor.magentaColor()
color[.Red]    // 1
color[.Green]  // 0
color[.Blue]   // 1
color[.Alpha]  // 1
```

I love how Swift enables you to declare and initialize all the variables at once, which you see in the implementation of the `channels` property. You can easily extend this implementation for other color spaces such as hue-saturation-brightness.

Parameter-less Subscripting

As well as supporting labels, Swift enables you to implement zero-argument subscripting. The following implementation mimics the custom *** print-and-pass-through operator described earlier in this chapter:

```
public protocol SubscriptPrintable {
    subscript() -> Self {get}
}

public extension SubscriptPrintable {
    subscript() -> Self {
        print(self); return self
    }
}
```

```
extension Int: SubscriptPrintable {}
5[] // whee!
```

Kevin Ballard, who discovered this little feature, had a slightly better use for it. He implemented a simple way to offer get-and-set access to an unsafe mutable pointer's memory:

```
extension UnsafeMutablePointer {
    subscript() -> T {
        get {
            return memory
        }
        nonmutating set {
            memory = newValue
        }
    }
}
```

String Utilities

String is a workhorse type, used throughout a programmer's day. The following sections introduce a variety of handy approaches to getting the most out of Swift's String type.

Repeat Initializers

Both strings and arrays allow you to construct new instances with a count and a value:

```
public init(count: Int, repeatedValue c: Character)
public init(count: Int, repeatedValue: Self.Generator.Element)
```

You pass a character to the string initializer and any legal element to the array one:

```
let s = String(count: 5, repeatedValue: Character("X")) // "XXXXX"
let a = Array(count: 3, repeatedValue: "X") // ["X", "X", "X"]
let a2 = Array(count: 2, repeatedValue: [1, 2]) // [[1, 2], [1, 2]]
```

Most typically, you use the array approach to construct a zero-initialized buffer:

```
let buffer = Array<Int8>(count: 512, repeatedValue: 0)
```

Strings and Radix

Swift's radix initializer enables you to convert integers into base-specific representations including binary, octal, and hex:

```
String(15, radix:2) // 1111
String(15, radix:8) // 17
String(15, radix:16) // f
```

Recipe 8-5 builds on this, creating string properties for integers and integer properties for strings that enable simple back-and-forth conversion.

Recipe 8-5   **Converting Strings to and from Base Systems**

```
extension String {
    var boolValue: Bool {return (self as NSString).boolValue}
}

// Support Swift prefixes (0b, 0o, 0x) and Unix (0, 0x / 0X)
extension String {
    var binaryValue: Int {
        return strtol(self.hasPrefix("0b") ?
            String(self.characters.dropFirst(2)) : self, nil, 2)}
    var octalValue: Int {
        return strtol(self.hasPrefix("0o") ?
            String(self.characters.dropFirst(2)) : self, nil, 8)}
    var hexValue: Int {
        return strtol(self, nil, 16)}

    var uBinaryValue: UInt {
        return strtoul(self.hasPrefix("0b") ?
            String(self.characters.dropFirst(2)) : self, nil, 2)}
    var uOctalValue: UInt {
        return strtoul(self.hasPrefix("0o") ?
            String(self.characters.dropFirst(2)) : self, nil, 8)}
    var uHexValue: UInt {
        return strtoul(self, nil, 16)}

    func pad(width: Int, character: Character) -> String {
        return String(
            count: width - self.characters.count,
            repeatedValue: character) + self
    }
}

extension Int {
    var binaryString: String {return String(self, radix:2)}
    var octalString: String {return String(self, radix:8)}
    var hexString: String {return String(self, radix:16)}
}
```

String Ranges

Many people consider ranges to be portable things. For example, Foundation's NSRange consists of a simple integer position and length and can be used with any object that supports integer-based indexing. Now consider the example in Figure 8-1, which fetches a Swift String. Index range from a string and then attempts to reuse that range to fetch items from other strings.

```
 5  // Fetch a range
 6  let string = "My String"                                                    "My String"
 7  let range = string.rangeOfString("Str")!                                    "3..<6"
 8
 9  let string2 = "Another String"                                              "Another String"
10  let result2 = string2.substringWithRange(range) // can seem to work         "the"
11
12  // It fails with a string that uses different backing traits
13  let string3 = "😀😀😀😀😀😀😀😈😀😀😀😀😀"                                        "😀😀😀😀😀😀..."
14  let result3 = string3.substringWithRange(range) // bzzt, returns "😀😀"        "◆😀"
```

Figure 8-1   Swift ranges are specific to characteristics of their sources.

You cannot apply the range returned from the initial string to string3 even though both items are typed String and their ranges are typed String.Index. The backing character stores do not match. You shouldn't assume that the range from "My String" works with "Another String" either. Even if strings are both ASCII, they can use different internal encodings. The range may appear to work with another string with the same basic properties, but this is not reliable, and it may just as easily misbehave.

Create range portability by abstracting ranges using startIndex, endIndex, and the distanceTo and advancedBy functions, as in Recipe 8-6.

Recipe 8-6   **Creating String Index Portability**

```
extension String {
    func toPortable(range: Range<String.Index>) -> Range<Int> {
        let start = self.startIndex.distanceTo(range.startIndex)
        let end = self.startIndex.distanceTo(range.endIndex)
        return start..< end
    }

    func fromPortable(range: Range<Int>) -> Range<String.Index> {
        let start = startIndex.advancedBy(range.startIndex)
        let end = startIndex.advancedBy(range.endIndex)
        return start..<end
    }
}
```

Cast ranges to portable form by using the original string. Then conform them to a specific string before using them to index that new string. Each portability cast operates in O(n), so use these advisedly. This recipe does not perform range checking or other safety checks. Using the right character stride length does not immunize you from errors, either. When you address indices outside string bounds, a string-adjusted range crashes just as nastily as a natively created range does:

```
let portableRange = string.toPortable(range)
let threeSpecific = string3.fromPortable(portableRange)
let result4 = string3.substringWithRange(threeSpecific) // correct
```

Always follow the golden rule of Swift String indices: "Never use `String.Index` with a string other than the string it belongs to." This generalizes to a don't-share-needles-or-indices rule for every index type. This recipe enables you to move indices to and away from the strings they represent, but it provides no further guarantees of safety.

String Splitting

Segmenting a string is a common task. You might split at word boundaries by finding spaces or line boundaries by checking for carriage returns. Although you can decompose a string into characters and split from there, I find it more convenient to use a string-level entry point for split operations. Recipe 8-7 builds two `String` functions. One mimics the signature of the character-specific split function. The other simply accepts a character as its parameter.

Recipe 8-7   **Splitting a String at Character Matches**

```
extension String {
    public func split(
        maxSplit: Int = .max,
        allowEmptySlices: Bool = false,
        @noescape isSeparator:
            (Character) throws -> Bool) rethrows -> [String] {
            return try self.characters.split(
                maxSplit,
                allowEmptySlices: allowEmptySlices,
                isSeparator: isSeparator)
                .map({String($0)})
    }

    public func split(character: Character) -> [String] {
        return self.split{$0 == character}
    }
}
```

String Subscripts

Recipe 8-8 extends the way you can look up and manipulate the contents of strings. It offers ways to retrieve information using integer-based indices that abstract away from the specifics of backing stores and internal implementations. The result is a general-purpose approach to get and set parts of a string as if it were a well-behaved sequence of characters instead of a wildly unpredictable data type.

This approach is not ideal, and I recommend that you avoid it where possible. Each integer-based operation is O(n), and you can trivially end up with O(n^2) or worse performance with this approach. Beyond the performance issues, you're basically fighting Swift and its best practices. I include this example solely as a nod to the fact that this is one of the backward-compatibility "moving to Swift" challenges that people approach me about over and over.

Recipe 8-8 Subscripting Strings

```
extension String {
    // Convert int range to string-specific range
    public func rangeFromIntRange(range: Range<Int>) ->
        Range<String.Index> {
        let start = startIndex.advancedBy(range.startIndex)
        let end = startIndex.advancedBy(range.endIndex)
        return start..<end
    }

    // Substring within range
    public func just(desiredRange: Range<Int>) -> String {
        return substringWithRange(rangeFromIntRange(desiredRange))
    }

    // Substring at one index
    public func at(desiredIndex: Int) -> String {
        return just(desiredIndex...desiredIndex)
    }

    // Substring excluding range
    public func except(range: Range<Int>) -> String {
        var copy = self
        copy.replaceRange(rangeFromIntRange(range), with:"")
        return copy
    }

    // The setters in the following two subscript do not enforce
    // length equality. You can replace 1...100 with, for example, "foo"
    public subscript (aRange: Range<Int>) -> String? {
        get {return just(aRange)}
        set {replaceRange(rangeFromIntRange(aRange), with:newValue ?? "")}
    }

    public subscript (i: Int) -> String? {
        get {return at(i)}
        set {self[i...i] = newValue}
    }
}
```

Foundation Interoperability

It's impossible to consider Swift without taking Cocoa and Foundation into account. Swift lives within the umbra of Apple's existing APIs, and it's "transparent" bridging between Swift strings and Foundation's `NSString` isn't always as seamless as one might wish. Recipe 8-9 offers ways to force strings into one world or the other, using simple property implementations.

Recipe 8-9   **Moving to and from Foundation**

```
extension String {
    public var ns: NSString {return self as NSString}
}

public extension NSString {
    public var swift: String {return self as String}
}
```

Joining and Extending

Swift's standard library offers several functions that help you combine items together. For example, you can easily calculate the nth factorial by reducing terms:

```
func factorial(n: Int) -> Int{return (1...n).reduce(1, combine:*)}
```

The `joinWithSeparator` function operates in a similar manner, specifying how to combine items in a sequence. For example, you might create comma-delineated strings or intersperse one array among others:

```
["a", "b", "c"].joinWithSeparator(", ") // "a, b, c"
print(Array([[1, 2], [1, 2], [1, 2]]
    .joinWithSeparator([0]))) // [1, 2, 0, 1, 2, 0, 1, 2]
```

The sequence must be composed of strings or items that are themselves of sequence type, so you can use this with arrays but not with, for example, integers. Both strings and arrays offer additional functions to insert, append, remove, and replace elements, courtesy of the Swift standard library.

Permutation Generator

Swift's Permutation Generator adapts a collection and a sequence of its indices to present collection members in a different order. As this generator isn't actually limited to strict permutations and can be used in ways that repeat or skip indices, it might be better called something like an "objects-at-indices" generator.

Recipe 8-10 demonstrates a common use case, randomly mixing up indices to scramble a collection. It demonstrates how you build a basic generator by passing collection elements and a sequence—in this case, a lazily generated random sequence. This implementation converts the scrambled index generator built with `anyGenerator` into a sequence using `AnySequence`, a simple solution for moving between the two.

Recipe 8-10   **Scrambled Collections**

```
extension CollectionType {
    // Return a scrambled index generator
    func generateScrambledIndices() -> AnyGenerator<Self.Index> {
        var indices = Array(self.startIndex..<self.endIndex)
        return anyGenerator {
            if indices.count == 0 {return nil}
            // Select a random index and remove it from future use
            let nextIndex = arc4random_uniform(UInt32(indices.count))
            let nextItem = indices.removeAtIndex(Int(nextIndex))
            return nextItem
        }
    }

    // Create a permutation generator to present the scrambled indices
    func generateScrambled() ->
        PermutationGenerator<Self,AnySequence<Self.Index>> {
        return PermutationGenerator(elements: self,
            indices: AnySequence(self.generateScrambledIndices()))
    }
}
```

Notice how the generator returned by `generateScrambledIndices()` holds onto the state declared in its creating scope, specifically the `indices` array. This generator-building function approach enables you to build generators with associated state.

The Permutation Generator isn't limited to random scrambles. You can use the same approach to build a strideable sequence. Striding enables you to traverse elements at set interval distances, as in Recipe 8-11, or to return members using any other computed walk-through.

Recipe 8-11   **Striding Indices with a Permutation Generator**

```
extension CollectionType {
    func generateWithStride(interval: Self.Index.Distance = 1) ->
        PermutationGenerator<Self,AnySequence<Self.Index>> {
        var index = startIndex
        let generator: AnyGenerator<Self.Index> = anyGenerator {
            // Return a value and advance by the stride interval
            defer { index = index.advancedBy(interval, limit: self.endIndex) }
            return index == self.endIndex ? nil : index
        }
```

```
        return PermutationGenerator(elements:self,
            indices: AnySequence(generator))
    }
}
```

The length of the returned collection needn't match that of the original. Recipe 8-12 generates multiple copies of each element, transforming, for example, a collection of *A, B, C* into *A, A, A, B, B, B, C, C, C,* using a custom multiplicity count supplied to the generator.

Recipe 8-12   **A Multiple-Instance Collection**

```
extension CollectionType {
    func generateMultiple(count count: Int = 1) ->
        PermutationGenerator<Self,AnySequence<Self.Index>> {
        var index = startIndex; var current = 0
        let generator:  AnyGenerator<Self.Index> = anyGenerator {
            defer {
                if (current + 1) == count {
                    index = index.advancedBy(1, limit: self.endIndex)
                }
                current = (current + 1) % count
            }
            return index == self.endIndex ? nil : index
        }
        return PermutationGenerator(elements:self,
            indices: AnySequence(generator))
    }
}
```

Wrap-up

This chapter provides just a taste of the many features Swift offers that extend beyond basic development. Learning Swift is a continuous experience both as the language itself grows and you push boundaries as a programmer. I encourage you to dive into Swift's documentation and its standard library to explore and discover the features available to you.

Index

W

X-Y-Z

Developer's Library

ESSENTIAL REFERENCES FOR PROGRAMMING PROFESSIONALS

Xcode Start to Finish

Fritz Anderson

ISBN-13: 978-0-13-405277-9

Mastering iOS Frameworks: Beyond the Basics, 2nd Edition

Kyle Richter
Joe Keeley

ISBN-13: 978-0-13-405249-6

The Gourmet iOS Developer's Cookbook

Erica Sadun

ISBN-13: 978-0-13-408622-4

Other Developer's Library Titles

TITLE	AUTHOR	ISBN-13
Objective-C Phrasebook Second Edition	David Chisnall	978-0-321-81375-6
Test-Driven iOS Development	Graham Lee	978-0-321-77418-7
Cocoa® Programming Developer's Handbook	David Chisnall	978-0-321-63963-9
Cocoa Design Patterns	Erik M. Buck / Donald A. Yacktman	978-0-321-53502-3

Developer's Library books are available at most retail and online bookstores. For more information or to order direct, visit our online bookstore at **informit.com/store**

Online editions of all Developer's Library titles are available by subscription from Safari Books Online at **safari.informit.com**

Addison
Wesley

Developer's Library

informit.com/devlibrary

REGISTER YOUR PRODUCT at informit.com/register
Access Additional Benefits and SAVE 35% on Your Next Purchase

- Download available product updates.

- Access bonus material when applicable.

- Receive exclusive offers on new editions and related products.
  (Just check the box to hear from us when setting up your account.)

- Get a coupon for 35% for your next purchase, valid for 30 days. Your code will
  be available in your InformIT cart. (You will also find it in the Manage Codes
  section of your account page.)

Registration benefits vary by product. Benefits will be listed on your account page
under Registered Products.

InformIT.com–The Trusted Technology Learning Source
InformIT is the online home of information technology brands at Pearson, the world's foremost
education company. At InformIT.com you can

- Shop our books, eBooks, software, and video training.
- Take advantage of our special offers and promotions (informit.com/promotions).
- Sign up for special offers and content newsletters (informit.com/newsletters).
- Read free articles and blogs by information technology experts.
- Access thousands of free chapters and video lessons.

Connect with InformIT–Visit informit.com/community
Learn about InformIT community events and programs.

informIT.com
the trusted technology learning source

Addison-Wesley · Cisco Press · IBM Press · Microsoft Press · Pearson IT Certification · Prentice Hall · Que · Sams · VMware Press

ALWAYS LEARNING   PEARSON